INSTANT POT PRO CRISP AIR FRYER COOKBOOK

+390 HEALTHY AND SAVORY RECIPES FOR YOUR AIR FRYER. EASY MEAL FOR BEGINNERS WITH TIPS & TRICKS TO FRY, GRILL, ROAST AND BAKE.

KIMBERLY TALBERT

CONTENTS

BREAKFAST

POULTRY

BEEF, PORK & LAMB

FISH & SEAFOOD

VEGETABLES & SIDE DISHES

SNACKS & APPETIZERS

DEHYDRATE

DESSERTS

INTRODUCTION

In this cookbook, we have introduced a new member which comes from the instant pot family known as instant pot pro crisp air fryer. It works on two different cooking techniques one is used for pressure cooking purposes and the other is used for air frying. The instant pot pro crisp air fryer comes with two lids one is for pressure cooker lid and another is an air fryer lid. It is one of the advanced cooking appliances loaded with 11 cooking functions. These functions are used with suitable lids only. If you are using a pressure cooker lid then use Pressure Cook, Slow Cook, Steam, Sous Vide, and Keep Warm functions. If you are using an air fryer lid then use Air Fry, Roast, Broil, Bake, and Dehydrate functions.

All the touch button functions given on the touch panel is easily customizable as per recipe needs. Almost every kind of tasty and delicious dish is made using instant pot pro crisp air fryer. The delay starts functions add a special advantage here, you can set delay time as per your convenience. It prepares your food as per your set time and you will get your food ready to serve hot. If you already have instant pot pro crisp at your home, then you have to move chapter 2 to check out healthy and delicious recipes

The Cookbook contains healthy, delicious, and mouth-watering recipes. The book includes all type of recipes start from breakfast and end with desserts. The recipes written in this cookbook are unique and written with step by step instructions. All the recipes written with their perfect preparation and cooking time. Every recipe ends with their exact nutritional values. This will help you to keep track of daily calorie consumption. The information on daily calorie intake will also help to keep you in a ketosis state. There are various cookbooks available on this topic, thanks for choosing my cookbook. I hope you love the healthy and delicious recipes written in this book.

BREAKFAST

1

BACON CHEESE QUICHE

Preparation Time: 10 minutes

Cooking Time: 20 minutes

Serve: 8

Ingredients:

•6 eggs

•1 1/2 cups Colby jack cheese, grated

•6 bacon slices, cooked & crumbled

•2/3 cup heavy whipping cream

•1/2 tsp pepper

•1/2 tsp salt

Directions:

1.In a bowl, whisk eggs with cream, cheese, pepper, and salt. Add bacon and stir well.

2.Place multi-functional rack into the instant pot.

3.Pour egg mixture into the greased cake pan and place the pan on top of the rack in the pot.

4.Secure pot with air fryer lid and cook on bake mode at 350 F for 20 minutes.

5.Slice and serve.

Nutritional Value (Amount per Serving):

- •Calories 242
- •Fat 19.2 g
- •Carbohydrates 1.6 g
- •Sugar 0.3 g
- •Protein 14.2 g
- •Cholesterol 171 mg

2

PEPPER ONION EGG MUFFINS

Preparation Time: 10 minutes

Cooking Time: 30 minutes

Serve: 6

Ingredients:

•6 eggs

•2 oz cheddar cheese, shredded

•1/4 cup almond milk

•1/4 cup bell peppers, chopped

•1/4 cup onion, chopped

•Pepper

•Salt

Directions:

1.Place the dehydrating tray in a multi-level air fryer basket.

2.In a bowl, whisk eggs with milk, pepper, and salt. Stir in cheese, pepper, and onion.

3.Pour egg mixture into the six silicone molds and place molds on dehydrating tray.

4.Place basket into the pot. Secure pot with air fryer lid and cook on bake mode at 350 F for 25-30 minutes.

5.Serve and enjoy.

Nutritional Value (Amount per Serving):

•Calories 128

•Fat 9.9 g

•Carbohydrates 1.9 g

•Sugar 1.2 g

•Protein 8.2 g

•Cholesterol 174 mg

3

SPINACH BREAKFAST QUICHE

Preparation Time: 10 minutes

Cooking Time: 25 minutes

Serve: 6

Ingredients:

•6 eggs

•1 cup cheddar cheese, shredded

•2 breakfast sausage links, chopped

•1 cup spinach, chopped

•1/3 cup heavy cream

•Pepper

•Salt

Directions:

1.In a bowl, whisk eggs with cream, pepper, and salt. Stir in 3/4 cup cheese, sausage, and spinach.

2.Place multi-functional rack into the instant pot.

3.Pour egg mixture into the greased cake pan and top with remaining cheese.

4.Place pan on top of the rack in the pot.

5.Secure pot with air fryer lid and cook on bake mode at 375 F for 25 minutes.

6.Slice and serve.

Nutritional Value (Amount per Serving):

•Calories 178

•Fat 14.3 g

•Carbohydrates 1 g

•Sugar 0.5 g

•Protein 11.4 g

•Cholesterol 196 mg

4

EASY OMELETTE MUFFINS

Preparation Time: 10 minutes

Cooking Time: 25 minutes

Serve: 6

Ingredients:

•4 eggs

•2 tbsp onion, diced

•1/4 cup zucchini, grated

•1/2 cup ham, cooked & chopped

•1/2 cup cheddar cheese, grated

•1/4 cup almond milk

•Pepper

•Salt

Directions:

1.Place the dehydrating tray in a multi-level air fryer basket.

2.In a bowl, whisk eggs with milk, pepper, and salt.

3.Add onion, zucchini, ham, and cheese and stir well.

4.Pour egg mixture into the six silicone muffin molds and place molds on dehydrating tray.

5.Place basket into the pot. Secure pot with air fryer lid and cook on bake mode at 350 F for 25-30 minutes.

6.Serve and enjoy.

Nutritional Value (Amount per Serving):

•Calories 123

•Fat 9.4 g

•Carbohydrates 1.8 g

•Sugar 0.8 g

•Protein 8.2 g

•Cholesterol 125 mg

5

ARTICHOKE SPINACH QUICHE

Preparation Time: 10 minutes

Cooking Time: 50 minutes

Serve: 8

Ingredients:

•6 eggs

•1 1/2 cups mozzarella cheese, shredded

•1 tbsp olive oil

•1 tsp garlic, minced

•6 oz can artichoke hearts, drained & chopped

•6 oz spinach, chopped

•1/2 cup heavy whipping cream

•1/2 cup sour cream

•Pepper

•Salt

Directions:

1.Heat oil in a pan over medium heat.

2.Add garlic and sauté for a minute. Add spinach and artichoke hearts and cook for 4 minutes. Remove pan from heat.

3.In a bowl, whisk eggs with sour cream, heavy cream, pepper, and salt. Add sautéed vegetables and 1 cup cheese and stir well.

4.Pour egg mixture into the greased cake pan and top with remaining cheese.

5.Place multi-functional rack into the instant pot.

6.Place pan on top of the rack in the pot.

7.Secure pot with air fryer lid and cook on bake mode at 350 F for 40-45 minutes.

8.Slice and serve.

Nutritional Value (Amount per Serving):

•Calories 146

•Fat 11.8 g

•Carbohydrates 3.2 g

•Sugar 0.6 g

•Protein 7.2 g

•Cholesterol 142 mg

6

HERB OMELETTE

Preparation Time: 10 minutes

Cooking Time: 15 minutes

Serve: 4

Ingredients:

•6 eggs

•1/2 cup almond milk

•3 tbsp parmesan cheese, grated

•5 oz cheddar cheese, grated

•5 oz plain yogurt

•1 lemon zest

•1 1/2 tsp fresh thyme, chopped

•1 1/2 tsp fresh mint, chopped

•1 1/2 tsp fresh rosemary, chopped

•1 1/2 tsp fresh basil, chopped

•Pepper

•Salt

Directions:

1.In a bowl, whisk eggs with milk, pepper, and salt.

2.Add parmesan cheese, cheddar cheese, yogurt, lemon zest, thyme, mint, rosemary, and basil and stir until well combined.

3.Pour egg mixture into the greased cake pan.

4.Place multi-functional rack into the instant pot.

5.Place pan on top of the rack in the pot.

6.Secure pot with air fryer lid and cook on bake mode at 400 F for 15 minutes.

7.Slice and serve.

Nutritional Value (Amount per Serving):

•Calories 235

•Fat 18 g

•Carbohydrates 4.8 g

•Sugar 3 g

•Protein 14.4 g

•Cholesterol 192 mg

7

HEALTHY BROCCOLI QUICHE

Preparation Time: 10 minutes

Cooking Time: 40 minutes

Serve: 6

Ingredients:

•6 eggs

•1 cup heavy cream

•1/3 cup onion, chopped

•8 oz cheddar cheese, shredded

•10 oz frozen broccoli, drained, chopped & cooked

•Pepper

•Salt

Directions:

1.In a bowl, whisk eggs with heavy cream, pepper, and salt.

2.Add onion, cheese, and broccoli and stir well.

3.Pour egg mixture into the greased cake pan.

4.Place multi-functional rack into the instant pot.

5.Place pan on top of the rack in the pot.

6.Secure pot with air fryer lid and cook on bake mode at 350 F for 35-40 minutes.

7.Slice and serve.

Nutritional Value (Amount per Serving):
•Calories 303
•Fat 24.5 g
•Carbohydrates 5.1 g
•Sugar 1.6 g
•Protein 16.8 g
•Cholesterol 231 mg

8

LIGHT & FLUFFY BAKED OMELETTE

Preparation Time: 10 minutes

Cooking Time: 35 minutes

Serve: 4

Ingredients:

- 5 eggs
- 4 oz ham, diced
- 1 cup cottage cheese
- 1 cup Monterey jack cheese, shredded
- 1/4 cup coconut flour
- Pepper
- Salt

Directions:

1. Add eggs, pepper, and salt into the mixing bowl and beat until light and fluffy.
2. Add ham, cottage cheese, Monterey jack cheese, and coconut flour and stir well.
3. Pour egg mixture into the greased cake pan.
4. Place multi-functional rack into the instant pot.
5. Place pan on top of the rack in the pot.

6.Secure pot with air fryer lid and cook on bake mode at 350 F for 35 minutes.

7.Slice and serve.

Nutritional Value (Amount per Serving):

•Calories 285

•Fat 17.7 g

•Carbohydrates 4.3 g

•Sugar 0.8 g

•Protein 26.4 g

•Cholesterol 250 mg

9

MEXICAN BREAKFAST CASSEROLE

Preparation Time: 10 minutes

Cooking Time: 35 minutes

Serve: 2

Ingredients:

•1 egg

•2 tbsp coconut flour

•1/3 cup almond milk

•1/4 cup cheddar cheese, shredded

•1/2 cup Monterey jack cheese, shredded

•1/2 tsp chili powder

•1/4 tsp oregano

•1/4 tsp ground cumin

•7 oz can green chilies, diced

•1/2 tsp garlic, minced

•1/4 onion, chopped

•1/2 lb ground beef

•1/2 tbsp olive oil

•Pepper

•Salt

Directions:

1.Heat oil in a pan over medium heat.

2.Add ground beef and cook for 5 minutes. Drain excess grease.

3.Add chili powder, oregano, cumin, green chilies, garlic, pepper, and salt and stir until well combined.

4.Remove pan from heat.

5.Add meat mixture into the greased cake pan. Sprinkle half cheese on top.

6.In a bowl, whisk egg, milk, and coconut flour.

7.Pour egg mixture on top of the cheese layer.

8.Place multi-functional rack into the instant pot.

9.Place pan on top of the rack in the pot.

10. Secure pot with air fryer lid and cook on bake mode at 325 F for 30 minutes.

11. Slice and serve.

Nutritional Value (Amount per Serving):

•Calories 504

•Fat 30 g

•Carbohydrates 10.5 g

•Sugar 2.4 g

•Protein 48.3 g

•Cholesterol 218 mg

10

CHEESY BREAKFAST CASSEROLE

Preparation Time: 10 minutes

Cooking Time: 25 minutes

Serve: 6

Ingredients:

•4 eggs
•1/2 tsp dried oregano
•1/4 tsp dried thyme
•1/2 tsp garlic powder
•1/2 tsp onion powder
•1/3 cup heavy cream
•6 bacon slices, cooked and chopped
•1 cup cheddar cheese, shredded
•3 tbsp water
•3 cups broccoli florets
•2 tbsp olive oil
•Pepper
•Salt

Directions:

1.Heat oil in a pan over medium heat.

2.Add broccoli and water and cook for 2-3 minutes or until broccoli softens. Remove pan from heat.

3.Drain broccoli and transfer into the greased cake pan. Top with bacon and shredded cheese and set aside.

4.In a bowl, whisk eggs with cream, oregano, thyme, garlic powder, onion powder, pepper, and salt.

5.Pour egg mixture over broccoli.

6.Place multi-functional rack into the instant pot.

7.Place pan on top of the rack in the pot.

8.Secure pot with air fryer lid and cook on bake mode at 350 F for 20 minutes.

9.Slice and serve.

Nutritional Value (Amount per Serving):

•Calories 301

•Fat 24.4 g

•Carbohydrates 4.4 g

•Sugar 1.3 g

•Protein 16.9 g

•Cholesterol 159 mg

11

HAM CHEESE EGG MUFFINS

Preparation Time: 10 minutes

Cooking Time: 20 minutes

Serve: 6

Ingredients:

•3 eggs

•1/2 cup cheddar cheese, shredded

•1/2 cup ham, chopped

•1/4 tsp baking powder

•2 tbsp heavy cream

•1/4 tsp salt

Directions:

1.Place the dehydrating tray in a multi-level air fryer basket.

2.In a bowl, whisk eggs with cream, baking powder, and salt.

3.Add cheese and ham and stir well.

4.Pour egg mixture into the six silicone muffin molds and place molds on dehydrating tray.

5.Place basket into the pot. Secure pot with air fryer lid and cook on bake mode at 350 F for 20 minutes.

6.Serve and enjoy.

Nutritional Value (Amount per Serving):

- Calories 57
- Fat 4.4 g
- Carbohydrates 0.5 g
- Sugar 0.1 g
- Protein 3.9 g
- Cholesterol 57 mg

12

TOMATO BREAKFAST QUICHE

Preparation Time: 10 minutes

Cooking Time: 40 minutes

Serve: 4

Ingredients:

•3 eggs

•1 tsp dried basil

•1 tomato, sliced

•1/4 cup scallions, sliced

•4 bacon slices, cooked & chopped

•1 cup broccoli florets, chopped

•5 oz almond milk

•2 cups cheddar cheese, shredded

•Pepper

•Salt

Directions:

1.Sprinkle 1/3 cheddar cheese into the greased cake pan. Spread broccoli on top.

2.Sprinkle 1/3 cheese on top of broccoli. Sprinkle scallions and bacon on top.

3.Sprinkle remaining cheese on top of the bacon layer.

4.In a bowl, whisk eggs with milk, pepper, and salt and pour over broccoli mixture.

5.Arrange tomato slices on top of the cheese layer.

6.Place multi-functional rack into the instant pot.

7.Place pan on top of the rack in the pot.

8.Secure pot with air fryer lid and cook on bake mode at 350 F for 40 minutes.

9.Slice and serve.

Nutritional Value (Amount per Serving):

•Calories 472

•Fat 38.5 g

•Carbohydrates 5.8 g

•Sugar 2.7 g

•Protein 27 g

•Cholesterol 203 mg

13

PERFECT SAUSAGE CHEESE BITES

Preparation Time: 10 minutes

Cooking Time: 20 minutes

Serve: 4

Ingredients:

•3 eggs, lightly beaten

•1/2 tsp baking powder

•1/3 cup coconut flour

•1 cup cheddar cheese, shredded

•4 oz cream cheese, softened

•1 lb breakfast sausage, cooked & drained

Directions:

1.Line multi-level air fryer basket with parchment paper.

2.Add all ingredients into the mixing bowl and mix until well combined.

3.Make small balls from the mixture and place it into the multi-level air fryer basket.

4.Place basket into the pot. Secure pot with air fryer lid and cook on bake mode at 350 F for 20 minutes.

5.Serve and enjoy.

Nutritional Value (Amount per Serving):

•Calories 650
•Fat 54.9 g
•Carbohydrates 2.3 g
•Sugar 0.5 g
•Protein 35.5 g
•Cholesterol 279 mg

14

EASY CHEESE EGG MUFFINS

Preparation Time: 10 minutes

Cooking Time: 30 minutes

Serve: 6

Ingredients:

•3 eggs, lightly beaten
•1/4 cup cheddar cheese, shredded
•1 bacon slice, cooked & crumbled
•1 1/2 tbsp water
•1/2 tsp baking powder
•5 tbsp almond flour
•2 tbsp coconut flour
•1/4 cup parmesan cheese, grated
•5 tbsp cottage cheese
•1/4 tsp salt

Directions:

1.Place the dehydrating tray in a multi-level air fryer basket.
2.In a bowl, whisk eggs with water, baking powder, and salt.
3.Add remaining ingredients and stir until well combined.
4.Pour egg mixture into the six silicone muffin molds and place molds on dehydrating tray.

5.Place basket into the pot. Secure pot with air fryer lid and cook on bake mode at 400 F for 25-30 minutes.

6.Serve and enjoy.

Nutritional Value (Amount per Serving):

•Calories 244

•Fat 18.4 g

•Carbohydrates 8.7 g

•Sugar 1.4 g

•Protein 13.6 g

•Cholesterol 94 mg

15

BREAKFAST BISCUITS

Preparation Time: 10 minutes
Cooking Time: 15 minutes
Serve: 6
Ingredients:

•2 eggs
•1 3/4 cup ham, chopped
•1 tbsp butter, melted
•1/4 cup heavy cream
•1 tsp baking powder
•2 cups almond flour
•1 cup cheddar cheese, shredded
•3 oz cream cheese
•1/4 tsp salt

Directions:

1.Line multi-level air fryer basket with parchment paper.

2.Add all ingredients into the mixing bowl and mix until well combined. Cover and place in the fridge for 15 minutes.

3.Make small balls from the mixture and place it into the multi-level air fryer basket.

4.Place basket into the pot. Secure pot with air fryer lid and cook on bake mode at 350 F for 15 minutes.

5.Serve and enjoy.

Nutritional Value (Amount per Serving):

•Calories 299

•Fat 24.5 g

•Carbohydrates 4.8 g

•Sugar 0.6 g

•Protein 16.3 g

•Cholesterol 124 mg

16

SAVORY BREAKFAST COOKIES

Preparation Time: 10 minutes

Cooking Time: 10 minutes

Serve: 1 2

Ingredients:

•3 eggs

•1 cup cheddar cheese, shredded

•1 tsp baking powder

•3/4 cup almond flour

•1/2 cup bell pepper, chopped

•1/2 cup onion, chopped

•4 oz pork sausage

•1/2 tsp pepper

•1/2 tsp salt

Directions:

1.Line multi-level air fryer basket with parchment paper.

2.Add sausage, bell pepper, and onion into the pan and cook over medium heat until onion is browned. Remove from heat and let it cool.

3.Add sausage mixture and remaining ingredients into the mixing bowl and mix until well combined.

4.Make small balls from the mixture and press down gently to form cookie shape then place it into the air fryer basket in batches.

5.Secure pot with air fryer lid and cook on bake mode at 375 F for 10 minutes.

6.Serve and enjoy.

Nutritional Value (Amount per Serving):

•Calories 100

•Fat 7.8 g

•Carbohydrates 1.7 g

•Sugar 0.6 g

•Protein 6.1 g

•Cholesterol 59 mg

17

ZUCCHINI MUFFINS

Preparation Time: 10 minutes

Cooking Time: 25 minutes

Serve: 6

Ingredients:

•3 eggs

•1/2 cup cheddar cheese, grated

•6 tbsp coconut flour

•1/2 tsp baking powder

•1 tbsp oregano, chopped

•1/4 cup butter, melted

•6 oz zucchini, grated

•Pepper

•Salt

Directions:

1.Place the dehydrating tray in a multi-level air fryer basket.

2.In a bowl, whisk eggs with melted butter, pepper, and salt.

3.Add remaining ingredients and stir until well combined.

4.Pour egg mixture into the six silicone muffin molds and place molds on dehydrating tray.

5.Place basket into the pot. Secure pot with air fryer lid and cook on bake mode at 350 F for 25 minutes.

6.Serve and enjoy.

Nutritional Value (Amount per Serving):

•Calories 205

•Fat 15.1 g

•Carbohydrates 9.9 g

•Sugar 1.8 g

•Protein 7.6 g

•Cholesterol 112 mg

18

CREAM CHEESE BLUEBERRY MUFFINS

Preparation Time: 10 minutes

Cooking Time: 20 minutes

Serve: 6

Ingredients:

•1 egg

•2 tbsp almonds, sliced

•2 tbsp blueberries

•1/4 tsp vanilla extract

•1/4 cup Swerve

•8 oz cream cheese

Directions:

1.Place the dehydrating tray in a multi-level air fryer basket.

2.In a bowl, beat cream cheese until smooth.

3.Add vanilla, egg, and sweetener and beat until well blended.

4.Add almonds and blueberries and fold well.

5.Pour mixture into the six silicone muffin molds and place molds on dehydrating tray.

6.Place basket into the pot. Secure pot with air fryer lid and cook on bake mode at 350 F for 20 minutes.

7.Serve and enjoy.

Nutritional Value (Amount per Serving):
•Calories 156
•Fat 14.9 g
•Carbohydrates 2 g
•Sugar 0.5 g
•Protein 4.2 g
•Cholesterol 69 mg

19

STUFFED OMELET PEPPERS

Preparation Time: 10 minutes

Cooking Time: 40 minutes

Serve: 4

Ingredients:

•8 eggs

•2 bell peppers, cut in half & remove seeds

•2 tbsp chives, chopped

•1 cup cheddar cheese, shredded

•4 bacon slices, cooked & crumbled

•1/4 cup almond milk

•Pepper

•Salt

Directions:

1.Place the dehydrating tray in a multi-level air fryer basket.

2.In a bowl, whisk eggs with milk, pepper, and salt. Add chives, cheese, and bacon and stir well.

3.Pour egg mixture into each bell pepper half.

4.Place bell peppers on dehydrating tray.

5.Place basket into the pot. Secure pot with air fryer lid and cook on bake mode at 400 F for 35-40 minutes.

6.Serve and enjoy.

Nutritional Value (Amount per Serving):

•Calories 397
•Fat 29.8 g
•Carbohydrates 6.7 g
•Sugar 4.4 g
•Protein 26.1 g
•Cholesterol 378 mg

20

CHEESY BAKED EGGS

Preparation Time: 10 minutes

Cooking Time: 10 minutes

Serve: 2

Ingredients:

- 4 eggs
- 1/4 cup basil, chopped
- 2 tbsp parmesan cheese, grated
- 1/4 cup cheddar cheese, shredded
- 1/4 cup almond milk
- 1 cup marinara sauce
- Pepper
- Salt

Directions:

1. Place the dehydrating tray in a multi-level air fryer basket.
2. Spray two ramekins with cooking spray.
3. Divide marinara sauce into the greased ramekins.
4. Top with eggs, almond milk, cheddar cheese, and parmesan cheese. Season with pepper and salt.
5. Place ramekins onto the dehydrating tray.

6.Place basket into the pot. Secure pot with air fryer lid and cook on bake mode at 400 F for 10 minutes.

7.Serve and enjoy.

Nutritional Value (Amount per Serving):

•Calories 384

•Fat 25.5 g

•Carbohydrates 20.1 g

•Sugar 12.8 g

•Protein 19.9 g

•Cholesterol 350 mg

21

BAKED CHEESE DIJON EGGS

Preparation Time: 10 minutes

Cooking Time: 15 minutes

Serve: 2

Ingredients:

•4 eggs

•2 tsp Dijon mustard

•1/2 cup cheddar cheese, shredded

•1/2 small tomato, diced

•Pepper

•Salt

Directions:

1.Place the dehydrating tray in a multi-level air fryer basket.

2.Spray two ramekins with cooking spray.

3.Break two eggs in each ramekin and season with pepper and salt. Add tomato on top.

4.Mix cheese and mustard and sprinkle evenly on top of eggs.

5.Place ramekins onto the dehydrating tray.

6.Place basket into the pot. Secure pot with air fryer lid and cook on bake mode at 350 F for 10-15 minutes.

7.Serve and enjoy.

Nutritional Value (Amount per Serving):

•Calories 247

•Fat 18.4 g

•Carbohydrates 2.2 g

•Sugar 1.5 g

•Protein 18.5 g

•Cholesterol 357 mg

22

CAPRESE EGG CUPS

Preparation Time: 10 minutes

Cooking Time: 8 minutes

Serve: 2

Ingredients:

•4 eggs

•2 tsp heavy cream

•8 basil leaves, chopped

•3 oz mozzarella cheese, chopped

•1 cup cherry tomatoes, cut in half

•Pepper

•Salt

Directions:

1.Place the dehydrating tray in a multi-level air fryer basket.

2.Spray two ramekins with cooking spray.

3.Add basil, cheese, and tomatoes evenly into the two ramekins.

4.Break 2 eggs into each ramekin and season with pepper and salt. Add 1 tsp heavy cream on top of the egg in each ramekin.

5.Place ramekins onto the dehydrating tray.

6.Place basket into the pot. Secure pot with air fryer lid and cook on bake mode at 350 F for 5-8 minutes.

7.Serve and enjoy.

Nutritional Value (Amount per Serving):

•Calories 280

•Fat 18.3 g

•Carbohydrates 5.9 g

•Sugar 3.1 g

•Protein 24 g

•Cholesterol 357 mg

23

ZUCCHINI COCONUT MUFFINS

Preparation Time: 10 minutes

Cooking Time: 25 minutes

Serve: 6

Ingredients:

•3 eggs

•1/4 cup walnuts, chopped

•3/4 cup zucchini, shredded

•1/2 tsp ground cinnamon

•1/8 tsp baking soda

•1/4 cup Swerve

•1/4 cup coconut flour

•2 1/2 tbsp olive oil

•Pepper

•Salt

Directions:

1.Place the dehydrating tray in a multi-level air fryer basket.

2.In a bowl, whisk eggs with oil, pepper, and salt.

3.Add remaining ingredients and stir until well combined.

4.Pour egg mixture into the six silicone muffin molds and place molds on dehydrating tray.

5.Place basket into the pot. Secure pot with air fryer lid and cook on bake mode at 350 F for 20-25 minutes.

6.Serve and enjoy.

Nutritional Value (Amount per Serving):

•Calories 140

•Fat 12.3 g

•Carbohydrates 4.4 g

•Sugar 1.5 g

•Protein 5.2 g

•Cholesterol 82 mg

24

EASY BREAKFAST CHEESE MUFFINS

Preparation Time: 10 minutes
Cooking Time: 20 minutes
Serve: 6
Ingredients:
- 1 egg, lightly beaten
- 6 tbsp heavy cream
- 2 tbsp butter, melted
- 1 cup cheddar cheese, shredded
- 3/4 tsp xanthan gum
- 1/2 tbsp Swerve
- 2 tbsp coconut flour
- 3/4 cup almond flour
- Pepper
- Salt

Directions:

1.Place the dehydrating tray in a multi-level air fryer basket.

2.In a bowl, whisk the egg with heavy cream, butter, pepper, and salt.

3.Add remaining ingredients and stir until well combined.

4.Pour egg mixture into the six silicone muffin molds and place molds on dehydrating tray.

5.Place basket into the pot. Secure pot with air fryer lid and cook on bake mode at 400 F for 20 minutes.

6.Serve and enjoy.

Nutritional Value (Amount per Serving):

•Calories 204

•Fat 18.7 g

•Carbohydrates 3.4 g

•Sugar 0.8 g

•Protein 7.2 g

•Cholesterol 78 mg

25

FLAVORFUL ZUCCHINI PEPPERONI MUFFINS

Preparation Time: 10 minutes

Cooking Time: 20 minutes

Serve: 6

Ingredients:

•2 eggs

•1 tsp garlic powder

•1/2 tsp thyme

•1/4 tsp baking powder

•3 tbsp coconut flour

•8 pepperoni slices, chopped

•1/2 cup cheddar cheese, shredded

•1 zucchini, grated & squeeze out all liquid

•Pepper

•Salt

Directions:

1.Place the dehydrating tray in a multi-level air fryer basket.

2.In a bowl, whisk eggs with garlic powder, thyme, baking powder, pepper, and salt.

3.Add remaining ingredients and stir until well combined.

4.Pour egg mixture into the six silicone muffin molds and place molds on dehydrating tray.

5.Place basket into the pot. Secure pot with air fryer lid and cook on bake mode at 400 F for 20 minutes.

6.Serve and enjoy.

Nutritional Value (Amount per Serving):

•Calories 120

•Fat 8.8 g

•Carbohydrates 4.1 g

•Sugar 1.6 g

•Protein 7.1 g

•Cholesterol 72 mg

26

GREEK SPINACH TOMATO FRITTATA

Preparation Time: 10 minutes

Cooking Time: 35 minutes

Serve: 3

Ingredients:

•6 eggs

•1/4 cup fresh basil, chopped

•1/2 cup baby spinach, chopped

•1/4 cup plain yogurt

•1/4 cup cheddar cheese, grated

•3/4 cups cherry tomatoes, cut in half

•Pepper

•Salt

Directions:

1.In a bowl, whisk eggs with yogurt, pepper, and salt.

2.Add spinach, basil, tomatoes, and cheese in greased cake pan.

3.Pour egg mixture over spinach mixture.

4.Place multi-functional rack into the instant pot.

5.Place pan on top of the rack in the pot.

6.Secure pot with air fryer lid and cook on bake mode at 390 F for 35 minutes.

7.Slice and serve.

Nutritional Value (Amount per Serving):

•Calories 188

•Fat 12.2 g

•Carbohydrates 4.2 g

•Sugar 3.4 g

•Protein 15.2 g

•Cholesterol 338 mg

27

EASY MEXICAN FRITTATA

Preparation Time: 10 minutes

Cooking Time: 25 minutes

Serve: 3

Ingredients:

- 4 eggs, scrambled
- 1/4 lb ground beef
- 1/4 cup salsa
- 1 tsp taco seasoning
- 1/2 tbsp olive oil
- 1/4 cup cheddar cheese, grated
- 2 scallions, chopped
- 1 tomato, sliced
- 1/2 green pepper, chopped
- Pepper
- Salt

Directions:

1. Heat oil in a pan over medium heat.
2. Add ground beef and cook until brown.
3. Add salsa, taco seasoning, scallions, and green pepper and stir well.

4.Transfer meat into the greased cake pan.

5.Arrange tomato slices on top of meat mixture.

6.In a bowl, whisk eggs with cheese, pepper, and salt.

7.Pour egg mixture over meat mixture.

8.Place multi-functional rack into the instant pot.

9.Place pan on top of the rack in the pot.

10. Secure pot with air fryer lid and cook on bake mode at 375 F for 25 minutes.

11. Slice and serve.

Nutritional Value (Amount per Serving):

•Calories 236

•Fat 14 g

•Carbohydrates 5.5 g

•Sugar 3 g

•Protein 22.4 g

•Cholesterol 262 mg

28

HEALTHY KALE MUFFINS

Preparation Time: 10 minutes

Cooking Time: 30 minutes

Serve: 4

Ingredients:

•3 eggs

•1/2 cup kale, chopped

•1/4 cup almond milk

•1/2 tsp garlic powder

•Pepper

•Salt

Directions:

1.Place the dehydrating tray in a multi-level air fryer basket.

2.In a bowl, whisk eggs with milk, garlic powder, pepper, and salt. Add kale and stir well.

3.Pour egg mixture into the four silicone muffin molds and place molds on dehydrating tray.

4.Place basket into the pot. Secure pot with air fryer lid and cook on bake mode at 350 F for 30 minutes.

5.Serve and enjoy.

Nutritional Value (Amount per Serving):

- •Calories 87
- •Fat 6.9 g
- •Carbohydrates 2.2 g
- •Sugar 0.8 g
- •Protein 4.8 g
- •Cholesterol 123 mg

29

VEGETABLE QUICHE CUPS

Preparation Time: 10 minutes

Cooking Time: 20 minutes

Serve: 6

Ingredients:

•4 eggs

•2 tbsp onion, chopped

•2 tbsp mushroom, diced

•1/4 cup cheddar cheese, shredded

•5 oz frozen spinach, chopped

•2 tbsp bell pepper, diced

•Pepper

•Salt

Directions:

1.Place the dehydrating tray in a multi-level air fryer basket.

2.In a bowl, whisk eggs with pepper and salt. Add remaining ingredients and stir until well combined.

3.Pour egg mixture into the six silicone muffin molds and place molds on dehydrating tray.

4.Place basket into the pot. Secure pot with air fryer lid and cook on bake mode at 375 F for 20 minutes.

5.Serve and enjoy.

Nutritional Value (Amount per Serving):

•Calories 81

•Fat 4.7 g

•Carbohydrates 4.5 g

•Sugar 2.5 g

•Protein 6 g

•Cholesterol 114 mg

30

SPINACH MUSHROOM FRITTATA

Preparation Time: 10 minutes

Cooking Time: 20 minutes

Serve: 2

Ingredients:

•6 eggs

•4 oz mushrooms, sliced & sautéed

•4 oz feta cheese, crumbled

•3 oz fresh spinach, sautéed

•Pepper

•Salt

Directions:

1.In a bowl, whisk eggs, pepper, and salt.

2.Add remaining ingredients and stir until well combined.

3.Pour egg mixture into the greased cake pan.

4.Place multi-functional rack into the instant pot.

5.Place pan on top of the rack in the pot.

6.Secure pot with air fryer lid and cook on bake mode at 350 F for 20 minutes.

7.Slice and serve.

Nutritional Value (Amount per Serving):

- •Calories 361
- •Fat 25.5 g
- •Carbohydrates 6.8 g
- •Sugar 4.5 g
- •Protein 27.7 g
- •Cholesterol 542 mg

31

PUMPKIN ALMOND MUFFINS

Preparation Time: 10 minutes

Cooking Time: 15 minutes

Serve: 4

Ingredients:

- 1 scoop vanilla protein powder
- 1/4 cup pumpkin puree
- 1/4 cup almond butter
- 1/2 tbsp cinnamon
- 1/4 cup almond flour
- 1/4 cup butter, melted
- 1/2 tsp baking powder

Directions:

1.Place the dehydrating tray in a multi-level air fryer basket.

2.In a bowl, mix all dry ingredients.

3.Add wet ingredients into the dry ingredients and stir to combine.

4.Pour batter into the four silicone muffin molds and place molds on a dehydrating tray.

5.Place basket into the pot. Secure pot with air fryer lid and cook on bake mode at 350 F for 15 minutes.

6.Serve and enjoy.

Nutritional Value (Amount per Serving):

•Calories 154

•Fat 13 g

•Carbohydrates 2.9 g

•Sugar 0.7 g

•Protein 7.7 g

•Cholesterol 31 mg

32

TUNA BREAKFAST MUFFINS

Preparation Time: 5 minutes

Cooking Time: 25 minutes

Serve: 6

Ingredients:

•2 eggs, lightly beaten

•1 can tuna, flaked

•1/4 cup sour cream

•1/4 cup mayonnaise

•1 tsp cayenne pepper

•1 1/2 cups cheddar cheese, shredded

•Pepper

•Salt

Directions:

1.Place the dehydrating tray in a multi-level air fryer basket.

2.Add all ingredients into the large bowl and mix until well combined.

3.Pour batter into the six silicone muffin molds and place molds on a dehydrating tray.

4.Place basket into the pot. Secure pot with air fryer lid and cook on bake mode at 350 F for 25 minutes.

5.Serve and enjoy.

Nutritional Value (Amount per Serving):

•Calories 250

•Fat 18.6 g

•Carbohydrates 3.4 g

•Sugar 0.9 g

•Protein 17.2 g

•Cholesterol 100 mg

33

JALAPENO MUFFINS

Preparation Time: 10 minutes

Cooking Time: 20 minutes

Serve: 4

Ingredients:

•3 eggs

•2 tbsp jalapenos, sliced

•2 tbsp almond milk

•2 1/2 tbsp olive oil

•1 1/2 tbsp Swerve

•5 tbsp coconut flour

•1 tsp baking powder

•Pepper

•Salt

Directions:

1.Place the dehydrating tray in a multi-level air fryer basket.

2.In a large bowl, mix coconut flour, baking powder, Swerve, pepper, and salt.

3.Stir in eggs, jalapenos, almond milk, and oil until well combined.

4.Pour egg mixture into the four silicone muffin molds and place molds on dehydrating tray.

5.Place basket into the pot. Secure pot with air fryer lid and cook on bake mode at 350 F for 20 minutes.

6.Serve and enjoy.

Nutritional Value (Amount per Serving):

•Calories 187

•Fat 16 g

•Carbohydrates 7.8 g

•Sugar 2.5 g

•Protein 6.2 g

•Cholesterol 123 mg

34

SIMPLE ASPARAGUS QUICHE

Preparation Time: 10 minutes

Cooking Time: 45 minutes

Serve: 4

Ingredients:

•5 eggs

•1 lb asparagus, trimmed, roasted & cut into pieces

•1/2 tsp garlic powder

•Pepper

•Salt

Directions:

1.In a bowl, whisk eggs with garlic powder, pepper, and salt.

2.Add asparagus in a greased cake pan.

3.Pour egg mixture over asparagus.

4.Place multi-functional rack into the instant pot.

5.Place pan on top of the rack in the pot.

6.Secure pot with air fryer lid and cook on bake mode at 400 F for 30 minutes.

7.Slice and serve.

Nutritional Value (Amount per Serving):

•Calories 103

- Fat 5.6 g
- Carbohydrates 5.1 g
- Sugar 2.6 g
- Protein 9.5 g
- Cholesterol 205 mg

35

CAULIFLOWER EGG CASSEROLE

Preparation Time: 10 minutes
Cooking Time: 45 minutes
Serve: 3
Ingredients:

•5 eggs
•2 cups cauliflower rice
•1/2 tsp paprika
•4 oz cheddar cheese, shredded
•6 oz bacon, cooked and crumbled
•1/4 cup heavy whipping cream
•Pepper
•Salt

Directions:

1.Spread cauliflower rice into the greased cake pan and top with half cheddar cheese.

2.In a bowl, whisk eggs with cream, paprika, pepper, and salt and pour over cauliflower.

3.Top with remaining cheese and bacon.

4.Place multi-functional rack into the instant pot.

5.Place pan on top of the rack in the pot.

6.Secure pot with air fryer lid and cook on bake mode at 350 F for 45 minutes.

7.Slice and serve.

Nutritional Value (Amount per Serving):

•Calories 637

•Fat 48.5 g

•Carbohydrates 6.8 g

•Sugar 3.5 g

•Protein 42.5 g

•Cholesterol 389 mg

36

SIMPLE & TASTY EGG BAKE

Preparation Time: 10 minutes

Cooking Time: 30 minutes

Serve: 4

Ingredients:

•4 eggs

•4 oz cream cheese

•1/3 cup half and half

•1/2 tsp garlic powder

•Pepper

•Salt

Directions:

1.Add eggs, half and half, cream cheese, garlic powder, pepper, and salt into the blender and blend until smooth.

2.Pour egg mixture into the greased cake pan.

3.Place multi-functional rack into the instant pot.

4.Place pan on top of the rack in the pot.

5.Secure pot with air fryer lid and cook on bake mode at 350 F for 30 minutes.

6.Slice and serve.

Nutritional Value (Amount per Serving):

- •Calories 189
- •Fat 16.6 g
- •Carbohydrates 2.2 g
- •Sugar 0.5 g
- •Protein 8.3 g
- •Cholesterol 202 mg

37

SPINACH ZUCCHINI EGG CASSEROLE

Preparation Time: 10 minutes

Cooking Time: 30 minutes

Serve: 4

Ingredients:

•5 eggs

•1/2 small zucchini, sliced into rounds

•1/4 cup spinach

•2 cherry tomatoes, halved

•1/4 cup mushrooms, sliced

•1/4 cup ham, chopped

•5 tbsp heavy cream

•Pepper

•Salt

Directions:

1.In a large bowl, whisk eggs with heavy cream, pepper, and salt.

2.Stir in tomatoes, mushrooms, ham, zucchini, and spinach.

3.Pour egg mixture into the greased cake pan.

4.Place multi-functional rack into the instant pot.

5.Place pan on top of the rack in the pot.

6.Secure pot with air fryer lid and cook on bake mode at 350 F for 30 minutes.

7.Slice and serve.

Nutritional Value (Amount per Serving):

•Calories 172

•Fat 13.3 g

•Carbohydrates 4.4 g

•Sugar 2.4 g

•Protein 9.6 g

•Cholesterol 235 mg

38

RANCH EGG QUICHE

Preparation Time: 10 minutes

Cooking Time: 55 minutes

Serve: 3

Ingredients:

•4 eggs

•1/2 cup sour cream

•1/2 lb ground Italian sausage

•1/2 tbsp ranch seasoning

•3/4 cups cheddar cheese, shredded

•Pepper

•Salt

Directions:

1.Brown the sausage in a pan over medium heat and drain well.

2.Transfer sausage into the greased cake pan.

3.In a bowl, whisk eggs with ranch seasoning, and sour cream. Stir in cheddar cheese.

4.Pour egg mixture over sausage.

5.Place multi-functional rack into the instant pot.

6.Place pan on top of the rack in the pot.

7.Secure pot with air fryer lid and cook on bake mode at 350 F for 55 minutes.

8.Slice and serve.

Nutritional Value (Amount per Serving):

•Calories 512

•Fat 40.6 g

•Carbohydrates 3.8 g

•Sugar 2 g

•Protein 29 g

•Cholesterol 318 mg

39

DELICIOUS CHICKEN QUICHE

Preparation Time: 10 minutes

Cooking Time: 45 minutes

Serve: 3

Ingredients:

•4 eggs

•1/8 cup mozzarella cheese, shredded

•2.5 oz cooked chicken breast, chopped

•1/8 tsp pepper

•1/4 tsp oregano

•1/8 tsp onion powder

•1/8 tsp garlic powder

•1/4 tsp salt

Directions:

1.In a bowl, whisk eggs with oregano, onion powder, pepper, and salt. Stir in cheese and chicken.

2.Pour egg mixture into the greased cake pan.

3.Place multi-functional rack into the instant pot.

4.Place pan on top of the rack in the pot.

5.Secure pot with air fryer lid and cook on bake mode at 350 F for 45 minutes.

6.Slice and serve.

Nutritional Value (Amount per Serving):

•Calories 116

•Fat 6.6 g

•Carbohydrates 0.8 g

•Sugar 0.5 g

•Protein 12.8 g

•Cholesterol 234 mg

40

ITALIAN BREAKFAST MUFFINS

Preparation Time: 10 minutes

Cooking Time: 15 minutes

Serve: 6

Ingredients:

•2 eggs

•4 egg whites

•1/4 cup feta cheese, crumbled

•1/4 cup olives, diced

•1/4 cup tomatoes, diced

•1/2 cup almond milk

•1/4 cup onion, diced

•Pepper

•Salt

Directions:

1.Place the dehydrating tray in a multi-level air fryer basket.

2.In a bowl, whisk eggs with milk, pepper, and salt.

3.Add remaining ingredients and stir everything well.

4.Pour egg mixture into the six silicone muffin molds and place molds on dehydrating tray.

5.Place basket into the pot. Secure pot with air fryer lid and cook on bake mode at 350 F for 15 minutes.

6.Serve and enjoy.

Nutritional Value (Amount per Serving):

•Calories 105

•Fat 8.2 g

•Carbohydrates 2.7 g

•Sugar 1.6 g

•Protein 5.8 g

•Cholesterol 60 mg

POULTRY

41

DRY RUB CHICKEN WINGS

Preparation Time: 10 minutes

Cooking Time: 20 minutes

Serve: 4

Ingredients:

•8 chicken wings

•1/4 tsp black pepper

•1/2 tsp chili powder

•1/2 tsp garlic powder

•1/4 tsp salt

Directions:

1.Line multi-level air fryer basket with parchment paper.

2.In a bowl, mix chili powder, garlic powder, pepper, and salt.

3.Add chicken wings to the bowl toss to coat.

4.Add chicken wings into the multi-level air fryer basket.

5.Place basket into the pot. Secure pot with air fryer lid and cook on air fry mode at 350 F for 20 minutes. Flip wings after 15 minutes.

6.Serve and enjoy.

Nutritional Value (Amount per Serving):

•Calories 557

•Fat 21.7 g
•Carbohydrates 0.5 g
•Sugar 0.1 g
•Protein 84.6 g
•Cholesterol 260 mg

42

SPICY CHICKEN WINGS

Preparation Time: 10 minutes

Cooking Time: 20 minutes

Serve: 3

Ingredients:

•6 chicken wings

•1 tbsp olive oil

•1 tsp smoked paprika

•Pepper

•Salt

Directions:

1.Line multi-level air fryer basket with parchment paper.

2.In a bowl, mix chicken wings, paprika, olive oil, pepper, and salt.

3.Place marinated chicken wings into the refrigerator for 1 hour.

4.Add marinated chicken wings into the basket.

5.Place basket into the pot. Secure pot with air fryer lid and cook on air fry mode at 390 F for 20 minutes. Flip wings after 12 minutes.

6.Serve and enjoy.

Nutritional Value (Amount per Serving):

•Calories 640

•Fat 27.3 g

•Carbohydrates 6 g

•Sugar 0 g

•Protein 85.5 g

•Cholesterol 260 mg

43

SOUTHWEST CHICKEN BREASTS

Preparation Time: 10 minutes

Cooking Time: 25 minutes

Serve: 2

Ingredients:

•1/2 lb chicken breasts, skinless and boneless

•1/4 tsp chili powder

•1/2 tbsp olive oil

•1 tbsp lime juice

•1/8 tsp garlic powder

•1/8 tsp onion powder

•1/4 tsp cumin

•1/8 tsp salt

Directions:

1.Line multi-level air fryer basket with parchment paper.

2.Add all ingredients into the zip-lock bag and shake well and place it in the refrigerator for 1 hour.

3.Add a marinated chicken wing into the basket.

4.Place basket into the pot. Secure pot with air fryer lid and cook on air fry mode at 400 F for 25 minutes. Turn halfway through.

5.Serve and enjoy.

Nutritional Value (Amount per Serving):

•Calories 254

•Fat 12 g

•Carbohydrates 2.4 g

•Sugar 0.5 g

•Protein 33 g

•Cholesterol 101 mg

44

CHICKEN BURGER PATTIES

Preparation Time: 10 minutes

Cooking Time: 18 minutes

Serve: 2

Ingredients:

•2 cups chicken minced

•1.75 oz almond flour

•1/2 tbsp oregano

•1 oz mozzarella cheese

•Pepper

•Salt

Directions:

1.Line multi-level air fryer basket with parchment paper.

2.Add all ingredients into the mixing bowl and mix until well combined.

3.Make two equal shapes of patties from the mixture and place it into the basket.

4.Place basket into the pot. Secure pot with air fryer lid and cook on air fry mode at 360 F for 18 minutes. Turn halfway through.

5.Serve and enjoy.

Nutritional Value (Amount per Serving):

•Calories 291

•Fat 22.7 g

•Carbohydrates 7.3 g

•Sugar 1.6 g

•Protein 17.9 g

•Cholesterol 50 mg

45

SIMPLE CHICKEN BREAST

Preparation Time: 10 minutes

Cooking Time: 12 minutes

Serve: 2

Ingredients:

•2 chicken breast, skinless & boneless

•2 tsp olive oil

•1/2 tsp garlic powder

•Pepper

•Salt

Directions:

1.Line multi-level air fryer basket with parchment paper.

2.Brush chicken breast with oil and season with garlic powder, pepper, and salt.

3.Place chicken breast into the basket.

4.Place basket into the pot. Secure pot with air fryer lid and cook on air fry mode at 375 F for 12 minutes. Turn halfway through.

5.Serve and enjoy.

Nutritional Value (Amount per Serving):

•Calories 170

- Fat 7.5 g
- Carbohydrates 0.5 g
- Sugar 0.2 g
- Protein 23.9 g
- Cholesterol 72 mg

46

PESTO CHICKEN DRUMSTICKS

Preparation Time: 10 minutes

Cooking Time: 20 minutes

Serve: 4

Ingredients:

•4 chicken drumsticks

•1 tbsp ginger, sliced

•8 garlic cloves

•1/2 jalapeno pepper

•1/2 cup cilantro

•2 tbsp lemon juice

•2 tbsp olive oil

•1 tsp salt

Directions:

1.Line multi-level air fryer basket with parchment paper.

2.Add all the ingredients except chicken into the blender and blend until smooth.

3.Pour blended mixture into the mixing bowl.

4.Add chicken drumsticks into the bowl and stir well to coat.

5.Place marinated chicken drumsticks in the refrigerator for 2 hours.

6.Place marinated chicken drumsticks into the basket.

7.Place basket into the pot. Secure pot with air fryer lid and cook on air fry mode at 390 F for 20 minutes. Turn halfway through.

8.Serve and enjoy.

Nutritional Value (Amount per Serving):

•Calories 154

•Fat 9.8 g

•Carbohydrates 3.3 g

•Sugar 0.4 g

•Protein 13.3 g

•Cholesterol 40 mg

47

HERB CHICKEN BREAST

Preparation Time: 10 minutes
Cooking Time: 25 minutes
Serve: 2
Ingredients:
•10 oz chicken breast halves
•1/4 tsp dried thyme
•1/4 tsp paprika
•1 tbsp butter
•1/4 tsp black pepper
•1/4 tsp garlic powder
•1/4 tsp dried rosemary
•1/4 tsp salt
Directions:
1.Line multi-level air fryer basket with parchment paper.
2.In a small bowl, combine together butter, black pepper, garlic powder, rosemary, thyme, paprika, and salt.
3.Rub chicken halves with butter mixture and place into the basket.
4.Place basket into the pot. Secure pot with air fryer lid and

cook on air fry mode at 375 F for 25 minutes. Turn halfway through.

5.Serve and enjoy.

Nutritional Value (Amount per Serving):

•Calories 324

•Fat 16.3 g

•Carbohydrates 0.7 g

•Sugar 0.1 g

•Protein 41.2 g

•Cholesterol 141 mg

48

TASTY BUFFALO CHICKEN WINGS

Preparation Time: 10 minutes

Cooking Time: 24 minutes

Serve: 2

Ingredients:

•1/2 lb chicken wings

•1/4 cup hot sauce

Directions:

1.Line multi-level air fryer basket with parchment paper.

2.Place chicken wings in the basket.

3.Place basket into the pot. Secure pot with air fryer lid and cook on air fry mode at 400 F for 24 minutes. Turn halfway through.

4.Transfer chicken wings to the bowl.

5.Add hot sauce and toss well.

6.Serve and enjoy.

Nutritional Value (Amount per Serving):

•Calories 219

•Fat 8.5 g

•Carbohydrates 0.5 g

- Sugar 0.4 g
- Protein 33 g
- Cholesterol 101 mg

49

MEATBALLS

Preparation Time: 10 minutes

Cooking Time: 10 minutes

Serve: 4

Ingredients:

•1 lb ground chicken

•1 egg, lightly beaten

•3 tbsp fresh parsley, chopped

•1 small onion, minced

•1/2 cup mozzarella cheese, shredded

•1 1/2 tbsp taco seasoning

•3 garlic cloves, minced

•Pepper

•Salt

Directions:

1.Line multi-level air fryer basket with parchment paper.

2.Add all ingredients into the large mixing bowl and mix until well combined.

3.Make small balls from the mixture and place them in the basket.

4.Place basket into the pot. Secure pot with air fryer lid and cook on air fry mode at 400 F for 10 minutes.

5.Serve and enjoy.

Nutritional Value (Amount per Serving):

•Calories 261

•Fat 10.6 g

•Carbohydrates 3.4 g

•Sugar 0.9 g

•Protein 36.1 g

•Cholesterol 145 mg

50

LEMON PEPPER CHICKEN WINGS

Preparation Time: 10 minutes

Cooking Time: 16 minutes

Serve: 4

Ingredients:

•1 lb chicken wings

•1 tbsp olive oil

•1 tsp lemon pepper seasoning

•1 tsp salt

Directions:

1.Line multi-level air fryer basket with parchment paper.

2.Add chicken wings and remaining ingredients into the large bowl and toss well.

3.Add chicken wings into the basket.

4.Place basket into the pot. Secure pot with air fryer lid and cook on air fry mode at 400 F for 16 minutes. Flip halfway through.

5.Serve and enjoy.

Nutritional Value (Amount per Serving):

•Calories 247

- Fat 11.9 g
- Carbohydrates 0.3 g
- Sugar 0 g
- Protein 32.9 g
- Cholesterol 101 mg

51

ASIAN CHICKEN TENDERS

Preparation Time: 10 minutes

Cooking Time: 10 minutes

Serve: 3

Ingredients:

•12 oz chicken tenders, skinless and boneless

•1 tbsp ginger, grated

•1/4 cup sesame oil

•1/2 cup soy sauce

•2 tbsp green onion, chopped

•3 garlic cloves, chopped

•2 tsp sesame seeds, toasted

•1/4 tsp pepper

Directions:

1.Line multi-level air fryer basket with parchment paper.

2.In a large bowl, mix green onion, garlic, sesame seeds, ginger, sesame oil, soy sauce, and pepper.

3.Add chicken tenders into the bowl and coat well and place it in the refrigerator overnight.

4.Add marinated chicken tenders into the basket.

5.Place basket into the pot. Secure pot with air fryer lid and

cook on air fry mode at 390 F for 10 minutes. Flip halfway through.

6.Serve and enjoy.

Nutritional Value (Amount per Serving):

•Calories 423

•Fat 27.7 g

•Carbohydrates 6.4 g

•Sugar 0.9 g

•Protein 36.3 g

•Cholesterol 101 mg

52

CURRIED TURKEY DRUMSTICKS

Preparation Time: 10 minutes

Cooking Time: 22 minutes

Serve: 2

Ingredients:

•2 turkey drumsticks

•1/4 tsp cayenne pepper

•2 tbsp red curry paste

•1/4 tsp pepper

•1/3 cup coconut milk

•1 1/2 tbsp ginger, minced

•1 tsp kosher salt

Directions:

1.Line multi-level air fryer basket with parchment paper.

2.Add all ingredients into the zip-lock bag, seal bag, and place in the refrigerator overnight.

3.Place marinated turkey drumsticks into the basket.

4.Place basket into the pot. Secure pot with air fryer lid and cook on air fry mode at 390 F for 22 minutes. Flip halfway through.

5.Serve and enjoy.

Nutritional Value (Amount per Serving):

•Calories 279

•Fat 18.3 g

•Carbohydrates 8.4 g

•Sugar 1.5 g

•Protein 20.4 g

•Cholesterol 0 mg

53

DIJON DRUMSTICKS

Preparation Time: 10 minutes

Cooking Time: 28 minutes

Serve: 2

Ingredients:

•4 turkey drumsticks

•1/2 tbsp ginger, minced

•2 tbsp Dijon mustard

•1/3 tsp paprika

•1/3 cup sherry wine

•1/3 cup coconut milk

•Pepper

•Salt

Directions:

1.Line multi-level air fryer basket with parchment paper.

2.Add all ingredients into the zip-lock bag, seal bag, and place in the refrigerator overnight.

3.Place marinated turkey drumsticks into the basket.

4.Place basket into the pot. Secure pot with air fryer lid and cook on air fry mode at 380 F for 28 minutes. Flip halfway through.

5.Serve and enjoy.

Nutritional Value (Amount per Serving):

•Calories 365

•Fat 18.3 g

•Carbohydrates 5.3 g

•Sugar 1.9 g

•Protein 39.8 g

•Cholesterol 0 mg

54

SPICY CHICKEN WINGS

Preparation Time: 10 minutes

Cooking Time: 25 minutes

Serve: 4

Ingredients:

•2 lbs chicken wings

•1/2 tsp Worcestershire sauce

•1/2 tsp Tabasco

•6 tbsp butter, melted

•12 oz hot sauce

Directions:

1.Line multi-level air fryer basket with parchment paper.

2.Add chicken wings into the basket.

3.Place basket into the pot. Secure pot with air fryer lid and cook on air fry mode at 380 F for 25 minutes. Flip halfway through.

4.Meanwhile, in a bowl, mix hot sauce, Worcestershire sauce, and butter. Set aside.

5.Add cooked chicken wings into the sauce and toss well.

6.Serve and enjoy.

Nutritional Value (Amount per Serving):

•Calories 594
•Fat 34.4 g
•Carbohydrates 1.6 g
•Sugar 1.2 g
•Protein 66.2 g
•Cholesterol 248 mg

55

DELICIOUS FAJITA CHICKEN

Preparation Time: 10 minutes

Cooking Time: 15 minutes

Serve: 4

Ingredients:

•4 chicken breasts, boneless & sliced

•1 bell pepper, sliced

•2 tbsp fajita seasoning

•2 tbsp olive oil

•1 onion, sliced

Directions:

1.Line multi-level air fryer basket with parchment paper.

2.In a bowl, add chicken and remaining ingredients and toss well.

3.Add chicken mixture into the basket.

4.Place basket into the pot. Secure pot with air fryer lid and cook on air fry mode at 380 F for 15 minutes. Flip halfway through.

5.Serve and enjoy.

Nutritional Value (Amount per Serving):

•Calories 374

- •Fat 17.9 g
- •Carbohydrates 8 g
- •Sugar 2.7 g
- •Protein 42.8 g
- •Cholesterol 130 mg

56

CHINESE CHICKEN WINGS

Preparation Time: 10 minutes

Cooking Time: 30 minutes

Serve: 2

Ingredients:

•4 chicken wings

•1 tbsp soy sauce

•1 tbsp Chinese spice

•1 tsp mixed spice

•Pepper

•Salt

Directions:

1.Line multi-level air fryer basket with parchment paper.

2.Add chicken wings and remaining ingredients into the mixing bowl and toss well.

3.Transfer chicken wings into the basket.

4.Place basket into the pot. Secure pot with air fryer lid and cook on air fry mode at 350 F for 30 minutes. Flip halfway through.

5.Serve and enjoy.

Nutritional Value (Amount per Serving):

- •Calories 567
- •Fat 22.1 g
- •Carbohydrates 0.9 g
- •Sugar 0.2 g
- •Protein 85.7 g
- •Cholesterol 260 mg

57

CARIBBEAN CHICKEN THIGHS

Preparation Time: 10 minutes

Cooking Time: 10 minutes

Serve: 8

Ingredients:

•3 lbs chicken thigh, skinless and boneless

•1 tbsp cayenne

•1 tbsp cinnamon

•1 tbsp coriander powder

•3 tbsp coconut oil, melted

•1/2 tsp ground nutmeg

•1/2 tsp ground ginger

•Pepper

•Salt

Directions:

1.Line multi-level air fryer basket with parchment paper.

2.In a small bowl, mix together all ingredients except chicken.

3.Rub bowl mixture all over the chicken thighs.

4.Add chicken thighs into the basket.

5.Place basket into the pot. Secure pot with air fryer lid and

cook on air fry mode at 390 F for 10 minutes. Flip halfway through.

6.Serve and enjoy.

Nutritional Value (Amount per Serving):

•Calories 373

•Fat 17.9 g

•Carbohydrates 1.2 g

•Sugar 0.1 g

•Protein 49.3 g

•Cholesterol 151 mg

58

GARLIC HERB CHICKEN BREASTS

Preparation Time: 10 minutes

Cooking Time: 15 minutes

Serve: 6

Ingredients:

•2 lbs chicken breasts, skinless and boneless

•3 garlic cloves, minced

•1/4 cup yogurt

•2 tsp garlic herb seasoning

•1 tsp onion powder

•1/4 cup mayonnaise

•1/4 tsp salt

Directions:

1.Line multi-level air fryer basket with parchment paper.

2.In a small bowl, mix mayonnaise, seasoning, onion powder, garlic, and yogurt.

3.Brush chicken with mayonnaise mixture and season with salt.

4.Place chicken breasts into the basket.

5.Place basket into the pot. Secure pot with air fryer lid and

cook on air fry mode at 380 F for 15 minutes. Flip halfway through.

6.Serve and enjoy.

Nutritional Value (Amount per Serving):

•Calories 336

•Fat 14.6 g

•Carbohydrates 3.9 g

•Sugar 1.5 g

•Protein 44.6 g

•Cholesterol 138 mg

59

CRISPY CHICKEN TENDERS

Preparation Time: 10 minutes

Cooking Time: 15 minutes

Serve: 6

Ingredients:

•8 oz chicken breast tenderloins

•1 egg, lightly beaten

•1 cup almond flour

•1/4 cup heavy whipping cream

•1 tsp pepper

•1 tsp salt

Directions:

1.Line multi-level air fryer basket with parchment paper.

2.In a bowl, whisk egg, heavy whipping cream, pepper, and salt.

3.In a shallow dish, add the almond flour.

4.Dip chicken in egg mixture then coats with almond flour mixture.

5.Place coated chicken into the basket.

6.Place basket into the pot. Secure pot with air fryer lid and

cook on air fry mode at 400 F for 15 minutes. Flip halfway through.

7.Serve and enjoy.

Nutritional Value (Amount per Serving):

•Calories 89

•Fat 5.1 g

•Carbohydrates 1.4 g

•Sugar 0.2 g

•Protein 9.5 g

•Cholesterol 58 mg

60

CHEESE HERB CHICKEN WINGS

Preparation Time: 10 minutes

Cooking Time: 15 minutes

Serve: 4

Ingredients:

•2 lbs chicken wings

•1/2 cup parmesan cheese, grated

•1 tsp herb de Provence

•1 tsp smoked paprika

•Salt

Directions:

1.Line multi-level air fryer basket with parchment paper.

2.In a small bowl, mix cheese, herb de Provence, paprika, and salt.

3.Coat chicken wings with cheese mixture and place it into the basket.

4.Place basket into the pot. Secure pot with air fryer lid and cook on air fry mode at 350 F for 15 minutes. Flip halfway through.

5.Serve and enjoy.

Nutritional Value (Amount per Serving):

- •Calories 472
- •Fat 19.5 g
- •Carbohydrates 0.7 g
- •Sugar 0.1 g
- •Protein 69.7 g
- •Cholesterol 210 mg

61

DELICIOUS MUSTARD CHICKEN TENDERS

Preparation Time: 10 minutes

Cooking Time: 20 minutes

Serve: 4

Ingredients:

•1 lbs chicken tenders

•1/2 tsp paprika

•1 garlic clove, minced

•2 tbsp fresh tarragon, chopped

•1/2 cup whole grain mustard

•1/2 oz fresh lemon juice

•1/2 tsp pepper

•1/4 tsp kosher salt

Directions:

1.Line multi-level air fryer basket with parchment paper.

2.Add all ingredients except chicken to the large bowl and mix well.

3.Add chicken to the bowl and stir until well coated.

4.Place coated chicken tenders into the multi-level air fryer basket.

5.Place basket into the pot. Secure pot with air fryer lid and cook on bake mode at 400 F for 15-20 minutes.

6.Serve and enjoy.

Nutritional Value (Amount per Serving):

•Calories 242

•Fat 9.5 g

•Carbohydrates 3.1 g

•Sugar 0.1 g

•Protein 33.2 g

•Cholesterol 101 mg

62

LEMON GARLIC CHICKEN DRUMSTICKS

Preparation Time: 10 minutes

Cooking Time: 40 minutes

Serve: 4

Ingredients:

•2 lbs chicken drumsticks

•2 tbsp parsley, chopped

•1 fresh lemon juice

•8 garlic cloves, sliced

•2 tbsp olive oil

•Pepper

•Salt

Directions:

1.Line multi-level air fryer basket with parchment paper.

2.Brush chicken drumsticks with lemon juice and oil.

3.Place chicken drumstick into the multi-level air fryer basket. Add parsley, garlic, pepper, and salt on top of chicken.

4.Place basket into the pot. Secure pot with air fryer lid and cook on bake mode at 400 F for 35-40 minutes.

5.Serve and enjoy.

Nutritional Value (Amount per Serving):

- Calories 456
- Fat 20.1 g
- Carbohydrates 2.4 g
- Sugar 0.3 g
- Protein 62.9 g
- Cholesterol 200 mg

63

BAKED CHICKEN TENDERS

Preparation Time: 10 minutes

Cooking Time: 35 minutes

Serve: 4

Ingredients:

•2 lbs chicken tenders

•2 tbsp olive oil

•3 dill sprigs

•1 large zucchini

•1 cup grape tomatoes

•For topping:

•1 tbsp fresh lemon juice

•1 tbsp fresh dill, chopped

•2 tbsp feta cheese, crumbled

•1 tbsp olive oil

Directions:

1.Line multi-level air fryer basket with parchment paper.

2.Coat chicken with oil and season with salt and place into the multi-level air fryer basket. Add zucchini, dill, and tomatoes on top of chicken.

3.Place basket into the pot. Secure pot with air fryer lid and cook on bake mode at 400 F for 30 minutes.

4.Meanwhile, in a small bowl, stir together all topping ingredients.

5.Place chicken onto the serving plate then top with vegetables and discard dill sprigs.

6.Sprinkle topping mixture on top of chicken and vegetables.

7.Serve and enjoy.

Nutritional Value (Amount per Serving):

•Calories 563

•Fat 28.7 g

•Carbohydrates 6.5 g

•Sugar 2.9 g

•Protein 68.3 g

•Cholesterol 206 mg

64

PAPRIKA CHICKEN BREASTS

Preparation Time: 10 minutes
Cooking Time: 35 minutes
Serve: 4
Ingredients:

- 4 chicken breasts, skinless and boneless, cut into chunks
- 2 tbsp smoked paprika
- 3 tbsp olive oil
- 2 tsp garlic, minced
- 2 tbsp lemon juice
- Pepper
- Salt

Directions:

1. Line multi-level air fryer basket with parchment paper.
2. In a small bowl, mix garlic, paprika, lemon juice, and olive oil.
3. Season chicken with pepper and salt and rub with garlic mixture.
4. Place chicken breasts into the multi-level air fryer basket.
5. Place basket into the pot. Secure pot with air fryer lid and cook on bake mode at 350 F for 30-35 minutes.

6.Serve and enjoy.

Nutritional Value (Amount per Serving):

•Calories 381

•Fat 21.8 g

•Carbohydrates 2.6 g

•Sugar 0.5 g

•Protein 42.9 g

•Cholesterol 130 mg

65

LEMON GARLIC CHICKEN DRUMSTICKS

Preparation Time: 10 minutes

Cooking Time: 40 minutes

Serve: 4

Ingredients:

•2 lbs chicken drumsticks

•10 garlic cloves, sliced

•2 tbsp olive oil

•1 fresh lemon juice

•2 tbsp parsley, chopped

Directions:

1.Line multi-level air fryer basket with parchment paper.

2.Place chicken in the multi-level air fryer basket.

3.Sprinkle parsley and garlic over the chicken.

4.Pour lemon juice and olive oil on top of chicken.

5.Place basket into the pot. Secure pot with air fryer lid and cook on bake mode at 400 F for 35-40 minutes.

6.Serve and enjoy.

Nutritional Value (Amount per Serving):

•Calories 458

- Fat 20.1 g
- Carbohydrates 2.9 g
- Sugar 0.4 g
- Protein 63 g
- Cholesterol 200 mg

66

CHICKEN BURGER PATTIES

Preparation Time: 10 minutes

Cooking Time: 25 minutes

Serve: 5

Ingredients:

•1 lb ground chicken

•1/8 tsp red pepper flakes

•1 egg, lightly beaten

•1 cup Monterey jack cheese, grated

•1 cup carrot, grated

•1 cup cauliflower, grated

•2 garlic cloves, minced

•1/2 cup onion, minced

•3/4 cup almond flour

•Pepper

•Salt

Directions:

1.Line multi-level air fryer basket with parchment paper.

2.Add all ingredients into the mixing bowl and mix until well combined.

3.Make equal shapes of patties from the mixture and place them in the multi-level air fryer basket.

4.Place basket into the pot. Secure pot with air fryer lid and cook on bake mode at 400 F for 25 minutes.

5.Serve and enjoy.

Nutritional Value (Amount per Serving):

•Calories 314

•Fat 16.6 g

•Carbohydrates 5.9 g

•Sugar 2.4 g

•Protein 34.6 g

•Cholesterol 134 mg

67

MEATBALLS

Preparation Time: 10 minutes

Cooking Time: 25 minutes

Serve: 4

Ingredients:

•1 lb ground chicken

•2 garlic cloves, minced

•1/2 cup parmesan cheese, grated

•1/2 cup almond flour

•1 egg, lightly beaten

•2 tbsp cilantro, chopped

•1 tbsp olive oil

•1/2 tsp red pepper flakes

•1/4 cup shallots, chopped

•Pepper

•Salt

Directions:

1.Line multi-level air fryer basket with parchment paper.

2.Add all ingredients into the mixing bowl and mix until well combined.

3.Make small balls from meat mixture and place in the multi-level air fryer basket.

4.Place basket into the pot. Secure pot with air fryer lid and cook on bake mode at 400 F for 25 minutes. Turn meatballs after 15 minutes.

5.Serve and enjoy.

Nutritional Value (Amount per Serving):

•Calories 328

•Fat 17.2 g

•Carbohydrates 3.6 g

•Sugar 0.3 g

•Protein 39 g

•Cholesterol 150 mg

68

TURKEY MEATBALLS

Preparation Time: 10 minutes

Cooking Time: 18 minutes

Serve: 6

Ingredients:

•1 lb ground turkey

•1 tsp cumin

•2 cups zucchini, grated

•1 tsp dried oregano

•1 tbsp garlic, minced

•1 tbsp nutritional yeast

•1 tbsp dried onion flakes

•2 eggs, lightly beaten

•1 tbsp basil, chopped

•1/3 cup coconut flour

•Pepper

•Salt

Directions:

1.Line multi-level air fryer basket with parchment paper.

2.Add all ingredients into the mixing bowl and mix until well combined.

3.Make small balls from meat mixture and place in the multi-level air fryer basket.

4.Place basket into the pot. Secure pot with air fryer lid and cook on bake mode at 400 F for 18 minutes.

5.Serve and enjoy.

Nutritional Value (Amount per Serving):

•Calories 219

•Fat 11.6 g

•Carbohydrates 7.6 g

•Sugar 2.4 g

•Protein 25.4 g

•Cholesterol 132 mg

69

PARMESAN CHICKEN MEATBALLS

Preparation Time: 10 minutes

Cooking Time: 20 minutes

Serve: 6

Ingredients:

•2 lbs ground chicken

•2 tbsp olive oil

•1/2 cup parmesan cheese, grated

•1 cup almond flour

•1 egg, lightly beaten

•1 tbsp fresh parsley, chopped

•1 tsp Italian seasoning

•1 tsp garlic, minced

Directions:

1.Line multi-level air fryer basket with parchment paper.

2.Add all ingredients into the bowl and mix until well combined.

3.Make balls from mixture and place in the multi-level air fryer basket.

4.Place basket into the pot. Secure pot with air fryer lid and cook on bake mode at 400 F for 20 minutes.

5.Serve and enjoy.

Nutritional Value (Amount per Serving):

•Calories 392

•Fat 20.8 g

•Carbohydrates 1.6 g

•Sugar 0.3 g

•Protein 48.1 g

•Cholesterol 168 mg

70

CHICKEN & MUSHROOMS

Preparation Time: 10 minutes

Cooking Time: 30 minutes

Serve: 4

Ingredients:

•2 lbs chicken breasts, halved

•1/3 cup sun-dried tomatoes

•8 oz mushrooms, sliced

•1 tsp salt

Directions:

1.Line multi-level air fryer basket with parchment paper.

2.Place chicken, tomatoes, mushrooms, and salt in a multi-level air fryer basket.

3.Place basket into the pot. Secure pot with air fryer lid and cook on bake mode at 400 F for 30 minutes.

4.Serve and enjoy.

Nutritional Value (Amount per Serving):

•Calories 446

•Fat 17 g

•Carbohydrates 2.4 g

- Sugar 1.4 g
- Protein 67.5 g
- Cholesterol 202 mg

71

MEATBALLS

Preparation Time: 10 minutes

Cooking Time: 25 minutes

Serve: 6

Ingredients:

•1 lb ground turkey

•1 tsp olive oil

•1 egg, lightly beaten

•2 tbsp chives, chopped

•2 tbsp almond flour

•1/2 tsp ground ginger

•1/2 tsp salt

Directions:

1.Line multi-level air fryer basket with parchment paper.

2.Add all ingredients into the mixing bowl and mix until well combined.

3.Make small balls from meat mixture and place in the multi-level air fryer basket.

4.Place basket into the pot. Secure pot with air fryer lid and cook on bake mode at 375 F for 25 minutes.

5.Serve and enjoy.

Nutritional Value (Amount per Serving):
•Calories 219
•Fat 14.5 g
•Carbohydrates 2.2 g
•Sugar 0.4 g
•Protein 23.6 g
•Cholesterol 104 mg

72

JUICY CHICKEN THIGHS

Preparation Time: 10 minutes

Cooking Time: 40 minutes

Serve: 6

Ingredients:

•2 lbs chicken thighs, skinless and boneless

•1 fresh lemon juice

•8 garlic cloves, sliced

•2 tbsp olive oil

•Pepper

•Salt

Directions:

1.Line multi-level air fryer basket with parchment paper.

2.Coat chicken with oil and lemon juice. Season with pepper and salt.

3.Place chicken and garlic in a multi-level air fryer basket.

4.Place basket into the pot. Secure pot with air fryer lid and cook on bake mode at 400 F for 30-40 minutes.

5.Serve and enjoy.

Nutritional Value (Amount per Serving):

•Calories 335

- •Fat 16 g
- •Carbohydrates 1.5 g
- •Sugar 0.2 g
- •Protein 44.1 g
- •Cholesterol 135 mg

73

TURKEY BREAST WITH VEGETABLES

Preparation Time: 10 minutes

Cooking Time: 45 minutes

Serve: 4

Ingredients:

•1 lb turkey breast, cut into 1-inch cubes

•1 tsp garlic powder

•2 tbsp olive oil

•1 cup mushrooms, cleaned

•1/2 lb Brussels sprouts, cut in half

•Pepper

•Salt

Directions:

1.Line multi-level air fryer basket with parchment paper.

2.Brush turkey breast with oil and season with garlic powder, pepper, and salt.

3.Place turkey breast, mushrooms, and Brussels sprouts in a multi-level air fryer basket.

4.Place basket into the pot. Secure pot with air fryer lid and cook on bake mode at 350 F for 45 minutes.

5.Serve and enjoy.

Nutritional Value (Amount per Serving):

•Calories 209

•Fat 9.1 g

•Carbohydrates 11 g

•Sugar 5.7 g

•Protein 22 g

•Cholesterol 49 mg

74

DRIED HERB CHICKEN BREASTS

Preparation Time: 10 minutes

Cooking Time: 10 minutes

Serve: 2

Ingredients:

•2 chicken breasts, boneless and skinless

•2 tsp garlic, minced

•1 tsp dried thyme

•1 tsp dried oregano

•1 tsp dried basil

•1 tbsp olive oil

•Pepper

•Salt

Directions:

1.Line multi-level air fryer basket with parchment paper.

2.Brush chicken breasts with oil and season with pepper and salt.

3.In a small bowl, mix garlic, thyme, oregano, and basil and rub all over chicken breasts.

4.Place chicken breasts in a multi-level air fryer basket.

5.Place basket into the pot. Secure pot with air fryer lid and cook on bake mode at 400 F for 10 minutes.

6.Serve and enjoy.

Nutritional Value (Amount per Serving):

•Calories 345

•Fat g

•Carbohydrates 0.5 g

•Sugar 0.1 g

•Protein 84.6 g

•Cholesterol 260 mg

75

DELICIOUS TURKEY PATTIES

Preparation Time: 10 minutes

Cooking Time: 22 minutes

Serve: 4

Ingredients:

•1 lb ground turkey

•1 tsp Italian seasoning

•1 tbsp olive oil

•1 tbsp garlic paste

•4 oz feta cheese, crumbled

•1 1/4 cup spinach, chopped

•Pepper

•Salt

Directions:

1.Line multi-level air fryer basket with parchment paper.

2.Add all ingredients into the mixing bowl and mix until well combined.

3.Make four equal shapes of patties from the mixture and place in the multi-level air fryer basket.

4.Place basket into the pot. Secure pot with air fryer lid and

cook on bake mode at 390 F for 22 minutes. Turn patties halfway through.

5.Serve and enjoy.

Nutritional Value (Amount per Serving):

•Calories 335

•Fat 22.4 g

•Carbohydrates 2.3 g

•Sugar 1.3 g

•Protein 35.5 g

•Cholesterol 142 mg

76

MEATBALLS

Preparation Time: 10 minutes

Cooking Time: 20 minutes

Serve: 4

Ingredients:

•1 lb ground turkey

•1 egg, lightly beaten

•1/2 cup almond flour

•1/2 tsp red pepper, crushed

•1 tbsp lemongrass, chopped

•1 1/2 tbsp fish sauce

•2 garlic cloves, minced

•1/4 cup basil, chopped

•3 tbsp scallions, chopped

Directions:

1.Line multi-level air fryer basket with parchment paper.

2.Add all ingredients into the mixing bowl and mix until well combined.

3.Make small balls from meat mixture and place in the multi-level air fryer basket.

4.Place basket into the pot. Secure pot with air fryer lid and cook on bake mode at 390 F for 20 minutes.

5.Serve and enjoy.

Nutritional Value (Amount per Serving):

•Calories 269

•Fat 15.4 g

•Carbohydrates 3.4 g

•Sugar 1.3 g

•Protein 33.9 g

•Cholesterol 157 mg

77

ITALIAN CHICKEN BREASTS

Preparation Time: 10 minutes

Cooking Time: 25 minutes

Serve: 4

Ingredients:

•4 chicken breasts, skinless & boneless

•1 tbsp olive oil

For rub:

•1 tsp oregano

•1 tsp thyme

•1 tsp parsley

•1 tsp onion powder

•1 tsp basil

•Pepper

•Salt

Directions:

1.Line multi-level air fryer basket with parchment paper.

2.Brush chicken breast with olive oil.

3.In a small bowl, mix together all rub ingredients and rub all over the chicken.

4.Place chicken in a multi-level air fryer basket.

5.Place basket into the pot. Secure pot with air fryer lid and cook on bake mode at 390 F for 25 minutes. Turn chicken halfway through.

6.Serve and enjoy.

Nutritional Value (Amount per Serving):

•Calories 312

•Fat 14.4 g

•Carbohydrates 0.9 g

•Sugar 0.2 g

•Protein 42.4 g

•Cholesterol 130 mg

78

DELICIOUS CHICKEN TENDERS

Preparation Time: 10 minutes

Cooking Time: 16 minutes

Serve: 4

Ingredients:

•1 lb chicken tenders

For rub:

•1 tbsp paprika

•1/2 tbsp onion powder

•1/2 tsp cayenne pepper

•1/2 tbsp dried thyme

•1 tbsp garlic powder

•Pepper

•Salt

Directions:

1.Line multi-level air fryer basket with parchment paper.

2.In a bowl, add all rub ingredients and mix well.

3.Add chicken tenders into the bowl and coat well with rub.

4.Place chicken tenders in a multi-level air fryer basket.

5.Place basket into the pot. Secure pot with air fryer lid and

cook on bake mode at 370 F for 16 minutes. Turn chicken tenders halfway through.

6.Serve and enjoy.

Nutritional Value (Amount per Serving):

•Calories 232

•Fat 8.7 g

•Carbohydrates 3.6 g

•Sugar 1 g

•Protein 33.6 g

•Cholesterol 101 mg

79

LEMON PEPPER CHICKEN THIGHS

Preparation Time: 10 minutes

Cooking Time: 35 minutes

Serve: 4

Ingredients:

•4 chicken thighs

•2 tbsp fresh lemon juice

•1/2 tsp paprika

•1/2 tsp Italian seasoning

•1/2 tsp onion powder

•1 tsp garlic powder

•1 tbsp lemon pepper seasoning

•2 tbsp olive oil

•1 tsp salt

Directions:

1.Line multi-level air fryer basket with parchment paper.

2.Add chicken to the bowl.

3.Mix lemon juice and olive oil and pour over chicken.

4.Mix paprika, Italian seasoning, onion powder, garlic powder, lemon pepper seasoning, and salt and rub all over the chicken.

5.Place chicken in a multi-level air fryer basket.

6.Place basket into the pot. Secure pot with air fryer lid and cook on bake mode at 400 F for 35 minutes.

7.Serve and enjoy.

Nutritional Value (Amount per Serving):

•Calories 349

•Fat 18.1 g

•Carbohydrates 2.2 g

•Sugar 0.5 g

•Protein 42.7 g

•Cholesterol 130 mg

80

BAKED CHICKEN FAJITAS

Preparation Time: 10 minutes

Cooking Time: 40 minutes

Serve: 6

Ingredients:

•2 lbs chicken thighs, skinless, boneless, and cut into strips

•1 large onion, sliced

•1 red bell pepper, sliced

•2 tbsp olive oil

•2 tbsp fajita seasoning

•2 tsp salt

Directions:

1.Line multi-level air fryer basket with parchment paper.

2.Add all ingredients into the large mixing bowl and toss well.

3.Add the chicken mixture to a multi-level air fryer basket.

4.Place basket into the pot. Secure pot with air fryer lid and cook on bake mode at 400 F for 35-40 minutes.

5.Serve and enjoy.

Nutritional Value (Amount per Serving):

•Calories 354

- •Fat 16 g
- •Carbohydrates 5.9 g
- •Sugar 2.1 g
- •Protein 44.2 g
- •Cholesterol 135 mg

81

JUICY SHREDDED CHICKEN

Preparation Time: 10 minutes

Cooking Time: 13 minutes

Serve: 2

Ingredients:

•1 lb chicken breasts

•1 cup chicken stock

•1/4 tsp black pepper

•1/2 tsp onion powder

•1/2 tsp garlic powder

•1/4 tsp salt

Directions:

1.Season chicken with onion powder, garlic powder, pepper, and salt and place into the instant pot.

2.Pour chicken stock over the chicken.

3.Secure pot with pressure cooking lid and cook on high for 13 minutes.

4.Once done, allow to release pressure naturally for 10 minutes then release remaining using quick release. Remove lid.

5.Shred the chicken using a fork and serve.

Nutritional Value (Amount per Serving):

•Calories 441
•Fat 17.1 g
•Carbohydrates 1.5 g
•Sugar 0.7 g
•Protein 66.2 g
•Cholesterol 202 mg

82

CREAMY CHICKEN BREASTS

Preparation Time: 10 minutes

Cooking Time: 25 minutes

Serve: 2

Ingredients:

•2 chicken breasts

•1 cup sour cream

•3 bacon slices, cooked and crumbled

•2 jalapeno peppers, chopped

•1 1/2 tbsp chili powder

•1 cup chicken broth

Directions:

1.Add chili powder, jalapeno peppers, and broth in the instant pot and stir well.

2.Add chicken into the pot and Secure pot with pressure cooking lid and cook on high for 25 minutes.

3.Once done, release pressure using quick release. Remove lid.

4.Stir in bacon and sour cream.

5.Serve and enjoy.

Nutritional Value (Amount per Serving):

- •Calories 721
- •Fat 48.7 g
- •Carbohydrates 9.9 g
- •Sugar 1.4 g
- •Protein 59.7 g
- •Cholesterol 212 mg

83

FLAVORFUL SALSA CHICKEN

Preparation Time: 10 minutes

Cooking Time: 8 minutes

Serve: 2

Ingredients:

•2 chicken breasts, boneless and skinless

•1 cup of salsa

•1/2 tsp red chili powder

•1/4 cup fresh lime juice

•1/2 cup feta cheese, crumbled

•1/2 tsp ground cumin

•1 tbsp olive oil

Directions:

1.Add oil into the instant pot and set the pot on sauté mode.

2.Place chicken in the pot and sauté until lightly brown. Transfer chicken to a plate.

3.Add cumin, chili powder, salsa, and lime juice to the pot and stir well.

4.Return the chicken into the pot.

5.Secure pot with pressure cooking lid and cook on high for 8 minutes.

6.Once done, release pressure using quick release. Remove lid.

7.Top with feta cheese and serve.

Nutritional Value (Amount per Serving):

•Calories 477

•Fat 26.2 g

•Carbohydrates 10.7 g

•Sugar 5.7 g

•Protein 49.8 g

•Cholesterol 163 mg

84

LEMON CHICKEN THIGHS

Preparation Time: 10 minutes

Cooking Time: 15 minutes

Serve: 2

Ingredients:

•1 lb chicken thighs

•2 tbsp white wine

•1/2 cup tangerine juice

•2 tbsp lemon juice

•1/8 tsp thyme, dried

•1/2 tsp fresh rosemary, chopped

•1 tsp garlic, minced

•Pepper

•Salt

Directions:

1.Place chicken into the instant pot.

2.In a bowl, mix tangerine juice, garlic, white wine, lemon juice, thyme, rosemary, pepper, and salt and pour over chicken.

3.Secure pot with pressure cooking lid and cook on high for 15 minutes.

4.Once done, allow to release pressure naturally. Remove lid.

5.Serve and enjoy.

Nutritional Value (Amount per Serving):

•Calories 473

•Fat 17 g

•Carbohydrates 7.4 g

•Sugar 6 g

•Protein 66.3 g

•Cholesterol 202 mg

85

HERB LEMON ORANGE CHICKEN

Preparation Time: 10 minutes

Cooking Time: 15 minutes

Serve: 2

Ingredients:

•1 lb chicken thighs

•1 tsp garlic, minced

•1/2 tsp fresh rosemary, chopped

•2 tbsp white wine

•2 tbsp lemon juice

•1/8 tsp thyme, dried

•1/2 cup orange juice

•Pepper

•Salt

Directions:

1.Place chicken into the instant pot.

2.In a bowl, mix orange juice, garlic, white wine, lemon juice, thyme, rosemary, pepper, and salt and pour over chicken.

3.Secure pot with pressure cooking lid and cook on high for 15 minutes.

4.Once done, allow to release pressure naturally. Remove lid.

5.Serve and enjoy.

Nutritional Value (Amount per Serving):

•Calories 478
•Fat 17.1 g
•Carbohydrates 7.9 g
•Sugar 5.7 g
•Protein 66.3 g
•Cholesterol 202 mg

86

JALAPENO CHICKEN DRUMSTICKS

Preparation Time: 10 minutes

Cooking Time: 25 minutes

Serve: 2

Ingredients:

•6 chicken drumsticks

•1/4 cup fresh cilantro, chopped

•1 1/2 cup tomatillo sauce

•1 tsp olive oil

•1 tsp oregano

•1 jalapeno pepper, chopped

•Pepper

•Salt

Directions:

1.Season chicken with pepper, oregano, and salt.

2.Add oil into the instant pot and set the pot on sauté mode.

3.Add chicken to the pot and cook until brown.

4.Stir in jalapeno, cilantro, and tomatillo sauce.

5.Secure pot with pressure cooking lid and cook on high for 20 minutes.

6.Once done, allow to release pressure naturally. Remove lid.

7.Serve and enjoy.

Nutritional Value (Amount per Serving):

•Calories 266

•Fat 10.3 g

•Carbohydrates 2.5 g

•Sugar 1 g

•Protein 38.2 g

•Cholesterol 121 mg

87

LEMON PEPPER CHICKEN THIGHS

Preparation Time: 10 minutes

Cooking Time: 15 minutes

Serve: 2

Ingredients:

•4 chicken thighs, bone-in

•1 tsp lemon pepper seasoning

•2 tbsp butter, melted

•1 lemon juice

•1/4 tsp oregano

•1 tsp parsley flakes

•4 garlic cloves, diced

•1 small onion, diced

•1 cup chicken broth

•1/4 tsp pepper

•1/2 tsp salt

Directions:

1.Place chicken in the instant pot.

2.Pour remaining ingredients on top of chicken.

3.Secure pot with pressure cooking lid and cook on high for 15 minutes.

4.Once done, allow to release pressure naturally for 5 minutes then release remaining using quick release. Remove lid.

5.Serve and enjoy.

Nutritional Value (Amount per Serving):

•Calories 709

•Fat 34.2 g

•Carbohydrates 7.2 g

•Sugar 2.4 g

•Protein 88.2 g

•Cholesterol 290 mg

88

DELICIOUS ARTICHOKE CHICKEN BREASTS

Preparation Time: 10 minutes

Cooking Time: 5 minutes

Serve: 4

Ingredients:

•4 chicken breasts, skinless and boneless

•14 oz can artichoke hearts, drained

•1/4 cup water

•1/2 tsp dried thyme

•14 oz chicken broth

•1/4 cup butter

•1/2 tsp smoked paprika

•1/2 tsp pepper

•1 tsp salt

Directions:

1.Add all ingredients except artichoke into the instant pot and stir well.

2.Secure pot with pressure cooking lid and cook on high for 2 minutes.

3.Once done, release pressure using quick release. Remove lid.

4.Add artichoke hearts and stir well.
5.Serve and enjoy.

Nutritional Value (Amount per Serving):

•Calories 148
•Fat 23 g
•Carbohydrates 5.7 g
•Sugar 1.2 g
•Protein 46.1 g
•Cholesterol 160 mg

89

BUFFALO CHICKEN BREASTS

Preparation Time: 10 minutes

Cooking Time: 12 minutes

Serve: 8

Ingredients:

•2 lbs chicken breasts, skinless and boneless

•1/2 cup celery, diced

•1/4 cup feta cheese, crumbled

•1/2 cup chicken broth

•1/2 cup buffalo wing sauce

•2/3 cup onion, chopped

Directions:

1.Add all ingredients except cheese into the instant pot and stir well.

2.Secure pot with pressure cooking lid and cook on high for 12 minutes.

3.Once done, allow to release pressure naturally. Remove lid.

4.Shred the chicken using a fork.

5.Top with crumbled cheese and serve.

Nutritional Value (Amount per Serving):

•Calories 235

- •Fat 9.5 g
- •Carbohydrates 1.4 g
- •Sugar 0.7 g
- •Protein 33.9 g
- •Cholesterol 105 mg

90

RANCH CHICKEN BREASTS

Preparation Time: 10 minutes

Cooking Time: 12 minutes

Serve: 8

Ingredients:

•2 lbs chicken breasts, skinless and boneless

•1 cup chicken broth

•1/4 cup bacon, cooked & chopped

•1 oz ranch packet seasoning

•4 oz cream cheese, cubed

Directions:

1.Add all ingredients into the instant pot and stir well.

2.Secure pot with pressure cooking lid and cook on high for 12 minutes.

3.Once done, release pressure using quick release. Remove lid.

4.Shred the chicken using a fork.

5.Serve and enjoy.

Nutritional Value (Amount per Serving):

•Calories 284

- •Fat 13.8 g
- •Carbohydrates 0.5 g
- •Sugar 0.1 g
- •Protein 34.7 g
- •Cholesterol 117 mg

91

EASY SALSA VERDE CHICKEN

Preparation Time: 5 minutes

Cooking Time: 12 minutes

Serve: 8

Ingredients:

•2 lbs chicken breasts, skinless and boneless

•3/4 cup onion, sliced

•1 cup salsa Verde

•Pepper

•Salt

Directions:

1.Add all ingredients into the instant pot and stir well.

2.Secure pot with pressure cooking lid and cook on high for 12 minutes.

3.Once done, release pressure using quick release. Remove lid.

4.Shred the chicken using a fork.

5.Serve and enjoy.

Nutritional Value (Amount per Serving):

•Calories 227

- •Fat 8.5 g
- •Carbohydrates 2.3 g
- •Sugar 0.9 g
- •Protein 33.3 g
- •Cholesterol 101 mg

92

CREAMY JALAPENO CHICKEN BREASTS

Preparation Time: 10 minutes

Cooking Time: 25 minutes

Serve: 2

Ingredients:

•2 chicken breasts, skinless and boneless

•2 jalapeno peppers, chopped

•1 1/2 tbsp chili powder

•3 bacon slices, cooked & chopped

•1 cup chicken stock

•1 cup sour cream

Directions:

1.Add chili powder, jalapeno peppers, and broth in the instant pot and stir well.

2.Place chicken into the pot and secure pot with pressure cooking lid and cook on high for 25 minutes.

3.Once done, release pressure using quick release. Remove lid.

4.Add sour cream and bacon, stir well.

5.Serve and enjoy.

Nutritional Value (Amount per Serving):

- •Calories 706
- •Fat 48.3 g
- •Carbohydrates 9.8 g
- •Sugar 1.4 g
- •Protein 57.7 g
- •Cholesterol 212 mg

93

TACO CHICKEN BREASTS

Preparation Time: 10 minutes

Cooking Time: 15 minutes

Serve: 4

Ingredients:

•1 lb chicken breasts, boneless

•6 oz can tomato paste

•15 oz can tomatoes, diced

•1 lb chicken thighs, boneless

•1/2 cup hot water

•1 packet taco seasoning

•Pepper

•Salt

Directions:

1.Add all ingredients into the instant pot and mix well.

2.Secure pot with pressure cooking lid and cook on high for 15 minutes.

3.Once done, allow to release pressure naturally. Remove lid.

4.Shred the chicken using a fork.

5.Serve and enjoy.

Nutritional Value (Amount per Serving):

- Calories 186
- Fat 2.6 g
- Carbohydrates 8.8 g
- Sugar 5.4 g
- Protein 34 g
- Cholesterol 101 mg

94

EASY CHICKEN FAJITAS

Preparation Time: 10 minutes

Cooking Time: 12 minutes

Serve: 6

Ingredients:

•2 lbs chicken tenders, boneless

•14 oz can tomatoes with green chilies, diced

•1 onion, diced

•3 bell peppers, sliced

•1 package taco seasoning

•Pepper

•Salt

Directions:

1.Add all ingredients into the instant pot and stir well.

2.Secure pot with pressure cooking lid and cook on high for 12 minutes.

3.Once done, release pressure using quick release. Remove lid.

4.Serve and enjoy.

Nutritional Value (Amount per Serving):

•Calories 328

- Fat 11.4 g
- Carbohydrates 9.1 g
- Sugar 5.5 g
- Protein 45.1 g
- Cholesterol 135 mg

95

TASTY CHICKEN CURRY

Preparation Time: 10 minutes

Cooking Time: 15 minutes

Serve: 6

Ingredients:

•2 lbs chicken breast, cut into pieces

•16 oz can tomato sauce

•2 garlic cloves, minced

•6 oz tomato paste

•1 cup onion, chopped

•6 oz can coconut milk

•2 tbsp curry powder

•1 tsp salt

Directions:

1.Add all ingredients except chicken into the instant pot and stir well.

2.Add chicken into the pot.

3.Secure pot with pressure cooking lid and cook on high for 15 minutes.

4.Once done, allow to release pressure naturally. Remove lid.

5.Stir well and serve.

Nutritional Value (Amount per Serving):
- •Calories 260
- •Fat 9.6 g
- •Carbohydrates 9 g
- •Sugar 5.2 g
- •Protein 34.2 g
- •Cholesterol 97 mg

96

CHILI LIME CHICKEN

Preparation Time: 10 minutes

Cooking Time: 10 minutes

Serve: 2

Ingredients:

•1 lb chicken thighs, skinless and boneless

•6 garlic cloves, minced

•1 tsp cumin

•1/4 tsp black pepper

•1 tbsp chili powder

•1 1/2 lime juice

•1/2 cup chicken broth

•1 tsp kosher salt

Directions:

1.Add all ingredients into the instant pot and stir well.

2.Secure pot with pressure cooking lid and cook on high for 10 minutes.

3.Once done, allow to release pressure naturally. Remove lid.

4.Shred the chicken using a fork.

5.Serve and enjoy.

Nutritional Value (Amount per Serving):

- •Calories 479
- •Fat 18.1 g
- •Carbohydrates 8.7 g
- •Sugar 1.1 g
- •Protein 68.2 g
- •Cholesterol 202 mg

97

DIJON CHICKEN BREASTS

Preparation Time: 10 minutes
Cooking Time: 13 minutes
Serve: 4
Ingredients:
•2 lbs chicken breasts, skinless and boneless
•1 cup almond milk
•1/2 tsp pepper
•1 tbsp Dijon mustard
•1 tsp sage, dried
•1 tbsp rosemary, dried
•1 tsp thyme, dried
•1/2 tsp salt
Directions:
1.In a bowl, add all ingredients and mix until chicken is well coated.
2.Place marinated chicken in the refrigerator for 1 hour.
3.Pour marinated chicken into the instant pot.
4.Secure pot with pressure cooking lid and cook on high for 13 minutes.

5.Once done, release pressure using quick release. Remove lid.

6.Serve and enjoy.

Nutritional Value (Amount per Serving):

•Calories 576

•Fat 31.5 g

•Carbohydrates 4.5 g

•Sugar 2 g

•Protein 67.3 g

•Cholesterol 202 mg

98

SPICY TURKEY LEGS

Preparation Time: 10 minutes

Cooking Time: 25 minutes

Serve: 4

Ingredients:

•2 turkey legs

•2 green onions, chopped

•2 tbsp orange zest

•2 tbsp chili sauce

•1/2 cup soy sauce

•1/2 tsp pepper

•1 cup chicken stock

•1 green chili, chopped

•1 tsp sea salt

Directions:

1.Season turkey legs with pepper and salt and place into the instant pot. Pour the stock into the pot.

2.Secure pot with pressure cooking lid and cook on high for 15 minutes.

3.Once done, release pressure using quick release. Remove lid.

4.Set pot on sauté mode.
5.Add chili sauce and soy sauce. Stir well.
6.Add onion, orange zest, and green chili.
7.Stir well and cook for 10 minutes,
8.Serve and enjoy.

Nutritional Value (Amount per Serving):

•Calories 100
•Fat 3.7 g
•Carbohydrates 4.2 g
•Sugar 1 g
•Protein 12.3 g
•Cholesterol 30 mg

99

TOMATO TURKEY BREASTS

Preparation Time: 10 minutes

Cooking Time: 20 minutes

Serve: 4

Ingredients:

•2 lbs ground turkey breast

•15 oz can tomatoes, diced

•2 bell pepper, chopped

•1 tbsp butter

•2 garlic cloves, chopped

•1 cup chicken broth

•1 onion, sliced

Directions:

1.Add butter into the instant pot and set the pot on sauté mode.

2.Add ground turkey and sauté for 5 minutes.

3.Add tomatoes, bell peppers, garlic, and broth into the pot and stir well.

4.Secure pot with pressure cooking lid and cook on high for 15 minutes.

5.Once done, release pressure using quick release. Remove lid.

6.Stir well and serve.

Nutritional Value (Amount per Serving):

•Calories 519

•Fat 20.2 g

•Carbohydrates 13.2 g

•Sugar 8 g

•Protein 68.3 g

•Cholesterol 175 mg

100

FLAVORFUL TERIYAKI CHICKEN

Preparation Time: 10 minutes

Cooking Time: 8 minutes

Serve: 6

Ingredients:

•2 lbs chicken thighs, skinless and boneless

•1 tbsp garlic, minced

•1/2 cup mirin

•1/2 cup soy sauce

•1 tbsp ginger, minced

Directions:

1.Add chicken, garlic, ginger, mirin, and soy sauce into the instant pot and stir well.

2.Secure pot with pressure cooking lid and cook on high for 8 minutes.

3.Once done, allow to release pressure naturally for 5 minutes then release remaining using quick release. Remove lid.

4.Stir well and serve.

Nutritional Value (Amount per Serving):

•Calories 308

- Fat 11.3 g
- Carbohydrates 3.6 g
- Sugar 0.8 g
- Protein 45.2 g
- Cholesterol 135 mg

101

FLAVORFUL HARISSA CHICKEN BREASTS

Preparation Time: 10 minutes

Cooking Time: 4 hours

Serve: 4

Ingredients:

•1 lb chicken breasts, skinless and boneless

•1/4 tsp garlic powder

•1/2 tsp ground cumin

•1 cup harissa sauce

•1/2 tsp kosher salt

Directions:

1.Season chicken with cumin, garlic powder, and salt and place into the instant pot.

2.Pour harissa sauce over the chicken.

3.Secure pot with a lid and select slow cook mode and cook on low for 4 hours.

4.Shred the chicken using a fork and serve.

Nutritional Value (Amount per Serving):

•Calories 232

•Fat 9.7 g

- Carbohydrates 1.3 g
- Sugar 0.1 g
- Protein 32.9 g
- Cholesterol 101 mg

102

TOMATILLO CHICKEN

Preparation Time: 10 minutes

Cooking Time: 6 hours

Serve: 6

Ingredients:

•6 chicken drumsticks, bone-in, and skin removed

•1 tbsp apple cider vinegar

•1 1/2 cups tomatillo sauce

•1 tsp olive oil

•1 tsp dried oregano

•Pepper

•Salt

Directions:

1.Add all ingredients into the instant pot and stir to combine.

2.Secure pot with a lid and select slow cook mode and cook on low for 6 hours.

3.Serve and enjoy.

Nutritional Value (Amount per Serving):

•Calories 147

•Fat 7.9 g

- Carbohydrates 4 g
- Sugar 1.8 g
- Protein 14.3 g
- Cholesterol 43 mg

103

DELICIOUS SALSA CHICKEN

Preparation Time: 10 minutes

Cooking Time: 2 hours

Serve: 6

Ingredients:

•1 1/2 lbs chicken tenders, skinless

•1/8 tsp oregano

•1/4 tsp garlic powder

•16 oz salsa

•1/8 tsp ground cumin

•Pepper

•Salt

Directions:

1.Place chicken tenders into the instant pot then pour remaining ingredients over chicken.

2.Secure pot with a lid and select slow cook mode and cook on high for 2 hours.

3.Shred the chicken using a fork and serve.

Nutritional Value (Amount per Serving):

•Calories 237

•Fat 8.5 g
•Carbohydrates 4.9 g
•Sugar 2.3 g
•Protein 34 g
•Cholesterol 101 mg

104

SHREDDED TURKEY BREASTS

Preparation Time: 10 minutes

Cooking Time: 7 hours

Serve: 24

Ingredients:

•4 lbs turkey breast, skinless, boneless, and halves

•1/2 cup butter, cubed

•12 oz chicken broth

•1 envelope onion soup mix

Directions:

1.Place turkey breast into the instant pot.

2.Mix butter, chicken broth, and onion soup mix and pour over turkey breast.

3.Secure pot with a lid and select slow cook mode and cook on low for 8 hours.

4.Shred the turkey using a fork and serve.

Nutritional Value (Amount per Serving):

•Calories 114

•Fat 5.1 g

•Carbohydrates 3.4 g

- Sugar 2.7 g
- Protein 13 g
- Cholesterol 43 mg

105

ROSEMARY GARLIC TURKEY BREAST

Preparation Time: 10 minutes

Cooking Time: 4 hours

Serve: 12

Ingredients:

•6 lbs turkey breast, bone-in

•4 fresh rosemary sprigs

•1/2 cup water

•4 garlic cloves, peeled

•Pepper

•Salt

Directions:

1.Place turkey breast into the instant pot. Season with pepper and salt.

2.Pour water, garlic, and rosemary on top of turkey breast.

3.Secure pot with a lid and select slow cook mode and cook on low for 4 hours.

4.Serve and enjoy.

Nutritional Value (Amount per Serving):

•Calories 241

- Fat 3.9 g
- Carbohydrates 10.6 g
- Sugar 8 g
- Protein 38.8 g
- Cholesterol 98 mg

106

TASTY CAESAR CHICKEN

Preparation Time: 10 minutes

Cooking Time: 6 hours

Serve: 2

Ingredients:

•2 chicken breasts, skinless and boneless

•1/4 cup creamy Caesar dressing

•1/4 tsp dried parsley

•2 tbsp fresh basil, chopped

•1/8 tsp black pepper

•1/8 tsp salt

Directions:

1.Add all ingredients into the instant pot and stir to combine.

2.Secure pot with a lid and select slow cook mode and cook on low for 6 hours.

3.Shred the chicken using a fork and serve.

Nutritional Value (Amount per Serving):

•Calories 378

•Fat 19.8 g

•Carbohydrates 3.2 g

- Sugar 2 g
- Protein 42.3 g
- Cholesterol 135 mg

107

SPINACH ARTICHOKE CHICKEN BREASTS

Preparation Time: 10 minutes

Cooking Time: 3 hours 30 minutes

Serve: 4

Ingredients:

•2 lbs chicken breasts, skinless and boneless

•1 1/2 cups can artichoke hearts, drained and sliced

•1 lemon, cut into wedges

•1 shallot, sliced

•2 garlic cloves, smashed

•3 oz baby spinach

•1/2 cup dry white wine

•1/2 cup chicken broth

•1/2 tsp black pepper

•3/4 tsp kosher salt

Directions:

1.Season chicken with pepper and salt and place into the instant pot.

2.Add artichoke, lemon wedges, shallot, and garlic.

3.Pour in broth and wine.

4.Secure pot with a lid and select slow cook mode and cook on low for 3 1/2 hours.

5.Transfer chicken to a dish.

6.Add spinach to the instant pot and stir with lemon and artichokes.

7.Transfer spinach artichoke mixture to the chicken dish.

8.Serve and enjoy.

Nutritional Value (Amount per Serving):

•Calories 493

•Fat 17 g

•Carbohydrates 8.3 g

•Sugar 0.8 g

•Protein 67.2 g

•Cholesterol 202 mg

108

FLAVORFUL SHREDDED CHICKEN

Preparation Time: 10 minutes

Cooking Time: 6 hours

Serve: 6

Ingredients:

•2 lbs chicken breasts

•3 garlic cloves, minced

•1/2 onion, diced

•1/4 cup cilantro

•15 oz coconut milk

•1 tsp turmeric

•1 tsp ginger, minced

•1 tbsp lime juice

•1/2 tsp pepper

•1 tsp salt

Directions:

1.Add all ingredients into the instant pot and stir well.

2.Secure pot with a lid and select slow cook mode and cook on low for 6 hours.

3.Shred the chicken using a fork and serve.

Nutritional Value (Amount per Serving):

- Calories 461
- Fat 28.2 g
- Carbohydrates 6.5 g
- Sugar 2.9 g
- Protein 45.7 g
- Cholesterol 135 mg

109

THAI CHICKEN BREASTS

Preparation Time: 10 minutes

Cooking Time: 6 hours

Serve: 6

Ingredients:

•4 chicken breasts

•2 tbsp Thai seasoning

•15 oz coconut milk

•2 carrots, chopped

•1/4 cup fresh cilantro, chopped

•Pepper

•Salt

Directions:

1.Place chicken breasts into the instant pot and sprinkle with seasoning.

2.Add cilantro and carrots on top of chicken.

3.Pour coconut milk. Secure pot with a lid and select slow cook mode and cook on low for 6 hours.

4.Serve and enjoy.

Nutritional Value (Amount per Serving):

•Calories 356

- •Fat 24.1 g
- •Carbohydrates 6 g
- •Sugar 3.4 g
- •Protein 30 g
- •Cholesterol 87 mg

110

LEMON PEPPER CHICKEN WINGS

Preparation Time: 10 minutes

Cooking Time: 6 hours

Serve: 4

Ingredients:

•2 lbs chicken wings

•1 1/2 tsp black pepper

•1 tsp lemon zest

•2 lemon juice

•1 lemon, sliced

•2 garlic cloves, minced

•1 cup chicken broth

Directions:

1.Add chicken wings into the instant pot.

2.In a small bowl, mix remaining ingredients and pour over chicken wings.

3.Secure pot with a lid and select slow cook mode and cook on low for 6 hours.

4.Serve and enjoy.

Nutritional Value (Amount per Serving):

•Calories 451

•Fat 17.4 g
•Carbohydrates 1.8 g
•Sugar 0.7 g
•Protein 67.2 g
•Cholesterol 202 mg

111

CHICKEN WITH MUSHROOMS

Preparation Time: 10 minutes

Cooking Time: 4 hours

Serve: 6

Ingredients:

•1 1/2 lbs chicken breasts, skinless & boneless

•1 onion, sliced

•16 oz crimini mushrooms, sliced

•2 tbsp olive oil

•1 1/2 cups chicken broth

•1/4 cup fresh parsley, chopped

•4 garlic cloves, minced

•Pepper

•Salt

Directions:

1.Add oil into the instant pot and set the pot on sauté mode.

2.Add chicken to the pot and cook until brown. Cancel sauté mode.

3.Pour remaining ingredients over chicken.

4.Secure pot with a lid and select slow cook mode and cook on low for 4 hours.

5.Stir well and serve.

Nutritional Value (Amount per Serving):

•Calories 297

•Fat 13.5 g

•Carbohydrates 5.9 g

•Sugar 2.3 g

•Protein 36.3 g

•Cholesterol 101 mg

112

GARLIC SPINACH CHICKEN

Preparation Time: 10 minutes

Cooking Time: 6 hours

Serve: 4

Ingredients:

•3/4 lb chicken breasts, skinless, boneless and cut into strips

•1 tbsp fresh parsley, minced

•1 tbsp fresh oregano, minced

•1/2 tsp black pepper

•5 oz baby spinach

•4 garlic cloves, minced

•1/4 cup balsamic vinegar

Directions:

1.Add all ingredients except spinach into the instant pot and stir well.

2.Secure pot with a lid and select slow cook mode and cook on low for 6 hours.

3.Stir in spinach and serve.

Nutritional Value (Amount per Serving):

•Calories 182

- Fat 6.6 g
- Carbohydrates 3.4 g
- Sugar 0.3 g
- Protein 26 g
- Cholesterol 76 mg

113

BASIL THYME CHICKEN THIGHS

Preparation Time: 10 minutes

Cooking Time: 4 hours

Serve: 6

Ingredients:

•2 lbs chicken thighs, skinless and boneless

•2 tbsp fresh oregano, minced

•1 onion, sliced

•1 tbsp fresh thyme

•1 garlic clove, minced

•1 tbsp fresh basil, minced

•Pepper

•Salt

Directions:

1.Season chicken with pepper and salt.

2.Add chicken, thyme, garlic, basil, and oregano into the large zip-lock bag and place it in the fridge for 1 hour.

3.Place onion slices into the instant pot.

4.Add marinated chicken into the pot.

5.Secure pot with a lid and select slow cook mode and cook on high for 4 hours.

6.Serve and enjoy.

Nutritional Value (Amount per Serving):

•Calories 301

•Fat 11.4 g

•Carbohydrates 3.2 g

•Sugar 0.9 g

•Protein 44.2 g

•Cholesterol 135 mg

114

TASTY CHICKEN CARNITAS

Preparation Time: 10 minutes

Cooking Time: 4 hours

Serve: 6

Ingredients:

•2 1/2 lbs chicken breasts, skinless and boneless

•1 tbsp garlic, minced

•1 tbsp chili powder

•1 1/2 tsp cumin powder

•1/4 cup cilantro, chopped

•3 tbsp fresh lime juice

•1/2 Tsp salt

Directions:

1.Place chicken into the instant pot.

2.Add remaining ingredients on top of chicken.

3.Secure pot with a lid and select slow cook mode and cook on high for 4 hours.

4.Shred the chicken using a fork and serve.

Nutritional Value (Amount per Serving):

•Calories 373

- Fat 14.4 g
- Carbohydrates 3.2 g
- Sugar 0.5 g
- Protein 55.1 g
- Cholesterol 168 mg

115

EASY CHICKEN TACOS

Preparation Time: 10 minutes

Cooking Time: 6 hours

Serve: 6

Ingredients:

•1 1/2 lbs chicken breasts, skinless and boneless

•14 oz tomatoes, diced

•1 packet taco seasoning

•Pepper

•Salt

Directions:

1.Place chicken into the instant pot and sprinkle with taco seasoning, pepper, and salt.

2.Pour tomatoes over chicken.

3.Secure pot with a lid and select slow cook mode and cook on low for 6 hours.

4.Shred the chicken using a fork and serve.

Nutritional Value (Amount per Serving):

•Calories 289

•Fat 12 g

- Carbohydrates 7 g
- Sugar 1.7 g
- Protein 36.8 g
- Cholesterol 110 mg

116

LEMON DILL CHICKEN

Preparation Time: 10 minutes

Cooking Time: 4 hours

Serve: 4

Ingredients:

•16 oz chicken breasts, skinless, boneless, and halves

•1 tbsp fresh dill, minced

•1 cup sour cream

•1 tsp lemon zest

•1 tsp lemon pepper seasoning

Directions:

1.In a bowl, mix lemon zest, lemon pepper seasoning, dill, and sour cream.

2.Pour half bowl mixture into the instant pot.

3.Place chicken into the pot then pours the remaining bowl mixture over the chicken.

4.Secure pot with a lid and select slow cook mode and cook on low for 4 hours.

5.Serve and enjoy.

Nutritional Value (Amount per Serving):

•Calories 342

- •Fat 20.5 g
- •Carbohydrates 3.3 g
- •Sugar 0.1 g
- •Protein 34.9 g
- •Cholesterol 126 mg

117

TARRAGON CHICKEN

Preparation Time: 10 minutes

Cooking Time: 8 hours

Serve: 4

Ingredients:

•8 oz chicken breasts

•1/4 tsp black pepper

•1 medium onion, sliced

•2 cups fresh tarragon

•1/4 tsp salt

Directions:

1.Place chicken into the instant pot. Pour remaining ingredients over chicken.

2.Secure pot with a lid and select slow cook mode and cook on low for 8 hours.

3.Discard onions and tarragon.

4.Serve and enjoy.

Nutritional Value (Amount per Serving):

•Calories 162

•Fat 5.3 g

- Carbohydrates 9.9 g
- Sugar 1.2 g
- Protein 20 g
- Cholesterol 50 mg

118

THAI CHICKEN CURRY

Preparation Time: 10 minutes

Cooking Time: 2 hours

Serve: 4

Ingredients:

•1 lb chicken thighs, skinless and boneless

•1 tbsp coconut amino

•1 tbsp curry paste

•2 garlic cloves, minced

•1 tbsp fish sauce

•1/2 cup chicken stock

•14 oz coconut milk

•Pepper

•Salt

Directions:

1.Add all ingredients into the instant pot and stir well.

2.Secure pot with a lid and select slow cook mode and cook on high for 2 hours.

3.Stir well and serve.

Nutritional Value (Amount per Serving):

•Calories 478

•Fat 34.3 g
•Carbohydrates 8.1 g
•Sugar 3.6 g
•Protein 35.7 g
•Cholesterol 101 mg

119

GREEN CHICKEN CURRY

Preparation Time: 10 minutes

Cooking Time: 4 hours

Serve: 6

Ingredients:

•3 lbs chicken thighs, skinless and boneless

•2 cups of coconut milk

•3 tbsp green curry paste

•Pepper

•Salt

Directions:

1.Add all ingredients into the instant pot and stir well.

2.Secure pot with a lid and select slow cook mode and cook on low for 6 hours.

3.Shred the chicken using a fork and serve.

Nutritional Value (Amount per Serving):

•Calories 637

•Fat 37.4 g

•Carbohydrates 6.7 g

•Sugar 2.7 g

- Protein 67.4 g
- Cholesterol 202 mg

120

SAUSAGE CHICKEN BREASTS

Preparation Time: 10 minutes

Cooking Time: 6 hours

Serve: 6

Ingredients:

•1 lb chicken breasts, skinless & boneless

•12 oz sausage, sliced into 1-inch pieces

•1 cup chicken broth

•1 tsp garlic, minced

•3 celery stalks, diced

•1 bell pepper, diced

•1 tbsp Cajun seasoning

•15 oz tomato sauce

•24 oz tomatoes, diced

•1/2 cup onion, diced

Directions:

1.Add chicken breasts into the instant pot.

2.Pour remaining ingredients over chicken and mix well.

3.Secure pot with a lid and select slow cook mode and cook on low for 6 hours.

4.Shred the chicken using a fork and serve.

Nutritional Value (Amount per Serving):

•Calories 376

•Fat 22.2 g

•Carbohydrates 7.7 g

•Sugar 4.9 g

•Protein 35.1 g

•Cholesterol 115 mg

BEEF, PORK & LAMB

121

LEMON PEPPER PORK CHOPS

Preparation Time: 10 minutes

Cooking Time: 15 minutes

Serve: 4

Ingredients:

•4 pork chops, boneless

•1 tsp lemon pepper seasoning

•Salt

Directions:

1.Line multi-level air fryer basket with parchment paper.

2.Season pork chops with lemon pepper seasoning, and salt and place into the multi-level air fryer basket.

3.Place basket into the pot. Secure pot with air fryer lid and cook on air fry mode at 400 F for 15 minutes.

4.Serve and enjoy.

Nutritional Value (Amount per Serving):

•Calories 257

•Fat 19.9 g

•Carbohydrates 0.3 g

•Sugar 0 g

- Protein 18 g
- Cholesterol 69 mg

122

MEATBALLS

Preparation Time: 10 minutes

Cooking Time: 15 minutes

Serve: 2

Ingredients:

•5 oz pork minced

•1/2 tsp mustard

•1/2 tsp honey

•1/2 tsp garlic paste

•1/2 tbsp cheddar cheese, grated

•1/2 tbsp fresh basil

•1/2 onion, diced

•Pepper

•Salt

Directions:

1.Line multi-level air fryer basket with parchment paper.

2.Add all ingredients into the large bowl and mix well to combine.

3.Make small balls from the mixture and place it into the multi-level air fryer basket.

4.Place basket into the pot. Secure pot with air fryer lid and cook on air fry mode at 390 F for 15 minutes.

5.Serve and enjoy.

Nutritional Value (Amount per Serving):

•Calories 248

•Fat 20.2 g

•Carbohydrates 6.8 g

•Sugar 2.7 g

•Protein 10.4 g

•Cholesterol 51 mg

123

CRISPY PORK CHOPS

Preparation Time: 10 minutes

Cooking Time: 12 minutes

Serve: 6

Ingredients:

•1 1/2 lbs pork chops, boneless

•1/4 cup parmesan cheese, grated

•1/3 cup almond flour

•1 tsp paprika

•1 tsp Creole seasoning

•1 tsp garlic powder

Directions:

1.Line multi-level air fryer basket with parchment paper.

2.Add all ingredients except pork chops in a zip-lock bag.

3.Add pork chops to the bag. Seal bag and shake well to coat pork chops.

4.Remove pork chops from the zip-lock bag and place it into the multi-level air fryer basket.

5.Place basket into the pot. Secure pot with air fryer lid and cook on air fry mode at 360 F for 12 minutes.

6.Serve and enjoy.

Nutritional Value (Amount per Serving):

- •Calories 386
- •Fat 29.8 g
- •Carbohydrates 1 g
- •Sugar 0.2 g
- •Protein 27.2 g
- •Cholesterol 100 mg

124

DIJON LAMB CHOPS

Preparation Time: 10 minutes

Cooking Time: 15 minutes

Serve: 4

Ingredients:

•8 lamb chops

•2 tbsp Dijon mustard

•1 tbsp lemon juice

•1 tsp tarragon

•1/2 tsp olive oil

•Pepper

•Salt

Directions:

1.Line multi-level air fryer basket with parchment paper.

2.In a small bowl, mix together mustard, lemon juice, tarragon, and olive oil.

3.Brush mustard mixture over lamb chops.

4.Place lamb chops into the multi-level air fryer basket.

5.Place basket into the pot. Secure pot with air fryer lid and cook on air fry mode at 390 F for 15 minutes.

6.Serve and enjoy.

Nutritional Value (Amount per Serving):

•Calories 291

•Fat 11.9 g

•Carbohydrates 0.6 g

•Sugar 0.2 g

•Protein 42.5 g

•Cholesterol 135 mg

125

MEATBALLS

Preparation Time: 10 minutes
Cooking Time: 15 minutes
Serve: 8
Ingredients:
•1 lb ground beef
•1/2 tsp Italian seasoning
•1 lb Italian sausage
•2 tbsp parsley, chopped
•2 garlic cloves, minced
•1/4 cup onion, minced
•1/2 tsp red pepper flakes
•1 1/2 cups parmesan cheese, grated
•2 egg, lightly beaten
•Pepper
•Salt

Directions:

1.Line multi-level air fryer basket with parchment paper.

2.Add all ingredients into the large mixing bowl and mix until well combined.

3.Make meatballs from the mixture and place it into the multi-level air fryer basket.

4.Place basket into the pot. Secure pot with air fryer lid and cook on air fry mode at 350 F for 15 minutes.

5.Serve and enjoy.

Nutritional Value (Amount per Serving):

•Calories 370

•Fat 24.3 g

•Carbohydrates 1.4 g

•Sugar 0.3 g

•Protein 35 g

•Cholesterol 151 mg

126

GEEK LAMB PATTIES

Preparation Time: 10 minutes

Cooking Time: 20 minutes

Serve: 4

Ingredients:

•1 1/2 lbs ground lamb

•1 tsp oregano

•1/4 tsp pepper

•1/3 cup feta cheese, crumbled

•1/2 tsp salt

Directions:

1.Line multi-level air fryer basket with parchment paper.

2.Add all ingredients into the bowl and mix until well combined.

3.Make the equal shape of patties from the meat mixture and place it into the multi-level air fryer basket.

4.Place basket into the pot. Secure pot with air fryer lid and cook on air fry mode at 375 F for 20 minutes. Flip patties halfway through.

5.Serve and enjoy.

Nutritional Value (Amount per Serving):

- •Calories 351
- •Fat 15.2 g
- •Carbohydrates 0.8 g
- •Sugar 0.5 g
- •Protein 49.6 g
- •Cholesterol 164 mg

127

CHEESY PORK CHOPS

Preparation Time: 10 minutes

Cooking Time: 8 minutes

Serve: 2

Ingredients:

•4 pork chops

•1/2 tsp garlic powder

•1/4 cup cheddar cheese, shredded

•1/2 tsp salt

Directions:

1.Line multi-level air fryer basket with parchment paper.

2.Rub pork chops with garlic powder and salt and place it into the multi-level air fryer basket.

3.Place basket into the pot. Secure pot with air fryer lid and cook on air fry mode at 350 F for 8 minutes. Flip halfway through.

4.Top with cheese and serve.

Nutritional Value (Amount per Serving):

•Calories 571

•Fat 44.5 g

- Carbohydrates 0.7 g
- Sugar 0.2 g
- Protein 39.6 g
- Cholesterol 152 mg

128

FLAVORFUL RIB EYE STEAK

Preparation Time: 10 minutes

Cooking Time: 14 minutes

Serve: 2

Ingredients:

•2 medium rib-eye steaks

•1/4 tsp onion powder

•1 tsp olive oil

•1/4 tsp garlic powder

•Pepper

•Salt

Directions:

1.Line multi-level air fryer basket with parchment paper.

2.Coat steaks with oil and season with garlic powder, onion powder, pepper, and salt.

3.Place steaks into the multi-level air fryer basket.

4.Place basket into the pot. Secure pot with air fryer lid and cook on air fry mode at 400 F for 14 minutes. Flip wings after 15 minutes. Turn halfway through.

5.Serve and enjoy.

Nutritional Value (Amount per Serving):

- •Calories 332
- •Fat 27.3 g
- •Carbohydrates 0.5 g
- •Sugar 0.2 g
- •Protein 20.1 g
- •Cholesterol 75 mg

129

BEEF & BROCCOLI

Preparation Time: 10 minutes

Cooking Time: 15 minutes

Serve: 3

Ingredients:

•1/2 lb steak, cut into strips

•2 tbsp soy sauce

•4 tbsp oyster sauce

•1 lb broccoli florets

•1 tbsp sesame seeds, toasted

•1 tsp garlic, minced

•1 tsp ginger, minced

•2 tbsp sesame oil

Directions:

1.Line multi-level air fryer basket with parchment paper.

2.Add all ingredients except sesame seeds into the large bowl and toss well.

3.Cover bowl and place in the refrigerator for 1 hour.

4.Add marinated steak and broccoli into the multi-level air fryer basket.

5.Place basket into the pot. Secure pot with air fryer lid and cook on air fry mode at 350 F for 15 minutes.

6.Sprinkle with sesame seeds and serve.

Nutritional Value (Amount per Serving):

•Calories 311

•Fat 14.9 g

•Carbohydrates 12.9 g

•Sugar 2.8 g

•Protein 32.9 g

•Cholesterol 68 mg

130

JUICY BEEF KABOBS

Preparation Time: 10 minutes

Cooking Time: 10 minutes

Serve: 4

Ingredients:

- 1 lb beef, cut into chunks
- 1/3 cup sour cream
- 1/2 onion, cut into 1-inch pieces
- 1 bell pepper, cut into 1-inch pieces
- 2 tbsp soy sauce

Directions:

1. Line multi-level air fryer basket with parchment paper.
2. In a medium bowl, mix together soy sauce and sour cream.
3. Add beef into the bowl and coat well and place it in the fridge overnight.
4. Thread marinated beef, bell peppers, and onions onto the soaked wooden skewers.
5. Place skewers into the multi-level air fryer basket.
6. Place basket into the pot. Secure pot with air fryer lid and cook on air fry mode at 400 F for 10 minutes. Turn halfway through.

7.Serve and enjoy.

Nutritional Value (Amount per Serving):

•Calories 271

•Fat 11.2g

•Carbohydrates 5 g

•Sugar 2.3 g

•Protein 36 g

•Cholesterol 110 mg

131

SIRLOIN STEAKS

Preparation Time: 10 minutes

Cooking Time: 20 minutes

Serve: 2

Ingredients:

•12 oz sirloin steaks

•1 1/2 tbsp soy sauce

•2 tbsp erythritol

•1 tbsp garlic, minced

•1 tbsp ginger, grated

•1/2 tbsp Worcestershire sauce

•Pepper

•Salt

Directions:

1.Line multi-level air fryer basket with parchment paper.

2.Add steaks in a large zip-lock bag along with the remaining ingredients.

3.Shake well and place it in the refrigerator overnight.

4.Place marinated steaks into the multi-level air fryer basket.

5.Place basket into the pot. Secure pot with air fryer lid and cook on air fry mode at 400 F for 20 minutes.

6.Serve and enjoy.

Nutritional Value (Amount per Serving):

•Calories 342
•Fat 10.8 g
•Carbohydrates 5 g
•Sugar 1.1 g
•Protein 52.9 g
•Cholesterol 152 mg

132

EASY BURGER PATTIES

Preparation Time: 10 minutes

Cooking Time: 12 minutes

Serve: 4

Ingredients:

•1 lb ground beef

•1/2 tsp Italian seasoning

•4 cheddar cheese slices

•Pepper

•Salt

Directions:

1.Line multi-level air fryer basket with parchment paper.

2.In a bowl, mix together ground beef, Italian seasoning, pepper, and salt.

3.Make four equal shapes of patties from the meat mixture and place it into the multi-level air fryer basket.

4.Place basket into the pot. Secure pot with air fryer lid and cook on air fry mode at 375 F for 12 minutes. Flip halfway through.

5.Place cheese slices on top of each patty and cook for 2 minutes more.

6.Serve and enjoy.

Nutritional Value (Amount per Serving):

•Calories 325

•Fat 16.5 g

•Carbohydrates 0.4 g

•Sugar 0.2 g

•Protein 41.4 g

•Cholesterol 131 mg

133

TASTY BEEF ROAST

Preparation Time: 10 minutes

Cooking Time: 35 minutes

Serve: 7

Ingredients:

•2 lbs beef roast

•2 tsp garlic powder

•1/4 tsp pepper

•1 tbsp olive oil

•1 tsp thyme

•1 tbsp kosher salt

Directions:

1.Line multi-level air fryer basket with parchment paper.

2.Brush roast with olive oil.

3.Mix thyme, garlic powder, pepper, and salt and rub all over roast.

4.Place roast into the multi-level air fryer basket.

5.Place basket into the pot. Secure pot with air fryer lid and cook on air fry mode at 400 F for 35 minutes. Flip after 15 minutes.

6.Serve and enjoy.

Nutritional Value (Amount per Serving):

•Calories 261

•Fat 10.1 g

•Carbohydrates 0.7 g

•Sugar 0.2 g

•Protein 39.5 g

•Cholesterol 116 mg

134

FLAVORFUL STEAK FAJITAS

Preparation Time: 10 minutes

Cooking Time: 15 minutes

Serve: 6

Ingredients:

•1 lb steak, sliced

•1/2 cup onion, sliced

•3 bell peppers, sliced

•1 tbsp olive oil

•1 tbsp fajita seasoning, gluten-free

Directions:

1.Line multi-level air fryer basket with parchment paper.

2.Add all ingredients to a large bowl and toss until well coated.

3.Transfer fajita mixture into the multi-level air fryer basket.

4.Place basket into the pot. Secure pot with air fryer lid and cook on air fry mode at 390 F for 15 minutes.

5.Serve and enjoy.

Nutritional Value (Amount per Serving):

•Calories 199

•Fat 6.3 g

- Carbohydrates 6.4 g
- Sugar 3.4 g
- Protein 28 g
- Cholesterol 68 mg

135

EASY PORK WITH MUSHROOMS

Preparation Time: 10 minutes

Cooking Time: 18 minutes

Serve: 4

Ingredients:

•1 lb pork chops, rinsed and pat dry

•2 tbsp butter, melted

•8 oz mushrooms, halved

•1/2 tsp garlic powder

•1 tsp soy sauce

•Pepper

•Salt

Directions:

1.Line multi-level air fryer basket with parchment paper.

2.Cut pork chops into the 3/4-inch cubes and place in a large mixing bowl.

3.Add remaining ingredients into the bowl and toss well.

4.Transfer pork and mushroom mixture into the multi-level air fryer basket.

5.Place basket into the pot. Secure pot with air fryer lid and cook on air fry mode at 400 F for 15-18 minutes.

6.Serve and enjoy.

Nutritional Value (Amount per Serving):

•Calories 428

•Fat 34.1 g

•Carbohydrates 2.2 g

•Sugar 1.1 g

•Protein 27.5 g

•Cholesterol 113 mg

136

PAPRIKA PORK CHOPS

Preparation Time: 10 minutes

Cooking Time: 14 minutes

Serve: 3

Ingredients:

•3 pork chops, rinsed and pat dry

•2 tsp olive oil

•1/4 tsp smoked paprika

•1/2 tsp garlic powder

•Pepper

•Salt

Directions:

1.Line multi-level air fryer basket with parchment paper.

2.Coat pork chops with olive oil and season with paprika, garlic powder, pepper, and salt.

3.Place pork chops

4.into the multi-level air fryer basket.

5.Place basket into the pot. Secure pot with air fryer lid and cook on air fry mode at 390 F for 14 minutes. Flip halfway through.

6.Serve and enjoy.

Nutritional Value (Amount per Serving):

•Calories 285

•Fat 23 g

•Carbohydrates 0.5 g

•Sugar 0.1 g

•Protein 18.1 g

•Cholesterol 69 mg

137

GARLIC AIR FRYER STEAK

Preparation Time: 10 minutes

Cooking Time: 18 minutes

Serve: 2

Ingredients:

•12 oz steaks, 3/4-inch thick

•1 tsp olive oil

•1 tsp garlic powder

•Pepper

•Salt

Directions:

1.Line multi-level air fryer basket with parchment paper.

2.Coat steaks with oil and season with garlic powder, pepper, and salt.

3.Place steaks into the multi-level air fryer basket.

4.Place basket into the pot. Secure pot with air fryer lid and cook on air fry mode at 400 F for 15-18 minutes. Flip halfway through.

5.Serve and enjoy.

Nutritional Value (Amount per Serving):

•Calories 363

- •Fat 10.9 g
- •Carbohydrates 1.1 g
- •Sugar 0.3 g
- •Protein 61.7 g
- •Cholesterol 153 mg

138

PARMESAN PAPRIKA PORK CHOPS

Preparation Time: 10 minutes

Cooking Time: 10 minutes

Serve: 4

Ingredients:

•4 pork chops, boneless

•2 tbsp olive oil

•1/2 tsp pepper

•1 tsp onion powder

•1 tsp smoked paprika

•1/2 cup parmesan cheese, grated

•1 tsp kosher salt

Directions:

1.Line multi-level air fryer basket with parchment paper.

2.Brush pork chops with olive oil.

3.In a bowl, mix together parmesan cheese and spices.

4.Coat pork chops with parmesan cheese mixture and places it into the multi-level air fryer basket.

5.Place basket into the pot. Secure pot with air fryer lid and cook on air fry mode at 375 F for 8 minutes. Flip wings after 15 minutes.

6.Serve and enjoy.

Nutritional Value (Amount per Serving):

•Calories 356

•Fat 29.4 g

•Carbohydrates 1.4 g

•Sugar 0.3 g

•Protein 21.8 g

•Cholesterol 77 mg

139

BEEF BURGER PATTIES

Preparation Time: 10 minutes

Cooking Time: 12 minutes

Serve: 2

Ingredients:

•1/2 lb ground beef

•1/4 tsp onion powder

•2 cheese slices

•1/4 tsp pepper

•1/8 tsp salt

Directions:

1.Line multi-level air fryer basket with parchment paper.

2.In a bowl, mix ground beef, onion powder, pepper, and salt.

3.Make two equal shapes of patties from the meat mixture and place it into the multi-level air fryer basket.

4.Place basket into the pot. Secure pot with air fryer lid and cook on air fry mode at 370 F for 12 minutes. Flip halfway through.

5.Serve and enjoy.

Nutritional Value (Amount per Serving):

•Calories 325

- •Fat 16.4 g
- •Carbohydrates 0.8 g
- •Sugar 0.3 g
- •Protein 41.4 g
- •Cholesterol 131 mg

140

TASTY BEEF FAJITAS

Preparation Time: 10 minutes

Cooking Time: 8 minutes

Serve: 4

Ingredients:

- 1 lb beef flank steak, sliced
- 1/2 tbsp chili powder
- 3 tbsp olive oil
- 2 bell peppers, sliced
- 1 tsp garlic powder
- 1 tsp paprika
- 1 1/2 tsp cumin
- Pepper
- Salt

Directions:

1. Line multi-level air fryer basket with parchment paper.
2. In a mixing bowl, toss sliced steak with remaining ingredients.
3. Add meat mixture into the multi-level air fryer basket.
4. Place basket into the pot. Secure pot with air fryer lid and cook on air fry mode at 390 F for 8 minutes. Stir halfway through.

5.Serve and enjoy.

Nutritional Value (Amount per Serving):

•Calories 330

•Fat 18.1 g

•Carbohydrates 6.2 g

•Sugar 3.3 g

•Protein 35.5 g

•Cholesterol 101 mg

141

MEATBALLS

Preparation Time: 10 minutes

Cooking Time: 20 minutes

Serve: 4

Ingredients:

•1 lb ground beef

•1/2 cup frozen spinach, thawed & chopped

•2 garlic cloves, finely chopped

•1/2 onion, finely chopped

•4 oz mushrooms, finely chopped

•2 tsp Italian seasoning

•1/4 cup almond flour

•1 egg, lightly beaten

•Pepper

•Salt

Directions:

1.Line multi-level air fryer basket with parchment paper.

2.Add all ingredients into the mixing bowl and mix until well combined.

3.Make small balls from the meat mixture and place it into the multi-level air fryer basket.

4.Place basket into the pot. Secure pot with air fryer lid and cook on bake mode at 380 F for 20 minutes. Flip halfway through.

5.Serve and enjoy.

Nutritional Value (Amount per Serving):

•Calories 258

•Fat 9.9 g

•Carbohydrates 3.6 g

•Sugar 1.5 g

•Protein 37.4 g

•Cholesterol 144 mg

142

BAKED KEBABS

Preparation Time: 10 minutes

Cooking Time: 15 minutes

Serve: 4

Ingredients:

•1 lb ground beef

•1/2 cup onion, minced

•1/4 tsp ground cinnamon

•1/4 tsp ground cardamom

•1/2 tsp turmeric

•1 tbsp ginger garlic paste

•1/4 cup cilantro, chopped

•1/2 tsp cayenne

•1 tsp salt

Directions:

1.Line multi-level air fryer basket with parchment paper.

2.Add meat and remaining ingredients into the large bowl and mix until well combined.

3.Make sausage shape kebabs and place them into the multi-level air fryer basket.

4.Place basket into the pot. Secure pot with air fryer lid and cook on bake mode at 350 F for 15 minutes. Flip halfway through.

5.Serve and enjoy.

Nutritional Value (Amount per Serving):

•Calories 225

•Fat 7.4 g

•Carbohydrates 2.6 g

•Sugar 0.7 g

•Protein 34.9 g

•Cholesterol 101 mg

143

BAKED BEEF & BROCCOLI

Preparation Time: 10 minutes

Cooking Time: 25 minutes

Serve: 2

Ingredients:

•1/2 lb beef stew meat, cut into pieces

•1 tbsp vinegar

•1 garlic clove, minced

•1 tbsp olive oil

•1/2 cup broccoli florets

•1 onion, sliced

•Pepper

•Salt

Directions:

1.Line multi-level air fryer basket with parchment paper.

2.Add meat and remaining ingredients into the large bowl and toss well and spread into the multi-level air fryer basket.

3.Place basket into the pot. Secure pot with air fryer lid and cook on bake mode at 390 F for 25 minutes.

4.Serve and enjoy.

Nutritional Value (Amount per Serving):

- •Calories 304
- •Fat 14.2 g
- •Carbohydrates 7.3 g
- •Sugar 2.8 g
- •Protein 35.8 g
- •Cholesterol 101 mg

144

MEATBALLS

Preparation Time: 10 minutes

Cooking Time: 12 minutes

Serve: 4

Ingredients:

•4 oz ground lamb meat

•1 egg, lightly beaten

•1 tbsp oregano, chopped

•1/2 tbsp lemon zest

•Pepper

•Salt

Directions:

1.Line multi-level air fryer basket with parchment paper.

2.Add all ingredients into the bowl and mix until well combined.

3.Make small balls from the meat mixture and place it into the multi-level air fryer basket.

4.Place basket into the pot. Secure pot with air fryer lid and cook on bake mode at 400 F for 12 minutes.

5.Serve and enjoy.

Nutritional Value (Amount per Serving):

- Calories 73
- Fat 3.7 g
- Carbohydrates 3.5 g
- Sugar 1 g
- Protein 5.9 g
- Cholesterol 56 mg

145

GREEK MEATBALLS

Preparation Time: 10 minutes

Cooking Time: 20 minutes

Serve: 4

Ingredients:

•1 lb ground beef

•1 egg, lightly beaten

•2 tbsp marinara sauce

•2 garlic cloves, minced

•1/4 cup parmesan cheese, grated

•1/2 cup almond flour

•1 tbsp fresh basil, chopped

•1 tbsp fresh parsley, chopped

•1 tbsp fresh rosemary, chopped

•Pepper

•Salt

Directions:

1.Line multi-level air fryer basket with parchment paper.

2.Add all ingredients into the mixing bowl and mix until well combined.

3.Make small balls from the meat mixture and place it into the multi-level air fryer basket.

4.Place basket into the pot. Secure pot with air fryer lid and cook on bake mode at 375 F for 22 minutes.

5.Serve and enjoy.

Nutritional Value (Amount per Serving):

•Calories 277

•Fat 11.5 g

•Carbohydrates 3.2 g

•Sugar 0.9 g

•Protein 38.7 g

•Cholesterol 146 mg

146

MEATBALLS

Preparation Time: 10 minutes

Cooking Time: 20 minutes

Serve: 4

Ingredients:

- 1 lb ground beef
- 1 egg, lightly beaten
- 2 garlic cloves, minced
- 1 tbsp basil, chopped
- 1/4 cup parmesan cheese, grated
- 1 tbsp Italian parsley, chopped
- 1 tbsp rosemary, chopped
- 2 tbsp almond milk
- 1/2 small onion, chopped
- 1/2 cup almond flour
- Pepper
- Salt

Directions:

1.Line multi-level air fryer basket with parchment paper.

2.Add all ingredients into the bowl and mix until well combined.

3.Make small balls from the meat mixture and place it into the multi-level air fryer basket.

4.Place basket into the pot. Secure pot with air fryer lid and cook on bake mode at 375 F for 20 minutes.

5.Serve and enjoy.

Nutritional Value (Amount per Serving):

•Calories 291

•Fat 13.1 g

•Carbohydrates 3.4 g

•Sugar 0.9 g

•Protein 38.8 g

•Cholesterol 146 mg

147

CHEESY BURGER PATTIES

Preparation Time: 10 minutes

Cooking Time: 15 minutes

Serve: 6

Ingredients:

•2 lbs ground beef

•1 cup mozzarella cheese, grated

•1 tsp onion powder

•1 tsp garlic powder

•Pepper

•Salt

Directions:

1.Line multi-level air fryer basket with parchment paper.

2.Add all ingredients into the large bowl and mix until well combined.

3.Make patties from meat mixture and place it into the multi-level air fryer basket.

4.Place basket into the pot. Secure pot with air fryer lid and cook on bake mode at 400 F for 15 minutes.

5.Serve and enjoy.

Nutritional Value (Amount per Serving):

- Calories 297
- Fat 10.3 g
- Carbohydrates 0.8 g
- Sugar 0.3 g
- Protein 47.3 g
- Cholesterol 138 mg

148

MEATBALLS

Preparation Time: 10 minutes

Cooking Time: 15 minutes

Serve: 4

Ingredients:

•1 lb ground lamb

•1 tsp onion powder

•1 tbsp garlic, minced

•1 tsp ground coriander

•1 tsp ground cumin

•Pepper

•Salt

Directions:

1.Line multi-level air fryer basket with parchment paper.

2.Add all ingredients into the large bowl and mix until well combined.

3.Make small balls from the meat mixture and place it into the multi-level air fryer basket.

4.Place basket into the pot. Secure pot with air fryer lid and cook on bake mode at 400 F for 15 minutes.

5.Serve and enjoy.

Nutritional Value (Amount per Serving):

•Calories 218

•Fat 8.5 g

•Carbohydrates 1.4 g

•Sugar 0.2 g

•Protein 32.1 g

•Cholesterol 102 mg

149

BEEF MEATBALLS

Preparation Time: 10 minutes

Cooking Time: 20 minutes

Serve: 6

Ingredients:

•16 oz ground beef

•1/2 onion, diced

•1 egg, lightly beaten

•1/4 cup parmesan cheese, grated

•1/2 cup almond flour

•1/4 cup parsley, chopped

•1 tsp garlic, minced

•Pepper

•Salt

Directions:

1.Line multi-level air fryer basket with parchment paper.

2.Add all ingredients into the large bowl and mix until well combined.

3.Make small balls from the meat mixture and place it into the multi-level air fryer basket.

4.Place basket into the pot. Secure pot with air fryer lid and cook on bake mode at 400 F for 20 minutes.

5.Serve and enjoy.

Nutritional Value (Amount per Serving):

•Calories 182

•Fat 7.4 g

•Carbohydrates 1.9 g

•Sugar 0.6 g

•Protein 25.8 g

•Cholesterol 1.9 mg

150

TASTY BURGER PATTIES

Preparation Time: 10 minutes

Cooking Time: 35 minutes

Serve: 6

Ingredients:

•2 lbs ground pork

•1/2 cup almond flour

•1 egg, lightly beaten

•1 onion, minced

•1 carrot, minced

•1 tsp garlic powder

•1 tsp paprika

•Pepper

•Salt

Directions:

1.Line multi-level air fryer basket with parchment paper.

2.Add all ingredients into the large bowl and mix until well combined.

3.Make small patties from the meat mixture and place it into the multi-level air fryer basket.

4.Place basket into the pot. Secure pot with air fryer lid and

cook on bake mode at 375 F for 35 minutes. Flip patties after 15 minutes.

5.Serve and enjoy.

Nutritional Value (Amount per Serving):

•Calories 254

•Fat 7.3 g

•Carbohydrates 3.8 g

•Sugar 1.6 g

•Protein 41.4 g

•Cholesterol 138 mg

151

EASY RANCH PORK CHOPS

Preparation Time: 10 minutes

Cooking Time: 35 minutes

Serve: 6

Ingredients:

•6 pork chops, boneless

•1 oz ranch seasoning

•2 tbsp olive oil

•1 tsp dried parsley

Directions:

1.Line multi-level air fryer basket with parchment paper.

2.Mix together oil, dried parsley, and ranch seasoning and rub over pork chops.

3.Place pork chops into the multi-level air fryer basket.

4.Place basket into the pot. Secure pot with air fryer lid and cook on bake mode at 400 F for 35 minutes.

5.Serve and enjoy.

Nutritional Value (Amount per Serving):

•Calories 311

•Fat 24.6 g

- •Carbohydrates 0 g
- •Sugar 0 g
- •Protein 18 g
- •Cholesterol 69 mg

152

HEALTHY BEEF PATTIES

Preparation Time: 10 minutes

Cooking Time: 35 minutes

Serve: 6

Ingredients:

•3/4 lb ground beef

•2 medium zucchini, grated and squeeze out all liquid

•1/2 tsp chili powder

•1 tsp curry powder

•1 cup almond flour

•2 eggs, lightly beaten

•1/2 onion, chopped

•Pepper

•Salt

Directions:

1.Line multi-level air fryer basket with parchment paper.

2.Add all ingredients into the large bowl and mix until well combined.

3.Make small patties from the meat mixture and place it into the multi-level air fryer basket.

4.Place basket into the pot. Secure pot with air fryer lid and

cook on bake mode at 400 F for 35 minutes. Flip pattie after 15 minutes.

5.Serve and enjoy.

Nutritional Value (Amount per Serving):

•Calories 142

•Fat 7.5 g

•Carbohydrates 4.5 g

•Sugar 1.8 g

•Protein 21 g

•Cholesterol 105 mg

153

JALAPENO LAMB PATTIES

Preparation Time: 10 minutes

Cooking Time: 8 minutes

Serve: 4

Ingredients:

•1 lb ground lamb

•1 cup feta cheese, crumbled

•1 tbsp garlic, minced

•1 jalapeno pepper, minced

•5 basil leaves, minced

•10 mint leaves, minced

•1/4 cup fresh parsley, chopped

•1 tsp dried oregano

•1/4 tsp pepper

•1/2 tsp kosher salt

Directions:

1.Line multi-level air fryer basket with parchment paper.

2.Add all ingredients into the mixing bowl and mix until well combined.

3.Make four equal shape patties from the meat mixture and place it into the multi-level air fryer basket.

4.Place basket into the pot. Secure pot with air fryer lid and cook on bake mode at 390 F for 8 minutes.

5.Serve and enjoy.

Nutritional Value (Amount per Serving):

•Calories 318

•Fat 16.4 g

•Carbohydrates 3.3 g

•Sugar 1.7 g

•Protein 37.6 g

•Cholesterol 135 mg

154

ROSEMARY PORK CHOPS

Preparation Time: 10 minutes

Cooking Time: 35 minutes

Serve: 4

Ingredients:

•4 pork chops, boneless and cut 1/2-inch thick

•2 garlic cloves, minced

•1 tsp dried rosemary, crushed

•1/4 tsp pepper

•1/4 tsp salt

Directions:

1.Line multi-level air fryer basket with parchment paper.

2.Season pork chops with pepper and salt.

3.In a small bowl, mix together garlic and rosemary and rub all over pork chops.

4.Place pork chops into the multi-level air fryer basket.

5.Place basket into the pot. Secure pot with air fryer lid and cook on bake mode at 350 F for 35 minutes.

6.Serve and enjoy.

Nutritional Value (Amount per Serving):

•Calories 260

- •Fat 19.9 g
- •Carbohydrates 0.8 g
- •Sugar 0 g
- •Protein 18.1 g
- •Cholesterol 69 mg

155

EASY STEAK TIPS

Preparation Time: 10 minutes

Cooking Time: 6 minutes

Serve: 3

Ingredients:

•1 1/2 lbs steak, cut into 3/4-inch cubes

•1/2 tsp garlic powder

•1 tsp olive oil

•1/8 tsp cayenne pepper

•1 tsp steak seasoning

•Pepper

•Salt

Directions:

1.Line multi-level air fryer basket with parchment paper.

2.Toss steak cubes with oil, cayenne, steak seasoning, garlic powder, pepper, and salt.

3.Add steak cubes into the multi-level air fryer basket.

4.Place basket into the pot. Secure pot with air fryer lid and cook on bake mode at 400 F for 6 minutes.

5.Serve and enjoy.

Nutritional Value (Amount per Serving):

- Calories 467
- Fat 12.9 g
- Carbohydrates 0.4 g
- Sugar 0.1 g
- Protein 82 g
- Cholesterol 204 mg

156

TASTY BAKED PORK CHOPS

Preparation Time: 10 minutes

Cooking Time: 18 minutes

Serve: 4

Ingredients:

•4 pork chops, boneless

•1 tsp onion powder

•1 tsp garlic powder

•1 tbsp smoked paprika

•2 tbsp olive oil

•1 tsp oregano

•Pepper

•Salt

Directions:

1.Line multi-level air fryer basket with parchment paper.

2.Brush pork chops with 1 tablespoon of olive oil.

3.Mix paprika, garlic powder, onion powder, oregano, pepper, and salt and rub all over pork chops.

4.Place pork chops into the multi-level air fryer basket.

5.Place basket into the pot. Secure pot with air fryer lid and cook on bake mode at 400 F for 18 minutes.

6.Serve and enjoy.

Nutritional Value (Amount per Serving):

•Calories 327

•Fat 27.2 g

•Carbohydrates 2.2 g

•Sugar 0.6 g

•Protein 18.5 g

•Cholesterol 69 mg

157

TENDER PORK CHOPS

Preparation Time: 10 minutes

Cooking Time: 15 minutes

Serve: 4

Ingredients:

•4 pork chops, boneless

•1 tsp smoked paprika

•4 tbsp olive oil

•1 tsp onion powder

•Pepper

•Salt

Directions:

1.Line multi-level air fryer basket with parchment paper.

2.Brush pork chops with oil and season with onion powder, paprika, pepper, and salt.

3.Place pork chops into the multi-level air fryer basket.

4.Place basket into the pot. Secure pot with air fryer lid and cook on bake mode at 400 F for 15 minutes.

5.Serve and enjoy.

Nutritional Value (Amount per Serving):

•Calories 380

- Fat 34 g
- Carbohydrates 0.8 g
- Sugar 0.3 g
- Protein 18.1 g
- Cholesterol 69 mg

158

CRISPY PARMESAN PORK CHOPS

Preparation Time: 10 minutes

Cooking Time: 45 minutes

Serve: 4

Ingredients:

•4 pork chops, boneless

•1 cup parmesan cheese, grated

•1 cup pork rinds, crushed

•1 tsp black pepper

•2 tbsp olive oil

•1 tsp garlic powder

Directions:

1.Line multi-level air fryer basket with parchment paper.

2.In a shallow dish, mix crushed pork rinds, black pepper, parmesan cheese, and garlic powder.

3.Brush pork chops with oil and coat with pork rind mixture.

4.Place coated pork chops into the multi-level air fryer basket.

5.Place basket into the pot. Secure pot with air fryer lid and cook on bake mode at 350 F for 40-45 minutes.

6.Serve and enjoy.

Nutritional Value (Amount per Serving):

- Calories 463
- Fat 36.2 g
- Carbohydrates 1.7 g
- Sugar 0.2 g
- Protein 33.4 g
- Cholesterol 103 mg

159

SIMPLE LEMON GARLIC PORK CHOPS

Preparation Time: 10 minutes

Cooking Time: 20 minutes

Serve: 4

Ingredients:

•4 pork chops

•1 tbsp garlic, minced

•1 lemon juice

•1 tbsp olive oil

•Pepper

•Salt

Directions:

1.Line multi-level air fryer basket with parchment paper.

2.Add pork chops and remaining ingredients into the zip-lock bag, seal bag, and place in the fridge overnight.

3.Place marinated pork chops into the multi-level air fryer basket.

4.Place basket into the pot. Secure pot with air fryer lid and cook on bake mode at 400 F for 15-20 minutes.

5.Serve and enjoy.

Nutritional Value (Amount per Serving):

- •Calories 292
- •Fat 23.5 g
- •Carbohydrates 1 g
- •Sugar 0.3 g
- •Protein 18.2 g
- •Cholesterol 69 mg

160

HERB LAMB CHOPS

Preparation Time: 10 minutes

Cooking Time: 15 minutes

Serve: 4

Ingredients:

•8 lamb chops

•2 tsp dried herb de Provence

•2 tbsp Dijon mustard

•2 garlic cloves, minced

•2 tbsp olive oil

•1/4 tsp salt

Directions:

1.Line multi-level air fryer basket with parchment paper.

2.In a small bowl, mix together garlic, oil, Dijon mustard, herb de Provence, and salt and rub all over pork chops.

3.Place pork chops into the multi-level air fryer basket.

4.Place basket into the pot. Secure pot with air fryer lid and cook on bake mode at 400 F for 15 minutes.

5.Serve and enjoy.

Nutritional Value (Amount per Serving):

•Calories 495

- •Fat 24.2 g
- •Carbohydrates 0.9 g
- •Sugar 0.1 g
- •Protein 64.8 g
- •Cholesterol 204 mg

161

LEMON PEPPER PORK CHOPS

Preparation Time: 10 minutes

Cooking Time: 15 minutes

Serve: 2

Ingredients:

•2 pork chops

•1/4 cup apple juice

•2 tbsp lemon pepper seasoning

•Salt

Directions:

1.Season pork chops with lemon pepper seasoning and salt and place into the instant pot.

2.Set pot on sauté mode and brown the pork chops. Cancel sauté mode.

3.Pour apple juice over the pork chops.

4.Secure pot with pressure cooking lid and cook on high for 10 minutes.

5.Once done, release pressure using quick release. Remove lid.

6.Serve and enjoy.

Nutritional Value (Amount per Serving):

- Calories 286
- Fat 20.1 g
- Carbohydrates 7.7 g
- Sugar 3 g
- Protein 18.7 g
- Cholesterol 69 mg

162

PORK CARNITAS

Preparation Time: 10 minutes
Cooking Time: 30 minutes
Serve: 4
Ingredients:
•1 lb pork shoulder
•1/4 cup of water
•1 cup chicken broth
•1/2 tbsp olive oil
•1 tsp garlic, minced
•1/2 tsp cumin
•1/2 tsp oregano
•1/2 onion, chopped
•1 lime juice
Directions:
1.Add oil into the instant pot and set the pot on sauté mode.
2.Add meat sauté until browned.
3.Add remaining ingredients to the pot and stir to combine.
4.Secure pot with pressure cooking lid and cook on high for 30 minutes.
5.Once done, allow to release pressure naturally. Remove lid.

6.Shred the meat using a fork.
7.Serve and enjoy.

Nutritional Value (Amount per Serving):

•Calories 364
•Fat 26.5 g
•Carbohydrates 2.9 g
•Sugar 1 g
•Protein 27.9 g
•Cholesterol 102 mg

163

SPICY PORK ROAST

Preparation Time: 10 minutes

Cooking Time: 45 minutes

Serve: 2

Ingredients:

•1 lb pork roast, cut into chunks

•3/4 cup beef broth

•1/2 tsp stevia

•1/2 tsp paprika

•1/2 tsp oregano

•1/2 tsp thyme

•1/2 tsp cumin

•1/2 tsp garlic powder

•1/4 tsp onion powder

•1/2 tsp ground ginger

•1/2 tbsp coconut oil

•1/4 tsp chili powder

•1/4 tsp pepper

Directions:

1.Add oil into the instant pot and set the pot on sauté mode.

2.Mix together all spices and herbs and rub over meat.

3.Place meat in the instant pot and cook until browned. Cancel sauté mode.

4.Pour broth over meat.

5.Secure pot with pressure cooking lid and cook on high for 45 minutes.

6.Once done, allow to release pressure naturally. Remove lid.

7.Serve and enjoy.

Nutritional Value (Amount per Serving):

•Calories 525

•Fat 25.7 g

•Carbohydrates 2.7 g

•Sugar 0.7 g

•Protein 67 g

•Cholesterol 195 mg

164

ITALIAN PORK CHOPS

Preparation Time: 10 minutes

Cooking Time: 15 minutes

Serve: 2

Ingredients:

•3.5 oz pork chops, boneless

•1/2 tbsp olive oil

•1/2 tbsp Italian seasoning

•3 oz feta cheese, crumbled

•3/4 cup chicken stock

•1/2 tsp garlic powder

•Pepper

•Salt

Directions:

1.Add oil into the instant pot and set the pot on sauté mode.

2.Season pork chops with Italian seasoning, garlic powder, pepper, and salt and place into the instant pot.

3.Cook pork chops until browned. Cancel sauté mode.

4.Pour stock over pork chops.

5.Secure pot with pressure cooking lid and cook on high for 10 minutes.

6.Once done, allow to release pressure naturally for 10 minutes then release remaining using quick release. Remove lid.

7.Transfer pork chops on a plate.

8.Add cheese into the instant pot and stir well.

9.Pour sauce over pork chops and serve.

Nutritional Value (Amount per Serving):

•Calories 318

•Fat 26.1 g

•Carbohydrates 2.9 g

•Sugar 2.5 g

•Protein 17.6 g

•Cholesterol 83 mg

165

QUICK & SMOKY PORK CHOPS

Preparation Time: 10 minutes

Cooking Time: 10 minutes

Serve: 2

Ingredients:

•2 pork chops

•1 tsp black pepper

•2 tbsp olive oil

•1 tbsp liquid smoke

•1 cup chicken broth

•2 tsp salt

Directions:

1.Season pork chops from both the side with pepper and salt.

2.Add oil into the instant pot and set the pot on sauté mode.

3.Add pork chops to the pot and cook until brown.

4.Remove pork chops from the pot and set aside.

5.Add liquid smoke and broth to the pot and stir well.

6.Return pork chops to the pot.

7.Secure pot with pressure cooking lid and cook on high for 10 minutes.

8.Once done, allow to release pressure naturally for 10 minutes then release remaining using quick release. Remove lid.

9.Serve and enjoy.

Nutritional Value (Amount per Serving):

•Calories 398

•Fat 34.6 g

•Carbohydrates 1.1 g

•Sugar 0.4 g

•Protein 20.5 g

•Cholesterol 69 mg

166

THYME GARLIC BEEF

Preparation Time: 10 minutes

Cooking Time: 45 minutes

Serve: 4

Ingredients:

•2 lbs beef roast

•1 tsp thyme

•4 garlic cloves

•1 tsp ginger, grated

•1 cup of water

•1 tsp garlic powder

•1/2 tsp salt

Directions:

1.Mix together all spices and rub over the meat.

2.Place meat into the instant pot.

3.Add garlic cloves on top.

4.Pour water around the meat.

5.Secure pot with pressure cooking lid and cook on high for 45 minutes.

6.Once done, release pressure using quick release. Remove lid.

7.Shred meat using a fork and serve.

Nutritional Value (Amount per Serving):

•Calories 430

•Fat 14.2 g

•Carbohydrates 2 g

•Sugar 0.2 g

•Protein 69.2 g

•Cholesterol 203 mg

167

PORK WITH BROCCOLI

Preparation Time: 10 minutes

Cooking Time: 20 minutes

Serve: 2

Ingredients:

•1 lb pork, cut into pieces

•1/2 tsp garlic powder

•1 tsp dried celery

•1 tbsp tomato paste

•1 tbsp Dijon mustard

•1 chili pepper, chopped

•1 cup broccoli, chopped

•1/4 cup celery stalk, chopped

•2 tbsp vinegar

•2 tbsp olive oil

•2 spring onions, chopped

•1/2 tsp pepper

•4 cup beef stock

•1 tsp sea salt

Directions:

1.Add oil into the pot and set the pot on sauté mode.

2.Season meat with pepper and salt and place into the pot.

3.Add vegetables, garlic powder, celery, tomato paste, and stock and stir well.

4.Secure pot with pressure cooking lid and cook on high for 20 minutes.

5.Once done, allow to release pressure naturally. Remove lid.

6.Serve and enjoy.

Nutritional Value (Amount per Serving):

•Calories 520

•Fat 23.6 g

•Carbohydrates 7.8 g

•Sugar 2.7 g

•Protein 67.4 g

•Cholesterol 166 mg

168

BEEF STROGANOFF

Preparation Time: 10 minutes

Cooking Time: 20 minutes

Serve: 2

Ingredients:

•1/2 lb beef sirloin steak, cut into strips

•1 bacon slice, diced

•1 garlic clove, crushed

•1/2 small onion, diced

•1/4 lb mushrooms, quartered

•1/4 cup sour cream

•1/2 cup beef broth

•1 1/2 tbsp tomato paste

•1/2 tsp paprika

Directions:

1.Add all ingredients except sour cream to the instant pot and stir well.

2.Secure pot with pressure cooking lid and cook on high for 20 minutes.

3.Once done, allow to release pressure naturally. Remove lid.

4.Stir in sour cream and serve.

Nutritional Value (Amount per Serving):

•Calories 366

•Fat 17.7 g

•Carbohydrates 8.2 g

•Sugar 3.5 g

•Protein 42.7 g

•Cholesterol 124 mg

169

GINGER GARLIC BEEF ROAST

Preparation Time: 10 minutes

Cooking Time: 45 minutes

Serve: 2

Ingredients:

- 1 lb beef roast
- 4 garlic cloves
- 1/2 tsp ginger, grated
- 1/2 cup beef stock
- 1/2 tsp garlic powder
- 1/4 tsp salt

Directions:

1. In a small bowl, mix all spices and rub over the meat.
2. Place meat into the pot.
3. Add garlic on top of the meat.
4. Pour stock around the meat.
5. Secure pot with pressure cooking lid and cook on high for 45 minutes.
6. Once done, release pressure using quick release. Remove lid.
7. Shred the meat using a fork and serve.

Nutritional Value (Amount per Serving):
•Calories 438
•Fat 14.3 g
•Carbohydrates 2.8 g
•Sugar 0.3 g
•Protein 70 g
•Cholesterol 203 mg

170

BEEF RIBS

Preparation Time: 10 minutes

Cooking Time: 35 minutes

Serve: 2

Ingredients:

•1 lb beef short ribs

•1 1/2 tsp garlic, minced

•2 tbsp swerve

•2 tbsp coconut aminos

•1/2 cup chicken broth

•1/2 tbsp ginger, grated

•1/2 tsp five-spice powder

Directions:

1.Add broth, five-spice powder, garlic, swerve, and coconut aminos in the instant pot and stir well.

2.Place beef ribs in the instant pot.

3.Secure pot with pressure cooking lid and cook on high for 35 minutes.

4.Once done, allow to release pressure naturally. Remove lid.

5.Serve and enjoy.

Nutritional Value (Amount per Serving):

- •Calories 502
- •Fat 20.9 g
- •Carbohydrates 6.9 g
- •Sugar 0.2 g
- •Protein 67 g
- •Cholesterol 206 mg

171

BEEF SHAWARMA

Preparation Time: 10 minutes

Cooking Time: 5 minutes

Serve: 4

Ingredients:

- 1 lb ground beef
- 1/2 tsp cinnamon
- 1 tsp oregano
- 2 cups cabbage, sliced
- 1 cup bell pepper, sliced
- 1/2 tsp ground coriander
- 1/2 tsp cumin
- 1/4 tsp cayenne pepper
- 1/4 tsp allspice
- 1 cup onion, chopped
- 1 tsp salt

Directions:

1.Add the meat into the instant pot and set the pot on sauté mode and cook for 2 minutes.

2.Add remaining ingredients and stir well.

3.Secure pot with pressure cooking lid and cook on high for 13 minutes.

4.Once done, allow to release pressure naturally. Remove lid.

5.Stir well and serve.

Nutritional Value (Amount per Serving):

•Calories 244

•Fat 7.4 g

•Carbohydrates 7.7 g

•Sugar 3.9 g

•Protein 35.6 g

•Cholesterol 101 mg

172

TACO MEAT

Preparation Time: 10 minutes

Cooking Time: 25 minutes

Serve: 6

Ingredients:

•2 lbs ground beef

•2 tsp onion powder

•2 tsp cumin

•2 tsp paprika

•2 cups chicken stock

•1/2 tsp chipotle powder

•1 tsp Ancho chili powder

•2 tsp garlic powder

•1 tsp salt

Directions:

1.Add all ingredients into the instant pot and stir well.

2.Secure pot with pressure cooking lid and cook on high for 25 minutes.

3.Once done, release pressure using quick release. Remove lid.

4.Stir and serve.

Nutritional Value (Amount per Serving):

•Calories 295
•Fat 9.9 g
•Carbohydrates 2.3 g
•Sugar 0.8 g
•Protein 46.6 g
•Cholesterol 135 mg

173

THAI BEEF ROAST

Preparation Time: 10 minutes

Cooking Time: 48 minutes

Serve: 8

Ingredients:

•3 lbs chuck roast

•1 tsp curry powder

•2 tbsp olive oil

•1 tsp garlic powder

•1/2 cup sweet chili sauce

•1/2 cup orange juice

•Pepper

•Salt

Directions:

1.Add olive oil into the instant pot and set the pot on sauté mode.

2.Add roast into the pot and cook until brown.

3.Add remaining ingredients into the pot and stir well.

4.Secure pot with pressure cooking lid and cook on high for 45 minutes.

5.Once done, release pressure using quick release. Remove lid.

6.Shred the meat using a fork and serve.

Nutritional Value (Amount per Serving):

•Calories 436

•Fat 17.7 g

•Carbohydrates 8 g

•Sugar 7.4 g

•Protein 56.4 g

•Cholesterol 172 mg

174

CREAMY STEAK

Preparation Time: 10 minutes

Cooking Time: 25 minutes

Serve: 2

Ingredients:

•1 lb flank steak

•1/2 tbsp Worcestershire sauce

•2 tbsp vinegar

•2 tbsp onion soup mix

•1/4 cup olive oil

Directions:

1.Place flank steak in the instant pot and sauté meat until brown.

2.Add olive oil, onion soup mix, vinegar, and Worcestershire sauce over the steak.

3.Secure pot with pressure cooking lid and cook on high for 25 minutes.

4.Once done, allow to release pressure naturally. Remove lid.

5.Serve and enjoy.

Nutritional Value (Amount per Serving):

•Calories 684

- •Fat 44.1 g
- •Carbohydrates 5.5 g
- •Sugar 1.1 g
- •Protein 63.6 g
- •Cholesterol 125 mg

175

BALSAMIC BEEF ROAST

Preparation Time: 10 minutes

Cooking Time: 30 minutes

Serve: 6

Ingredients:

•3 lbs beef roast, boneless and cut into pieces

•1/2 tsp red pepper flakes

•1 tbsp soy sauce

•1 tbsp Worcestershire sauce

•1/2 cup balsamic vinegar

•1 cup chicken stock

•4 garlic cloves, chopped

Directions:

1.Place the beef roast into the instant pot.

2.In a bowl, mix remaining ingredients and pour over beef roast.

3.Secure pot with pressure cooking lid and cook on high for 30 minutes.

4.Once done, allow to release pressure naturally. Remove lid.

5.Stir and serve.

Nutritional Value (Amount per Serving):

- Calories 435
- Fat 14.3 g
- Carbohydrates 1.8 g
- Sugar 0.8 g
- Protein 69.2 g
- Cholesterol 203 mg

176

SALSA PORK CHOPS

Preparation Time: 10 minutes

Cooking Time: 15 minutes

Serve: 8

Ingredients:

•3 lbs pork chops

•1/4 cup fresh lime juice

•1/2 cup salsa

•3 tbsp butter

•1/2 tsp pepper

•1/2 tsp garlic powder

•1/2 tsp ground cumin

•1/2 tsp salt

Directions:

1.Mix together lemon juice and salsa and set aside.

2.In a small bowl, mix garlic powder, cumin, pepper, and salt and rub all over the pork chops.

3.Add butter into the instant pot and set the pot on sauté mode.

4.Add pork chops to the pot and sauté until brown.

5.Pour salsa over the pork chops.

6.Secure pot with pressure cooking lid and cook on high for 15 minutes.

7.Once done, release pressure using quick release. Remove lid.

8.Serve and enjoy.

Nutritional Value (Amount per Serving):

•Calories 589

•Fat 46.7 g

•Carbohydrates 1.4 g

•Sugar 0.6 g

•Protein 38.6 g

•Cholesterol 158 mg

177

ASIAN PORK CUBES

Preparation Time: 10 minutes

Cooking Time: 25 minutes

Serve: 6

Ingredients:

•2 lbs pork belly, cut into 1.5-inch cubes

•1 tbsp ginger, grated

•1/3 cup bone broth

•2 tbsp coconut aminos

•1 tbsp blackstrap molasses

•3 tbsp sherry

•2 tbsp swerve

•1 tsp sea salt

Directions:

1.Add all ingredients into the instant pot and stir well.

2.Secure pot with pressure cooking lid and cook on high for 25 minutes.

3.Once done, allow to release pressure naturally. Remove lid.

4.Cook on sauté mode until sauce is thickened.

5.Stir and serve.

Nutritional Value (Amount per Serving):

- •Calories 726
- •Fat 40.8 g
- •Carbohydrates 4.8 g
- •Sugar 1.9 g
- •Protein 71 g
- •Cholesterol 174 mg

178

SALSA PORK SHOULDER

Preparation Time: 10 minutes

Cooking Time: 55 minutes

Serve: 4

Ingredients:

•2 lbs pork shoulder

•1 1/2 cups salsa verde

•1/2 tsp oregano

•1/4 tsp smoked paprika

•1 tbsp olive oil

•1/2 cup water

•1/4 tsp garlic powder

•1/2 tsp black pepper

•1/2 tsp kosher salt

Directions:

1.Mix all spices and rub over meat.

2.Add olive oil into the instant pot and set the pot on sauté mode.

3.Add pork into the pot and sauté until brown.

4.Add remaining ingredients into the instant pot and stir well.

5.Secure pot with pressure cooking lid and cook on high for 55 minutes.

6.Once done, allow to release pressure naturally. Remove lid.

7.Shred the meat using a fork and serve.

Nutritional Value (Amount per Serving):

•Calories 717

•Fat 52.3 g

•Carbohydrates 4.4 g

•Sugar 1.4 g

•Protein 54.1 g

•Cholesterol 204 mg

179

DELICIOUS PORK LOIN

Preparation Time: 10 minutes

Cooking Time: 45 minutes

Serve: 4

Ingredients:

•2 lb pork loin

•1 tsp ground ginger

•1/2 cup water

•1/4 cup soy sauce

•1 cup chicken stock

•2 garlic cloves, crushed

•1 tsp onion powder

Directions:

1.In a small bowl, mix all ingredients except meat and stock. Pour the stock into the instant pot.

2.Place meat into the pot then pours bowl mixture over the pork.

3.Secure pot with pressure cooking lid and cook on high for 45 minutes.

4.Once done, allow to release pressure naturally. Remove lid.

5.Serve and enjoy.

Nutritional Value (Amount per Serving):
•Calories 566
•Fat 31.8 g
•Carbohydrates 2.7 g
•Sugar 0.7 g
•Protein 63.3 g
•Cholesterol 181 mg

180

COUNTRY STYLE RIBS

Preparation Time: 10 minutes

Cooking Time: 45 minutes

Serve: 4

Ingredients:

•3 lbs country-style pork ribs

•3/4 cup beef stock

•For rub:

•1 tsp cumin

•1 tsp pepper

•1 tsp paprika

•1 tsp onion powder

•1 tsp garlic powder

•1/4 tsp cayenne pepper

•1 tsp salt

Directions:

1.In a small bowl, mix all rub ingredients and rub over meat.

2.Pour the stock into the instant pot then place the meat into the pot.

3.Secure pot with pressure cooking lid and cook on high for 45 minutes.

4.Once done, allow to release pressure naturally. Remove lid.
5.Serve and enjoy.

Nutritional Value (Amount per Serving):

•Calories 645
•Fat 39.5 g
•Carbohydrates 1.9 g
•Sugar 0.5 g
•Protein 67.2 g
•Cholesterol 256 mg

181

TASTY CHILI LIME BEEF

Preparation Time: 10 minutes

Cooking Time: 6 hours

Serve: 4

Ingredients:

•1 lb beef chuck roast

•1 fresh lime juice

•1 garlic clove, crushed

•1 tsp chili powder

•2 cups lemon-lime soda

•1/2 tsp salt

Directions:

1.Place beef chuck roast into the instant pot.

2.Season roast with garlic, chili powder, and salt.

3.Pour lemon-lime soda over the roast.

4.Secure pot with a lid and select slow cook mode and cook on low for 6 hours.

5.Shred the meat using a fork.

6.Pour lime juice over the shredded meat and serve.

Nutritional Value (Amount per Serving):

•Calories 439

- Fat 31.7 g
- Carbohydrates 7 g
- Sugar 5.4 g
- Protein 29.8 g
- Cholesterol 117 mg

182

EASY BEEF STROGANOFF

Preparation Time: 10 minutes

Cooking Time: 8 hours

Serve: 2

Ingredients:

•1/2 lb beef stew meat

•10 oz mushroom soup

•1 medium onion, chopped

•1/2 cup sour cream

•2.5 oz mushrooms, sliced

•Pepper and salt

Directions:

1.Add all ingredients except sour cream into the instant pot and stir well.

2.Secure pot with a lid and select slow cook mode and cook on low for 8 hours.

3.Stir in cream and serve.

Nutritional Value (Amount per Serving):

•Calories 354

•Fat 19.5 g

- •Carbohydrates 4.7 g
- •Sugar 0.7 g
- •Protein 37.5 g
- •Cholesterol 127 mg

183

ROASTED PORK SHOULDER

Preparation Time: 10 minutes

Cooking Time: 8 hours

Serve: 8

Ingredients:

•4 lbs pork shoulder

•1/2 tsp black pepper

•1 tsp garlic powder

•1/2 cup water

•1/2 tsp sea salt

Directions:

1.Season pork with garlic powder, pepper, and salt and place in the instant pot. Add water.

2.Secure pot with a lid and select slow cook mode and cook on low for 8 hours.

3.Shred the meat using a fork and serve.

Nutritional Value (Amount per Serving):

•Calories 664

•Fat 48.5 g

•Carbohydrates 0.3 g

- Sugar 0.1 g
- Protein 52.9 g
- Cholesterol 204 mg

184

TASTY GARLIC PORK CHOPS

Preparation Time: 10 minutes

Cooking Time: 4 hours

Serve: 4

Ingredients:

•4 pork chops

•2 garlic cloves, minced

•1/4 cup olive oil

•1 cup chicken broth

•1 tbsp poultry seasoning

•Pepper

•Salt

Directions:

1.In a bowl, whisk together olive oil, poultry seasoning, garlic, broth, pepper, and salt.

2.Pour olive oil mixture into the instant pot then place pork chops into the pot.

3.Secure pot with a lid and select slow cook mode and cook on high for 4 hours.

4.Serve and enjoy.

Nutritional Value (Amount per Serving):

- Calories 379
- Fat 32.9 g
- Carbohydrates 1.4 g
- Sugar 0.2 g
- Protein 19.4 g
- Cholesterol 69 mg

185

STEAK FAJITAS

Preparation Time: 10 minutes

Cooking Time: 6 hours

Serve: 6

Ingredients:

•2 lbs beef, sliced

•20 oz salsa

•1 large onion, sliced

•1 bell pepper, sliced

•2 tbsp fajita seasoning

Directions:

1.Add salsa into the instant pot.

2.Add remaining ingredients on top of the salsa and stir well.

3.Secure pot with a lid and select slow cook mode and cook on low for 6 hours.

4.Stir well and serve.

Nutritional Value (Amount per Serving):

•Calories 333

•Fat 9.7 g

•Carbohydrates 11.9 g

- Sugar 5 g
- Protein 47.8 g
- Cholesterol 135 mg

186

GARLIC LAMB CHOPS

Preparation Time: 10 minutes

Cooking Time: 6 hours

Serve: 8

Ingredients:

•8 lamb chops

•1/2 tsp dried thyme

•1 medium onion, sliced

•1 tsp dried oregano

•2 garlic cloves, minced

•Pepper

•Salt

Directions:

1.Add sliced onion into the instant pot.

2.Mix thyme, oregano, pepper, and salt and rub over lamb chops.

3.Place lamb chops in instant pot and top with garlic.

4.Pour 1/4 cup water around the lamb chops.

5.Secure pot with a lid and select slow cook mode and cook on low for 6 hours.

6.Serve and enjoy.

Nutritional Value (Amount per Serving):

•Calories 218

•Fat 8.3 g

•Carbohydrates 1.7 g

•Sugar 0.6 g

•Protein 32.1 g

•Cholesterol 102 mg

187

TACO MEAT

Preparation Time: 10 minutes

Cooking Time: 6 hours

Serve: 12

Ingredients:

•1 lb ground beef

•1 envelope taco seasoning

•10 oz can tomatoes with green chilies

Directions:

1.Add all ingredients into the instant pot and stir well.

2.Secure pot with a lid and select slow cook mode and cook on low for 6 hours.

3.Serve and enjoy.

Nutritional Value (Amount per Serving):

•Calories 105

•Fat 4.1 g

•Carbohydrates 3.1 g

•Sugar 0 g

•Protein 13.4 g

•Cholesterol 38 mg

188

BALSAMIC LAMB CHOPS

Preparation Time: 10 minutes

Cooking Time: 6 hours

Serve: 6

Ingredients:

•3 lbs lamb chops, trimmed off

•2 tbsp balsamic vinegar

•4 garlic cloves, minced

•1 large onion, sliced

•1/2 tsp ground black pepper

•2 tbsp rosemary

•1/2 tsp salt

Directions:

1.Add onion into the instant pot.

2.Add lamb chops on top of onions, then add rosemary, vinegar, garlic, pepper, and salt.

3.Secure pot with a lid and select slow cook mode and cook on low for 6 hours.

4.Serve and enjoy.

Nutritional Value (Amount per Serving):

•Calories 440

- Fat 16.8 g
- Carbohydrates 3.9 g
- Sugar 1.1 g
- Protein 64.2 g
- Cholesterol 204 mg

189

TASTY ONION PORK CHOPS

Preparation Time: 10 minutes

Cooking Time: 6 hours

Serve: 6

Ingredients:

•2 lbs pork chops, boneless

•1 large onion, sliced

•1/8 tsp red pepper flakes

•1 tbsp olive oil

•1/4 tsp garlic powder

•1 tbsp vinegar

•2 tbsp Worcestershire sauce

•1/3 cup butter, sliced

•1/4 tsp pepper

•1/4 tsp salt

Directions:

1.Heat olive oil into the instant pot and set pot on sauté mode.

2.Brown pork chops in the instant pot. Cancel sauté mode.

3.Add remaining ingredients into the pot and stir well.

4.Secure pot with a lid and select slow cook mode and cook on low for 6 hours.

5.Serve and enjoy.

Nutritional Value (Amount per Serving):

•Calories 611

•Fat 50.2 g

•Carbohydrates 3.5 g

•Sugar 2.1 g

•Protein 34.4 g

•Cholesterol 157 mg

190

HERBED LAMB CHOPS

Preparation Time: 10 minutes

Cooking Time: 4 hours

Serve: 4

Ingredients:

•8 lamb loin chops

•1/2 tsp dried thyme

•1 tsp dried oregano

•1 medium onion, sliced

•2 garlic cloves, minced

•1/8 tsp black pepper

•1/2 tsp garlic powder

•1/4 tsp salt

Directions:

1.In a small bowl, mix together oregano, garlic powder, thyme, pepper, and salt.

2.Rub herb mixture over the lamb chops.

3.Place lamb chops into the instant pot.

4.Top lamb chops with garlic and sliced onion.

5.Secure pot with a lid and select slow cook mode and cook on low for 4 hours.

6.Serve and enjoy.

Nutritional Value (Amount per Serving):

•Calories 332

•Fat 12.6 g

•Carbohydrates 3.7 g

•Sugar 1.3 g

•Protein 48.3 g

•Cholesterol 153 mg

191

THYME GARLIC LAMB CHOPS

Preparation Time: 10 minutes

Cooking Time: 6 hours

Serve: 4

Ingredients:

•2 lamb shoulder chops, bone-in

•1/2 cup red wine

•1 cup beef broth

•1/4 cup fresh thyme

•1 tsp garlic paste

•Pepper

•Salt

Directions:

1.Add all ingredients into the instant pot and stir well.

2.Secure pot with a lid and select slow cook mode and cook on low for 6 hours.

3.Serve and enjoy.

Nutritional Value (Amount per Serving):

•Calories 118

•Fat 3.6 g

- Carbohydrates 3.2 g
- Sugar 0.5 g
- Protein 13 g
- Cholesterol 38 mg

192

LAMB SHOULDERS

Preparation Time: 10 minutes

Cooking Time: 4 hours

Serve: 4

Ingredients:

•2 lbs lamb shoulder

•1/4 lb carrots

•2 tbsp spice rub

•1/4 cup beef broth

•1/4 cup fresh mint

•1/4 cup onion, chopped

Directions:

1.Pour beef broth into the instant pot.

2.Rub spice on all over lamb shoulder and place lamb shoulder into the pot.

3.Add remaining ingredients into the pot.

4.Secure pot with a lid and select slow cook mode and cook on high for 4 hours.

5.Shred the meat using a fork and serve.

Nutritional Value (Amount per Serving):

•Calories 441

- Fat 16.8 g
- Carbohydrates 4 g
- Sugar 1.7 g
- Protein 64.5 g
- Cholesterol 204 mg

193

ADOBO PULLED PORK

Preparation Time: 10 minutes

Cooking Time: 8 hours

Serve: 4

Ingredients:

•2 lbs pork

•7 oz chipotle peppers in adobo sauce

•1 can chicken broth

•1 tbsp ground cumin

•1 tbsp garlic, minced

Directions:

1.Add all ingredients into the instant pot and stir well.

2.Secure pot with a lid and select slow cook mode and cook on low for 8 hours.

3.Shred the meat using a fork and serve.

Nutritional Value (Amount per Serving):

•Calories 381

•Fat 11.1 g

•Carbohydrates 3.9 g

•Sugar 0.5 g

- Protein 64.7 g
- Cholesterol 175 mg

194

EASY RANCH PORK CHOPS

Preparation Time: 10 minutes

Cooking Time: 6 hours

Serve: 8

Ingredients:

•3 lbs pork chops

•1 oz onion soup mix

•22.5 oz cream of mushroom soup

•1/2 tsp black pepper

•1 tsp garlic powder

•1 oz ranch dressing mix

Directions:

1.Add all ingredients into the instant pot and stir well.

2.Secure pot with a lid and select slow cook mode and cook on low for 6 hours.

3.Serve and enjoy.

Nutritional Value (Amount per Serving):

•Calories 591

•Fat 44.6 g

•Carbohydrates 5.4 g

- Sugar 0.9 g
- Protein 39.2 g
- Cholesterol 146 mg

195

SIMPLE KALUA PORK

Preparation Time: 10 minutes

Cooking Time: 8 hours

Serve: 8

Ingredients:

•4 lbs pork shoulder roast

•1 tbsp liquid smoke

•2 tsp sea salt

Directions:

1.Place pork roast into the instant pot.

2.Pour liquid smoke and sea salt all over pork roast.

3.Secure pot with a lid and select slow cook mode and cook on low for 8 hours.

4.Shred the meat using a fork and serve.

Nutritional Value (Amount per Serving):

•Calories 582

•Fat 46.2 g

•Carbohydrates 0 g

•Sugar 0 g

•Protein 38.1 g

•Cholesterol 161 mg

196

CUBAN PORK SHOULDER

Preparation Time: 10 minutes

Cooking Time: 8 hours

Serve: 6

Ingredients:

•2 lbs pork shoulder, cut into 4-inch pieces

•1 1/2 tsp cumin

•1/4 cup orange juice

•3 garlic cloves, chopped

•2 tbsp fresh cilantro, chopped

•1/4 tsp red pepper flakes

•1 1/2 tsp paprika

•1 tbsp lime juice

•1 small onion, chopped

•1 1/2 tsp chili powder

•1 tbsp dry oregano

•1/2 tsp salt

Directions:

1.Add all ingredients into the instant pot and stir well.

2.Secure pot with a lid and select slow cook mode and cook on low for 8 hours.

3.Shred meat using a fork and serve.

Nutritional Value (Amount per Serving):

•Calories 463

•Fat 32.8 g

•Carbohydrates 4.7 g

•Sugar 1.7 g

•Protein 35.9 g

•Cholesterol 136 mg

197

PEPPER ONION STEAK

Preparation Time: 10 minutes

Cooking Time: 6 hours

Serve: 6

Ingredients:

•2 lbs sirloin top, sliced

•1 small onion, sliced

•2 garlic cloves, minced

•2 green bell peppers, sliced

For sauce:

•1 tbsp vinegar

•1/3 cup coconut aminos

•1/2 tsp black pepper

•1/2 tsp ground ginger

•1 tsp Dijon mustard

•1 tbsp olive oil

Directions:

1.Add steak, bell pepper, garlic, and onion into the instant pot.

2.In a small bowl, mix all sauce ingredients and pour them into the instant pot.

3.Secure pot with a lid and select slow cook mode and cook on low for 6 hours.

4.Stir well and serve.

Nutritional Value (Amount per Serving):

•Calories 335

•Fat 11.9 g

•Carbohydrates 7.4 g

•Sugar 2.5 g

•Protein 46.5 g

•Cholesterol 135 mg

198

DELICIOUS BEEF BRISKET

Preparation Time: 10 minutes

Cooking Time: 8 hours

Serve: 8

Ingredients:

•3 lbs beef brisket

•2 tbsp garlic salt

For sauce:

•1/2 tsp parsley

•1/4 cup dried onion flakes

•1/2 cup beef broth

•28 oz tomatoes, diced

•1/8 tsp pepper

•1/8 tsp paprika

•1/4 tsp onion powder

Directions:

1.Place beef brisket in the instant pot.

2.Pour remaining ingredients over the beef brisket.

3.Secure pot with a lid and select slow cook mode and cook on low for 8 hours.

4.Shred meat using a fork and serve.

Nutritional Value (Amount per Serving):

•Calories 350

•Fat 10.9 g

•Carbohydrates 7 g

•Sugar 3.8 g

•Protein 53.3 g

•Cholesterol 152 mg

199

BEEF HEART

Preparation Time: 10 minutes

Cooking Time: 4 hours

Serve: 4

Ingredients:

•1 lb beef heart, cut into cubes

•1/4 tsp garlic powder

•1/4 tsp pepper

•1/2 onion, sliced

•1/2 tsp dried oregano

•1/2 tsp salt

Directions:

1.Add all ingredients into the instant pot and stir well.

2.Secure pot with a lid and select slow cook mode and cook on high for 4 hours.

3.Serve and enjoy.

Nutritional Value (Amount per Serving):

•Calories 194

•Fat 5.4 g

•Carbohydrates 1.8 g

- Sugar 0.6 g
- Protein 32.5 g
- Cholesterol 240 mg

200

TASTY JALAPENO BEEF

Preparation Time: 10 minutes

Cooking Time: 8 hours

Serve: 8

Ingredients:

•2 lbs beef chuck roast

•4 jalapeno pepper, sliced

•1 onion, sliced

•12 oz roasted red bell peppers, drained and chopped

•1/2 cup beef broth

•1/2 tsp black pepper

•1/2 cup Worcestershire sauce

•1 tsp salt

Directions:

1.Place chuck roast in the instant pot.

2.Pour remaining ingredients over the roast.

3.Secure pot with a lid and select slow cook mode and cook on low for 8 hours.

4.Shred the meat using a fork and serve.

Nutritional Value (Amount per Serving):

•Calories 464

- Fat 33.7 g
- Carbohydrates 8.8 g
- Sugar 5.2 g
- Protein 31.6 g
- Cholesterol 117 mg

FISH & SEAFOOD

201

EASY TUNA NOODLE CASSEROLE

Preparation Time: 10 minutes

Cooking Time: 15 minutes

Serve: 4

Ingredients:

•2 cans tuna, drained

•2 cups mozzarella cheese, shredded

•4 oz cream cheese, cubed

•1/2 cup parmesan cheese, grated

•1 cup almond milk

•3 tbsp ranch dressing mix

•3 cups vegetable broth

•8 oz egg noodles

Directions:

1.Add noodles, broth, and ranch dressing mix into the instant pot and stir well.

2.Secure pot with pressure cooking lid and cook on high for 4 hours.

3.Once done, release pressure using quick release. Remove lid.

4.Add milk, tuna, mozzarella cheese, and cream cheese and stir well.

5.Sprinkle grated parmesan cheese on top.

6.Secure pot with air fryer lid and cook on broil mode for 3-4 minutes.

7.Serve and enjoy.

Nutritional Value (Amount per Serving):

•Calories 589

•Fat 38.5 g

•Carbohydrates 20.5 g

•Sugar 3.1 g

•Protein 41.1 g

•Cholesterol 91 mg

202

QUICK BROILED TILAPIA

Preparation Time: 10 minutes

Cooking Time: 8 minutes

Serve: 2

Ingredients:

•2 tilapia fillets

•1/8 tsp dried basil

•1/8 tsp old bay seasoning

•2 tbsp mayonnaise

•1 tbsp butter

•1/2 cup parmesan cheese, grated

•Pepper

•Salt

Directions:

1.Line multi-level air fryer basket with parchment paper.

2.Season tilapia with pepper and salt and place into the multi-level air fryer basket.

3.Place basket into the pot. Secure pot with air fryer lid and cook on broil mode for 4 minutes.

4.In a small bowl, mix mayonnaise, cheese, butter, old bay seasoning, and basil and spread on top of tilapia fillets.

5.Place basket into the pot. Secure pot with air fryer lid and cook on broil mode for 4 minutes more.

6.Serve and enjoy.

Nutritional Value (Amount per Serving):

•Calories 274

•Fat 16.5 g

•Carbohydrates 4.4 g

•Sugar 0.9 g

•Protein 28.5 g

•Cholesterol 90 mg

203

FLAVORFUL BROILED HADDOCK

Preparation Time: 10 minutes

Cooking Time: 8 minutes

Serve: 2

Ingredients:

•1 lb haddock fillets

•1/2 tbsp butter, cut into pieces

•1/8 tsp cayenne pepper

•1/4 tsp garlic powder

•1/4 tsp paprika

•1/4 tsp onion powder

•Pepper

•Salt

Directions:

1.Line multi-level air fryer basket with parchment paper.

2.Place haddock fillets into the multi-level air fryer basket.

3.Mix cayenne, garlic powder, paprika, onion powder, pepper, and salt and sprinkle over fish fillets. Top with butter.

4.Place basket into the pot. Secure pot with air fryer lid and cook on broil mode for 8 minutes.

5.Serve and enjoy.

Nutritional Value (Amount per Serving):

•Calories 283

•Fat 5 g

•Carbohydrates 0.7 g

•Sugar 0.2 g

•Protein 55.2 g

•Cholesterol 175 mg

204

PERFECT BROILED HALIBUT

Preparation Time: 10 minutes

Cooking Time: 10 minutes

Serve: 2

Ingredients:

•1 lb halibut fillets

•1 tbsp lemon juice

•1 1/2 tbsp mayonnaise

•2 tbsp butter, softened

•1/4 cup parmesan cheese, grated

•Pepper

•Salt

Directions:

1.Line multi-level air fryer basket with parchment paper.

2.Season halibut fillets with pepper and salt and place into the multi-level air fryer basket.

3.Secure pot with air fryer lid and cook on broil mode for 8 minutes.

4.Mix parmesan cheese, butter, mayonnaise, and lemon juice and spread on top of halibut fillets.

5.Place basket into the pot. Secure pot with air fryer lid and cook on broil mode for 2 minutes.

6.Serve and enjoy.

Nutritional Value (Amount per Serving):

•Calories 435

•Fat 23 g

•Carbohydrates 3.2 g

•Sugar 0.9 g

•Protein 51.7 g

•Cholesterol 114 mg

205

FLAVORFUL SALMON PATTIES

Preparation Time: 10 minutes

Cooking Time: 20 minutes

Serve: 4

Ingredients:

•12 oz can salmon, skinless, boneless & drained

•2 eggs, lightly beaten

•1/2 cup breadcrumbs

•1/2 tsp pepper

•1 tbsp Dijon mustard

•1 tsp garlic powder

•2 tbsp parsley, chopped

•1/2 cup celery, diced

•1/2 cup bell pepper, diced

•1/2 cup onion, diced

Directions:

1.Line multi-level air fryer basket with parchment paper.

2.Add all ingredients into the mixing bowl and mix until well combined.

3.Make 8 patties from mixture and place in multi-level air fryer basket in batches.

4.Place basket into the pot. Secure pot with air fryer lid and cook on bake mode at 400 F for 20 minutes. Flip patties halfway through.

5.Serve and enjoy.

Nutritional Value (Amount per Serving):

•Calories 222

•Fat 8.3 g

•Carbohydrates 13.8 g

•Sugar 2.8 g

•Protein 22.2 g

•Cholesterol 129 mg

206

ZESTY SCALLOPS

Preparation Time: 10 minutes

Cooking Time: 12 minutes

Serve: 2

Ingredients:

•12 scallops, pat dry

•1 tbsp lemon juice

•2 tbsp olive oil

•Pepper

•Salt

Directions:

1.Line multi-level air fryer basket with parchment paper.

2.Mix lemon juice, oil, pepper, and salt and brush over scallops.

3.Place scallops into the multi-level air fryer basket.

4.Place basket into the pot. Secure pot with air fryer lid and cook on broil mode for 12 minutes. Flip scallops halfway through.

5.Serve and enjoy.

Nutritional Value (Amount per Serving):

•Calories 280

- Fat 15.4 g
- Carbohydrates 4.4 g
- Sugar 0.2 g
- Protein 30.3 g
- Cholesterol 59 mg

207

SALMON MEATBALLS

Preparation Time: 10 minutes

Cooking Time: 18 minutes

Serve: 4

Ingredients:

•1 lb salmon, skinless & cut into chunks

•1/2 tsp oregano

•1/2 tsp paprika

•1/2 tsp pepper

•1 tsp garlic, minced

•1 egg white

•3 tbsp cilantro, minced

•6 tbsp breadcrumbs

•1/2 medium onion, grated

•3/4 tsp salt

Directions:

1.Line multi-level air fryer basket with parchment paper.

2.Add salmon into the food processor and process until finely chopped.

3.Transfer salmon and remaining ingredients into the mixing bowl and mix until well combined.

4.Make small balls from mixture and place in multi-level air fryer basket in batches.

5.Place basket into the pot. Secure pot with air fryer lid and cook on bake mode at 350 F for 15-18 minutes.

6.Serve and enjoy.

Nutritional Value (Amount per Serving):

•Calories 203

•Fat 7.6 g

•Carbohydrates 9.3 g

•Sugar 1.3 g

•Protein 24.6 g

•Cholesterol 50 mg

208

HONEY DIJON SALMON

Preparation Time: 10 minutes

Cooking Time: 20 minutes

Serve: 4

Ingredients:

•1 lb salmon fillet

•1 tsp garlic, minced

•1 tbsp Dijon mustard

•2 tbsp honey

•2 tbsp olive oil

•3 tbsp soy sauce

Directions:

1.Line multi-level air fryer basket with parchment paper.

2.Place salmon in a multi-level air fryer basket.

3.In a small bowl, mix soy sauce, oil, honey, Dijon mustard, and garlic.

4.Brush salmon with soy sauce mixture.

5.Place basket into the pot. Secure pot with air fryer lid and cook on bake mode at 400 F for 15 minutes.

6.Brush salmon with remaining soy sauce mixture and bake for 5 minutes more.

7.Serve and enjoy.

Nutritional Value (Amount per Serving):

•Calories 252

•Fat 14.2 g

•Carbohydrates 10 g

•Sugar 8.9 g

•Protein 8.9 g

•Cholesterol 23 mg

209

MOIST & JUICY SRIRACHA SALMON

Preparation Time: 10 minutes

Cooking Time: 15 minutes

Serve: 2

Ingredients:

•1 lb salmon fillet

•1 tbsp soy sauce

•1 tbsp honey

•1 tsp sriracha

•1 tbsp lime juice

Directions:

1.Line multi-level air fryer basket with parchment paper.

2.In a small bowl, mix soy sauce, honey, sriracha, and lime juice. Brush salmon with soy sauce mixture and place it into the multi-level air fryer basket.

3.Place basket into the pot. Secure pot with air fryer lid and cook on bake mode at 375 F for 15 minutes.

4.Serve and enjoy.

Nutritional Value (Amount per Serving):

•Calories 344

- Fat 14 g
- Carbohydrates 11.6 g
- Sugar 9.1 g
- Protein 44.6 g
- Cholesterol 100 mg

210

HONEY LIME SALMON

Preparation Time: 10 minutes

Cooking Time: 20 minutes

Serve: 2

Ingredients:

•2 salmon fillets

•1/2 tbsp garlic, minced

•2 tbsp honey

•1 lime juice

•1/4 cup butter, melted

•Pepper

•Salt

Directions:

1.Line multi-level air fryer basket with parchment paper.

2.In a small bowl, mix honey, lime juice, butter, garlic, pepper, and salt.

3.Brush salmon with honey mixture and place it into the multi-level air fryer basket.

4.Place basket into the pot. Secure pot with air fryer lid and cook on bake mode at 350 F for 15-20 minutes.

5.Serve and enjoy.

Nutritional Value (Amount per Serving):
•Calories 506
•Fat 34 g
•Carbohydrates 19.9 g
•Sugar 17.7 g
•Protein 35.1 g
•Cholesterol 140 mg

211

CAJUN SHRIMP

Preparation Time: 10 minutes

Cooking Time: 10 minutes

Serve: 4

Ingredients:

•12 oz shrimp, peeled & deveined

•1/4 tsp oregano

•1/2 tsp thyme

•1/2 tsp cayenne

•1 tbsp garlic powder

•1 tbsp onion powder

•1 tbsp paprika

•1 tbsp olive oil

•1 1/2 tsp salt

Directions:

1.Line multi-level air fryer basket with parchment paper.

2.Add shrimp and remaining ingredients into the mixing bowl and toss until well coated.

3.Add shrimp into the multi-level air fryer basket.

4.Place basket into the pot. Secure pot with air fryer lid and cook on bake mode at 350 F for 10 minutes.

5.Serve and enjoy.

Nutritional Value (Amount per Serving):

•Calories 150

•Fat 5.3 g

•Carbohydrates 5.5 g

•Sugar 1.3 g

•Protein 20.2 g

•Cholesterol 179 mg

212

SPICY BAKED SHRIMP

Preparation Time: 10 minutes

Cooking Time: 8 minutes

Serve: 2

Ingredients:

•1 lb shrimp, peeled & deveined

•1/8 tsp cayenne pepper

•1/2 tsp garlic powder

•1 tbsp chili powder

•1 tbsp olive oil

•1/2 tsp kosher salt

Directions:

1.Line multi-level air fryer basket with parchment paper.

2.Add shrimp and remaining ingredients into the bowl and toss well.

3.Transfer shrimp into the multi-level air fryer basket.

4.Place basket into the pot. Secure pot with air fryer lid and cook on bake mode at 400 F for 8 minutes.

5.Serve and enjoy.

Nutritional Value (Amount per Serving):

•Calories 344

- Fat 11.5 g
- Carbohydrates 6.1 g
- Sugar 0.5 g
- Protein 52.3 g
- Cholesterol 478 mg

213

QUICK BLACKENED SHRIMP

Preparation Time: 10 minutes

Cooking Time: 10 minutes

Serve: 6

Ingredients:

•1 lb shrimp, cleaned & deveined

•1 tbsp olive oil

•2 tsp blackened seasoning

•1/4 tsp pepper

•1/4 tsp salt

Directions:

1.Line multi-level air fryer basket with parchment paper.

2.Add shrimp and remaining ingredients into the bowl and toss well.

3.Add shrimp into the multi-level air fryer basket.

4.Place basket into the pot. Secure pot with air fryer lid and cook on bake mode at 400 F for 8-10 minutes.

5.Serve and enjoy.

Nutritional Value (Amount per Serving):

•Calories 110

- Fat 3.6 g
- Carbohydrates 1.2 g
- Sugar 0 g
- Protein 17.2 g
- Cholesterol 159 mg

214

PARMESAN BAKED SHRIMP

Preparation Time: 10 minutes

Cooking Time: 8 minutes

Serve: 4

Ingredients:

- 1 lb shrimp, peeled & deveined
- 1/4 cup parmesan cheese, grated
- 1/2 tsp paprika
- 1 tsp garlic powder
- 1/4 tsp pepper
- 1/4 cup butter, melted
- 1/2 tsp kosher salt

Directions:

1.Line multi-level air fryer basket with parchment paper.

2.Add shrimp and remaining ingredients into the zip-lock bag, seal bag and shake until shrimp is well coated.

3.Add shrimp into the multi-level air fryer basket.

4.Place basket into the pot. Secure pot with air fryer lid and cook on bake mode at 400 F for 8 minutes.

5.Serve and enjoy.

Nutritional Value (Amount per Serving):

- •Calories 258
- •Fat 14.7 g
- •Carbohydrates 2.7 g
- •Sugar 0.2 g
- •Protein 27.9 g
- •Cholesterol 273 mg

215

DELICIOUS CRAB CAKES

Preparation Time: 10 minutes

Cooking Time: 12 minutes

Serve: 8

Ingredients:

•16 oz lump crab meat

•1 lemon juice

•1/4 cup parsley, chopped

•2 tbsp yogurt

•2 tbsp mayonnaise

•1/4 cup bell pepper, minced

•2 scallions, chopped

•1 egg, lightly beaten

•2 egg whites lightly beaten

•1 cup crackers, crushed

•1 cup corn kernels

•Pepper

•Salt

Directions:

1.Line multi-level air fryer basket with parchment paper.

2.Add all ingredients into the mixing bowl and mix until well combined.

3.Make 8 equal shapes of patties from the mixture and place in the refrigerator for 1 hour.

4.After 1-hour place patties into the multi-level air fryer basket in batches.

5.Place basket into the pot. Secure pot with air fryer lid and cook on air fry mode at 370 F for 10-12 minutes. Turn patties halfway through.

6.Serve and enjoy.

Nutritional Value (Amount per Serving):

•Calories 128

•Fat 8.7 g

•Carbohydrates 11.3 g

•Sugar 1.7 g

•Protein 11 g

•Cholesterol 54 mg

216

AIR FRY SHRIMP SAUSAGE & PEPPER

Preparation Time: 10 minutes

Cooking Time: 12 minutes

Serve: 4

Ingredients:

•1/2 lb shrimp, peeled & deveined

•1/2 bell pepper, diced

•1/2 onion, diced

•1/2 zucchini, sliced

•1/2 squash, sliced

•1/2 smoked sausage, sliced

•1 tsp old bay seasoning

•1 tbsp olive oil

Directions:

1.Line multi-level air fryer basket with parchment paper.

2.Add all ingredients into the mixing bowl and toss well.

3.Transfer shrimp mixture into the multi-level air fryer basket.

4.Place basket into the pot. Secure pot with air fryer lid and cook on air fry mode at 400 F for 12 minutes.

5.Serve and enjoy.

Nutritional Value (Amount per Serving):

- Calories 121
- Fat 5.1 g
- Carbohydrates 4.9 g
- Sugar 2.2 g
- Protein 14.1 g
- Cholesterol 121 mg

217

SIMPLE AIR FRYER SRIRACHA SALMON

Preparation Time: 10 minutes

Cooking Time: 12 minutes

Serve: 2

Ingredients:

•2 salmon fillets

•1 tbsp soy sauce

•2 tbsp sriracha

•2 tbsp honey

Directions:

1.Line multi-level air fryer basket with parchment paper.

2.Mix soy sauce, sriracha, and honey in a small bowl.

3.Brush salmon fillets with soy sauce mixture and place it into the multi-level air fryer basket.

4.Place basket into the pot. Secure pot with air fryer lid and cook on air fry mode at 400 F for 12 minutes.

5.Serve and enjoy.

Nutritional Value (Amount per Serving):

•Calories 319

•Fat 11 g

- •Carbohydrates 20.9 g
- •Sugar 17.4 g
- •Protein 35.1 g
- •Cholesterol 78 mg

218

OLD BAY SEASONED SHRIMP

Preparation Time: 10 minutes

Cooking Time: 10 minutes

Serve: 4

Ingredients:

•1 lb shrimp, peeled & deveined

•1 tbsp old bay seasoning

•1/2 tbsp garlic, minced

•1/2 tbsp lemon juice

•1/2 tbsp olive oil

Directions:

1.Line multi-level air fryer basket with parchment paper.

2.Add shrimp and remaining ingredients into the mixing bowl and toss well.

3.Add shrimp into the multi-level air fryer basket.

4.Place basket into the pot. Secure pot with air fryer lid and cook on air fry mode at 390 F for 10 minutes.

5.Serve and enjoy.

Nutritional Value (Amount per Serving):

•Calories 152

- Fat 3.7 g
- Carbohydrates 2.1 g
- Sugar 0.1 g
- Protein 25.9 g
- Cholesterol 239 mg

219

SHRIMP WITH ZUCCHINI & PEPPERS

Preparation Time: 10 minutes

Cooking Time: 15 minutes

Serve: 4

Ingredients:

•1 lb shrimp, peeled & deveined

•1/4 cup parmesan cheese, grated

•1 tbsp Italian seasoning

•1 tbsp garlic, minced

•1 tbsp olive oil

•1 bell pepper, sliced

•1 zucchini, sliced

•Pepper

•Salt

Directions:

1.Line multi-level air fryer basket with parchment paper.

2.Add shrimp and remaining ingredients into the large bowl and toss well.

3.Add shrimp mixture into the multi-level air fryer basket.

4.Place basket into the pot. Secure pot with air fryer lid and

cook on air fry mode at 390 F for 15 minutes. Stir halfway through.

5.Serve and enjoy.

Nutritional Value (Amount per Serving):

•Calories 214

•Fat 7.9 g

•Carbohydrates 6.9 g

•Sugar 2.7 g

•Protein 28.7 g

•Cholesterol 245 mg

220

EASY TUNA CAKES

Preparation Time: 10 minutes

Cooking Time: 12 minutes

Serve: 12

Ingredients:

•12 oz can tuna chunks, drained

•1/2 onion, diced

•2 tbsp lemon juice

•4 tbsp mayonnaise

•1/2 cup breadcrumbs

•2 eggs, lightly beaten

•Pepper

•Salt

Directions:

1.Line multi-level air fryer basket with parchment paper.

2.Add all ingredients into the mixing bowl and mix until well combined.

3.Make equal shapes of patties from mixture and place into the multi-level air fryer basket in batches

4.Place basket into the pot. Secure pot with air fryer lid and

cook on air fry mode at 375 F for 12 minutes. Turn patties halfway through.

5.Serve and enjoy.

Nutritional Value (Amount per Serving):

•Calories 80

•Fat 2.7 g

•Carbohydrates 5 g

•Sugar 0.9 g

•Protein 9 g

•Cholesterol 37 mg

221

HEALTHY BAKED SALMON

Preparation Time: 10 minutes

Cooking Time: 18 minutes

Serve: 6

Ingredients:

•4 salmon fillets

•1 tsp Italian seasoning

•2 tsp garlic, minced

•1/4 tsp pepper

•2 tbsp olive oil

•1/2 tsp salt

Directions:

1.Line multi-level air fryer basket with parchment paper.

2.Coat salmon fillets with oil and season with Italian seasoning, garlic, pepper, and salt.

3.Place salmon fillets into the multi-level air fryer basket.

4.Place basket into the pot. Secure pot with air fryer lid and cook on bake mode at 400 F for 15-18 minutes.

5.Serve and enjoy.

Nutritional Value (Amount per Serving):

•Calories 201

- •Fat 12.2 g
- •Carbohydrates 0.5 g
- •Sugar 0.1 g
- •Protein 23.1 g
- •Cholesterol 53 mg

222

LEMON PEPPER FISH FILLETS

Preparation Time: 10 minutes

Cooking Time: 12 minutes

Serve: 4

Ingredients:

•4 basa fish fillets

•2 1/2 tbsp olive oil

•2 tbsp fresh parsley, chopped

•1/2 tsp garlic powder

•1/4 tsp lemon pepper seasoning

•4 tbsp fresh lemon juice

•Pepper

•Salt

Directions:

1.Line multi-level air fryer basket with parchment paper.

2.Coat fish fillets with lemon juice and oil and season with garlic powder, lemon pepper seasoning, pepper, and salt.

3.Place fish fillets into the multi-level air fryer basket.

4.Place basket into the pot. Secure pot with air fryer lid and cook on bake mode at 400 F for 10-12 minutes.

5.Garnish with parsley and serve.

Nutritional Value (Amount per Serving):
•Calories 301
•Fat 20.8 g
•Carbohydrates 5 g
•Sugar 3.2 g
•Protein 24 g
•Cholesterol 0 mg

223

BAKED ROSEMARY SHRIMP

Preparation Time: 10 minutes

Cooking Time: 10 minutes

Serve: 4

Ingredients:

•1 lb shrimp, peeled and deveined

•1/2 tbsp fresh rosemary, chopped

•1 tsp garlic, minced

•1 tbsp olive oil

•Pepper

•Salt

Directions:

1.Line multi-level air fryer basket with parchment paper.

2.Add shrimp and remaining ingredients in a large bowl and toss well.

3.Add shrimp mixture into the multi-level air fryer basket.

4.Place basket into the pot. Secure pot with air fryer lid and cook on bake mode at 400 F for 10 minutes.

5.Serve and enjoy.

Nutritional Value (Amount per Serving):

•Calories 167

- •Fat 5.5 g
- •Carbohydrates 2.2 g
- •Sugar 0 g
- •Protein 25.9 g
- •Cholesterol 239 mg

224

EASY BAKED HALIBUT

Preparation Time: 10 minutes

Cooking Time: 15 minutes

Serve: 4

Ingredients:

•1 lb halibut fillets

•1/4 cup olive oil

•1/4 tsp garlic powder

•1/2 tsp sweet paprika

•Pepper

•Salt

Directions:

1.Line multi-level air fryer basket with parchment paper.

2.In a small bowl, mix oil, garlic powder, paprika, pepper, and salt.

3.Brush fish fillets with oil mixture and place them into the multi-level air fryer basket.

4.Place basket into the pot. Secure pot with air fryer lid and cook on bake mode at 400 F for 12-15 minutes.

5.Serve and enjoy.

Nutritional Value (Amount per Serving):

- Calories 235
- Fat 15.3 g
- Carbohydrates 0.3 g
- Sugar 0.1 g
- Protein 23.9 g
- Cholesterol 36 mg

225

FLAVORFUL HERB SALMON

Preparation Time: 10 minutes

Cooking Time: 15 minutes

Serve: 4

Ingredients:

•1 lb salmon fillets

•1/2 tbsp dried rosemary

•1 tbsp olive oil

•1/4 tsp dried basil

•1 tbsp dried chives

•Pepper

•Salt

Directions:

1.Line multi-level air fryer basket with parchment paper.

2.Mix olive oil, basil, chives, and rosemary in a small bowl and brush over salmon.

3.Place salmon fillets into the multi-level air fryer basket.

4.Place basket into the pot. Secure pot with air fryer lid and cook on air fry mode at 400 F for 15 minutes.

5.Serve and enjoy.

Nutritional Value (Amount per Serving):

- Calories 182
- Fat 10.6 g
- Carbohydrates 0.3 g
- Sugar 0 g
- Protein 22 g
- Cholesterol 50 mg

226

ITALIAN SALMON

Preparation Time: 10 minutes

Cooking Time: 20 minutes

Serve: 4

Ingredients:

•1 lb salmon fillets

•1/3 cup artichoke hearts

•1/4 cup sun-dried tomatoes, drained

•1 tbsp fresh dill, chopped

•1/4 cup olives, pitted and chopped

•1/3 cup basil pesto

•1/4 cup capers

•1 tsp paprika

•1/4 tsp salt

Directions:

1.Line multi-level air fryer basket with parchment paper.

2.Place salmon fillets into the air fryer basket and season with paprika and salt.

3.Spread pesto on top of salmon fillets.

4.Add remaining ingredients on top of salmon.

5.Place basket into the pot. Secure pot with air fryer lid and cook on bake mode at 400 F for 20 minutes.

6.Serve and enjoy.

Nutritional Value (Amount per Serving):

•Calories 174

•Fat 8.1 g

•Carbohydrates 3.6 g

•Sugar 0.5 g

•Protein 23.1 g

•Cholesterol 50 mg

227

EASY & HEALTHY TILAPIA

Preparation Time: 10 minutes

Cooking Time: 15 minutes

Serve: 4

Ingredients:

•1 lb tilapia fillets

•2 tbsp garlic, minced

•2 tbsp olive oil

•Pepper

•Salt

Directions:

1.Line multi-level air fryer basket with parchment paper.

2.In a small bowl, mix oil and garlic.

3.Brush fish fillets with oil mixture and place them into the multi-level air fryer basket.

4.Place basket into the pot. Secure pot with air fryer lid and cook on bake mode at 400 F for 15 minutes.

5.Serve and enjoy.

Nutritional Value (Amount per Serving):

•Calories 160

- •Fat 8 g
- •Carbohydrates 1.4 g
- •Sugar 0 g
- •Protein 21.4 g
- •Cholesterol 55 mg

228

BLACKENED BAKED FISH FILLETS

Preparation Time: 10 minutes

Cooking Time: 15 minutes

Serve: 4

Ingredients:

•1 lb tilapia fillets

•1 tsp chili powder

•2 tsp onion powder

•2 tbsp paprika

•2 tbsp olive oil

•1/2 tsp garlic powder

•1/2 tsp dried thyme

•1/2 tsp oregano

•1 tsp pepper

•1/2 tsp salt

Directions:

1.Line multi-level air fryer basket with parchment paper.

2.Brush fish fillets with oil.

3.Mix together spices and rub all over the fish fillets.

4.Place fish fillets into the multi-level air fryer basket.

5.Place basket into the pot. Secure pot with air fryer lid and cook on bake mode at 400 F for 12-15 minutes.

6.Serve and enjoy.

Nutritional Value (Amount per Serving):

•Calories 173

•Fat 8.6 g

•Carbohydrates 4 g

•Sugar 0.9 g

•Protein 22 g

•Cholesterol 55 mg

229

PARMESAN COD

Preparation Time: 10 minutes

Cooking Time: 15 minutes

Serve: 4

Ingredients:

•4 cod fillets, wash & pat dry

•1/2 tbsp olive oil

•1/2 cup parmesan cheese, grated

•1 tsp parsley

•1 tsp sweet paprika

•Pepper

•Salt

Directions:

1.Line multi-level air fryer basket with parchment paper.

2.Brush fish fillets with oil and season with pepper and salt.

3.In a dish, mix parmesan cheese, paprika, and parsley.

4.Coat fish fillets with cheese mixture and place them into the multi-level air fryer basket.

5.Place basket into the pot. Secure pot with air fryer lid and cook on bake mode at 400 F for 15 minutes.

6.Serve and enjoy.

Nutritional Value (Amount per Serving):

•Calories 143

•Fat 5.2 g

•Carbohydrates 0.7 g

•Sugar 0.1 g

•Protein 23.7 g

•Cholesterol 63 mg

230

WHITE FISH FILLET WITH ROASTED PEPPER

Preparation Time: 10 minutes

Cooking Time: 30 minutes

Serve: 1

Ingredients:

•8 oz frozen white fish fillet

•1 1/2 tbsp olive oil

•1 tbsp lemon juice

•1 tbsp roasted red pepper, diced

•1/2 tsp Italian seasoning

Directions:

1.Line multi-level air fryer basket with parchment paper.

2.Coat fish fillet with oil and lemon juice and season with Italian seasoning.

3.Place fish fillet into the multi-level air fryer basket. Add roasted pepper on top of the fish fillet.

4.Place basket into the pot. Secure pot with air fryer lid and cook on bake mode at 400 F for 30 minutes.

5.Serve and enjoy.

Nutritional Value (Amount per Serving):

•Calories 384

- Fat 22.5 g
- Carbohydrates 1.3 g
- Sugar 1.1 g
- Protein 46.5 g
- Cholesterol 2 mg

231

GREEK PESTO SALMON

Preparation Time: 10 minutes

Cooking Time: 20 minutes

Serve: 4

Ingredients:

- 1 lb salmon fillets
- 1/4 cup olives, pitted and chopped
- 1 tbsp fresh dill, chopped
- 1/4 cup capers
- 1/3 cup basil pesto
- 1/4 cup sun-dried tomatoes, drained
- 1/3 cup artichoke hearts
- 1 tsp paprika
- 1/4 tsp salt

Directions:

1.Line multi-level air fryer basket with parchment paper.

2.Season salmon fillets with paprika and salt and place into the multi-level air fryer basket.

3.Spread pesto on top of fish fillets.

4.Add remaining ingredients on top of salmon.

5.Place basket into the pot. Secure pot with air fryer lid and cook on bake mode at 400 F for 20 minutes.

6.Serve and enjoy.

Nutritional Value (Amount per Serving):

•Calories 173

•Fat 8.1 g

•Carbohydrates 3.3 g

•Sugar 0.5 g

•Protein 23 g

•Cholesterol 50 mg

232

HEALTHY TUNA MUFFINS

Preparation Time: 10 minutes

Cooking Time: 25 minutes

Serve: 4

Ingredients:

•1 egg, lightly beaten

•3/4 cup cheddar cheese, shredded

•2 tbsp sour cream

•1/2 can tuna, flaked

•1/2 tsp cayenne pepper

•2 tbsp mayonnaise

•Pepper

•Salt

Directions:

1.Place the dehydrating tray in a multi-level air fryer basket.

2.In a bowl, whisk eggs with sour cream, mayonnaise, cayenne, pepper, and salt.

3.Add remaining ingredients and stir until well combined.

4.Pour egg mixture into the four silicone muffin molds and place molds on dehydrating tray.

5.Place basket into the pot. Secure pot with air fryer lid and cook on bake mode at 350 F for 25 minutes.

6.Serve and enjoy.

Nutritional Value (Amount per Serving):

•Calories 185

•Fat 13.7 g

•Carbohydrates 2.5 g

•Sugar 0.7 g

•Protein 12.9 g

•Cholesterol 75 mg

233

COD & VEGETABLES

Preparation Time: 10 minutes

Cooking Time: 15 minutes

Serve: 4

Ingredients:

•1 lb cod fillets

•1/2 tsp lemon pepper seasoning

•1/2 tsp paprika

•2 tbsp olive oil

•8 oz asparagus, chopped

•3 cups broccoli, chopped

•2 tbsp lemon juice

•1 tsp salt

Directions:

1.Line multi-level air fryer basket with parchment paper.

2.Coat fish fillets with lemon juice, oil, paprika, lemon pepper seasoning, and salt.

3.Place fish fillets into the multi-level air fryer basket.

4.Add broccoli and asparagus on top of fish fillets.

5.Place basket into the pot. Secure pot with air fryer lid and cook on bake mode at 400 F for 15 minutes.

6.Serve and enjoy.

Nutritional Value (Amount per Serving):

•Calories 189

•Fat 8.4 g

•Carbohydrates 7.2 g

•Sugar 2.4 g

•Protein 23.5 g

•Cholesterol 56 mg

234

TASTY BLACKENED MAHI-MAHI

Preparation Time: 10 minutes

Cooking Time: 15 minutes

Serve: 4

Ingredients:

•4 Mahi Mahi fillets

•1 tsp paprika

•1 tsp cumin

•3 tbsp olive oil

•1 tsp onion powder

•1/2 cayenne

•1/2 tsp pepper

•1 tsp garlic powder

•1/2 tsp salt

Directions:

1.Line multi-level air fryer basket with parchment paper.

2.In a small bowl, mix cumin, paprika, onion powder, cayenne, garlic powder, pepper, and salt.

3.Brush fish fillets with oil and rub with spice mixture.

4.Place fish fillets into the multi-level air fryer basket.

5.Place basket into the pot. Secure pot with air fryer lid and cook on bake mode at 400 F for 12-15 minutes.

6.Serve and enjoy.

Nutritional Value (Amount per Serving):

•Calories 189

•Fat 11.7 g

•Carbohydrates 2.1 g

•Sugar 0.5 g

•Protein 19.4 g

•Cholesterol 86 mg

235

HONEY ORANGE SALMON

Preparation Time: 10 minutes

Cooking Time: 25 minutes

Serve: 2

Ingredients:

•1 lb salmon fillets

•1 orange juice

•1 orange zest

•2 tbsp honey

•3 tbsp soy sauce

Directions:

1.Line multi-level air fryer basket with parchment paper.

2.In a small bowl, whisk together honey, soy sauce, orange juice, and orange zest.

3.Brush salmon fillets with honey mixture and place them into the multi-level air fryer basket.

4.Place basket into the pot. Secure pot with air fryer lid and cook on bake mode at 400 F for 25 minutes. Flip fish fillets after 15 minutes.

5.Serve and enjoy.

Nutritional Value (Amount per Serving):

- •Calories 399
- •Fat 14.1 g
- •Carbohydrates 24.4 g
- •Sugar 21.3 g
- •Protein 45.9 g
- •Cholesterol 100 mg

236

EASY BAKED HALIBUT

Preparation Time: 10 minutes

Cooking Time: 12 minutes

Serve: 4

Ingredients:

- 1 lb halibut fillets
- 1/2 tsp smoked paprika
- 2 tbsp olive oil
- 1/4 tsp garlic powder
- Pepper
- Salt

Directions:

1.Line multi-level air fryer basket with parchment paper.

2.Brush fish fillets with oil and season with paprika, garlic powder, pepper, and salt.

3.Place fish fillets into the multi-level air fryer basket.

4.Place basket into the pot. Secure pot with air fryer lid and cook on bake mode at 400 F for 10-12 minutes.

5.Serve and enjoy.

Nutritional Value (Amount per Serving):

- Calories 187

- Fat 9.7 g
- Carbohydrates 0.3 g
- Sugar 0.1 g
- Protein 23.9 g
- Cholesterol 36 mg

237

CAJUN SALMON

Preparation Time: 10 minutes

Cooking Time: 12 minutes

Serve: 1

Ingredients:

•1 lb salmon fillets

•1 tsp paprika

•2 tsp onion powder

•2 tsp garlic powder

•3 tbsp olive oil

•1 lemon juice

•1/8 tsp cayenne pepper

•2 tsp Cajun seasonings

•Pepper

•Salt

Directions:

1.Line multi-level air fryer basket with parchment paper.

2.In a small bowl, mix together Cajun seasoning, pepper, garlic powder, onion powder, paprika, cayenne pepper, and salt.

3.Brush fillets with oil and rub with spice mixture.

4.Place fish fillets into the multi-level air fryer basket.

5.Place basket into the pot. Secure pot with air fryer lid and cook on bake mode at 400 F for 10-12 minutes.

6.Serve and enjoy.

Nutritional Value (Amount per Serving):

•Calories 845

•Fat 45.5 g

•Carbohydrates 10.3 g

•Sugar 4.3 g

•Protein 2.2 g

•Cholesterol 0 mg

238

BAKED CATFISH FILLETS

Preparation Time: 10 minutes

Cooking Time: 15 minutes

Serve: 4

Ingredients:

•1 lb catfish fillets, cut 1/2-inch thick

•2 tsp onion powder

•1 tbsp dried oregano, crushed

•1/2 tsp ground cumin

•1/2 tsp chili powder

•1 tsp crushed red pepper

•Pepper

•Salt

Directions:

1.Line multi-level air fryer basket with parchment paper.

2.In a small bowl, mix together cumin, chili powder, crushed red pepper, onion powder, oregano, pepper, and salt.

3.Rub fish fillets with the spice mixture and place it into the multi-level air fryer basket.

4.Place basket into the pot. Secure pot with air fryer lid and cook on bake mode at 350 F for 15 minutes.

5.Serve and enjoy.

Nutritional Value (Amount per Serving):

•Calories 164

•Fat 8.9 g

•Carbohydrates 2.3 g

•Sugar 0.6 g

•Protein 18 g

•Cholesterol 53 mg

239

HEALTHY SALMON PATTIES

Preparation Time: 10 minutes

Cooking Time: 10 minutes

Serve: 2

Ingredients:

•1 egg

•14 oz salmon

•1 tsp dill, chopped

•1/2 cup breadcrumbs

•1/4 cup onion, diced

•Pepper

•Salt

Directions:

1.Line multi-level air fryer basket with parchment paper.

2.Add all ingredients into the mixing bowl and mix until well combined.

3.Make patties from mixture and place in multi-level air fryer basket in batches.

4.Place basket into the pot. Secure pot with air fryer lid and cook on air fry mode at 375 F for 10 minutes.

5.Serve and enjoy.

Nutritional Value (Amount per Serving):

•Calories 408

•Fat 15.9 g

•Carbohydrates 21.3 g

•Sugar 2.5 g

•Protein 45.1 g

•Cholesterol 169 mg

240

WALNUT CHEESE SALMON

Preparation Time: 10 minutes

Cooking Time: 15 minutes

Serve: 4

Ingredients:

•4 salmon fillets

•1/4 cup parmesan cheese, grated

•1/4 cup walnuts

•1 tsp olive oil

Directions:

1.Line multi-level air fryer basket with parchment paper.

2.Add walnuts into the blender and blend until ground.

3.Mix together walnuts, cheese, oil, and spread on top of salmon fillets.

4.Place salmon fillets into the multi-level air fryer basket.

5.Place basket into the pot. Secure pot with air fryer lid and cook on bake mode at 400 F for 15 minutes.

6.Serve and enjoy.

Nutritional Value (Amount per Serving):

•Calories 312

- •Fat 18 g
- •Carbohydrates 1 g
- •Sugar 0.1 g
- •Protein 38.2 g
- •Cholesterol 90 mg

241

SIMPLE SALMON PATTIES

Preparation Time: 10 minutes

Cooking Time: 7 minutes

Serve: 2

Ingredients:

- 1 egg, lightly beaten
- 8 oz salmon fillet, minced
- 1/4 tsp onion powder
- 1/4 tsp garlic powder
- 1/4 tsp paprika
- Pepper
- Salt

Directions:

1. Line multi-level air fryer basket with parchment paper.
2. Add all ingredients into the mixing bowl and mix until well combined.
3. Make patties from mixture and place in multi-level air fryer basket in batches.
4. Place basket into the pot. Secure pot with air fryer lid and cook on air fry mode at 400 F for 7 minutes.
5. Serve and enjoy.

Nutritional Value (Amount per Serving):

- •Calories 185
- •Fat 9.2 g
- •Carbohydrates 0.8 g
- •Sugar 0.4 g
- •Protein 24.9 g
- •Cholesterol 132 mg

242

TOMATO GARLIC SHRIMP

Preparation Time: 10 minutes

Cooking Time: 25 minutes

Serve: 4

Ingredients:

•1 lb shrimp, peeled

•1 tbsp olive oil

•1 tbsp garlic, sliced

•2 cups cherry tomatoes

•Pepper

•Salt

Directions:

1.Line multi-level air fryer basket with parchment paper.

2.Add shrimp and remaining ingredients into the bowl and toss well.

3.Add shrimp mixture into the multi-level air fryer basket.

4.Place basket into the pot. Secure pot with air fryer lid and cook on bake mode at 400 F for 25 minutes.

5.Serve and enjoy.

Nutritional Value (Amount per Serving):

•Calories 184

- •Fat 5.6 g
- •Carbohydrates 5.9 g
- •Sugar 2.4 g
- •Protein 26.8 g
- •Cholesterol 239 mg

243

STEAK SEASONED SHRIMP

Preparation Time: 10 minutes

Cooking Time: 6 minutes

Serve: 4

Ingredients:

•1 lb shrimp

•1 tsp steak seasoning

•1/4 tsp red pepper flakes

•2 garlic cloves, minced

•2 tsp olive oil

•1 tbsp parsley, chopped

•2 tsp fresh lemon juice

•1 tsp lemon zest, grated

•Pepper

•Salt

Directions:

1.Line multi-level air fryer basket with parchment paper.

2.Add shrimp and remaining ingredients into the mixing bowl and toss well.

3.Add shrimp mixture into the multi-level air fryer basket.

4.Place basket into the pot. Secure pot with air fryer lid and cook on air fry mode at 400 F for 6 minutes.

5.Serve and enjoy.

Nutritional Value (Amount per Serving):

•Calories 159

•Fat 4.3 g

•Carbohydrates 2.5 g

•Sugar 0.1 g

•Protein 26 g

•Cholesterol 239 mg

244

CRISPY CRAB CAKES

Preparation Time: 10 minutes

Cooking Time: 10 minutes

Serve: 4

Ingredients:

•18 oz can crab meat, drained

•1 tsp Old bay seasoning

•1 1/2 tbsp Dijon mustard

•1/4 cup breadcrumbs

•1 1/2 tsp dried parsley

•1 tbsp dried celery

•2 1/2 tbsp mayonnaise

•2 eggs, lightly beaten

•Pepper

•Salt

Directions:

1.Line multi-level air fryer basket with parchment paper.

2.Add all ingredients into the mixing bowl and mix until well combined.

3.Make small patties from crab mixture and place it into the multi-level air fryer basket.

4.Place basket into the pot. Secure pot with air fryer lid and cook on air fry mode at 320 F for 10 minutes.

5.Serve and enjoy.

Nutritional Value (Amount per Serving):

•Calories 173

•Fat 5.9 g

•Carbohydrates 9.8 g

•Sugar 3.4 g

•Protein 21 g

•Cholesterol 159 mg

245

SWEET & SPICY FISH FILLETS

Preparation Time: 10 minutes

Cooking Time: 12 minutes

Serve: 3

Ingredients:

•3 salmon fillets

•1/2 tsp chili powder

•1/4 cup honey

•1 tsp coriander

•1 tbsp red pepper flakes

•1/2 tsp turmeric

•Pepper

•Salt

Directions:

1.Line multi-level air fryer basket with parchment paper.

2.Add honey to microwave-safe bowl and microwave for 20 seconds.

3.Add red pepper flakes, chili powder, coriander, pepper, turmeric and salt in honey and stir well.

4.Spread honey mixture over salmon and place them into the multi-level air fryer basket.

5.Place basket into the pot. Secure pot with air fryer lid and cook on air fry mode at 400 F for 12 minutes.

6.Serve and enjoy.

Nutritional Value (Amount per Serving):

•Calories 330

•Fat 11.4 g

•Carbohydrates 24.8 g

•Sugar 23.4 g

•Protein 34.9 g

•Cholesterol 78 mg

246

AIR FRY EASY CAJUN SALMON

Preparation Time: 10 minutes

Cooking Time: 8 minutes

Serve: 4

Ingredients:

•4 salmon fillets

•1 tsp Cajun seasoning

•1/4 cup olive oil

Directions:

1.Line multi-level air fryer basket with parchment paper.

2.Brush salmon fillets with oil and season with Cajun seasoning.

3.Place salmon fillets into the multi-level air fryer basket.

4.Place basket into the pot. Secure pot with air fryer lid and cook on air fry mode at 375 F for 8 minutes.

5.Serve and enjoy.

Nutritional Value (Amount per Serving):

•Calories 343

•Fat 23.6 g

•Carbohydrates 0 g

- Sugar 0 g
- Protein 34.5 g
- Cholesterol 78 mg

247

MARINATED SALMON

Preparation Time: 10 minutes

Cooking Time: 10 minutes

Serve: 2

Ingredients:

•2 salmon fillets, skinless and boneless

•For marinade:

•1 tbsp olive oil

•2 tbsp scallions, minced

•1 tbsp ginger, grated

•2 garlic cloves, minced

•2 tbsp mirin

•2 tbsp soy sauce

Directions:

1.Line multi-level air fryer basket with parchment paper.

2.Add all marinade ingredients into the zip-lock bag and mix well.

3.Add salmon in a zip-lock bag, seal bag shake well and place in the fridge for 30 minutes.

4.Arrange marinated salmon fillets into the multi-level air fryer basket.

5.Place basket into the pot. Secure pot with air fryer lid and cook on air fry mode at 360 F for 10 minutes.

6.Serve and enjoy.

Nutritional Value (Amount per Serving):

•Calories 345

•Fat 18.2 g

•Carbohydrates 11.6 g

•Sugar 4.5 g

•Protein 36.1 g

•Cholesterol 78 mg

248

HONEY GLAZED SALMON

Preparation Time: 10 minutes

Cooking Time: 8 minutes

Serve: 4

Ingredients:

•4 salmon fillets

•1 tbsp honey

•2 tsp soy sauce

•1 tsp sesame seeds, toasted

•Pepper

•Salt

Directions:

1.Line multi-level air fryer basket with parchment paper.

2.Brush salmon with soy sauce and season with pepper and salt.

3.Place salmon into the multi-level air fryer basket.

4.Place basket into the pot. Secure pot with air fryer lid and cook on air fry mode at 375 F for 8 minutes.

5.Brush salmon with honey and sprinkle with sesame seeds.

6.Serve and enjoy.

Nutritional Value (Amount per Serving):

- •Calories 257
- •Fat 11.4 g
- •Carbohydrates 4.7 g
- •Sugar 4.4 g
- •Protein 34.9 g
- •Cholesterol 78 mg

249

ROSEMARY PRAWNS

Preparation Time: 10 minutes

Cooking Time: 10 minutes

Serve: 8

Ingredients:

•8 prawns

•1 tbsp rosemary, chopped

•1/2 tbsp olive oil

•Pepper

•Salt

Directions:

1.Line multi-level air fryer basket with parchment paper.

2.Add prawns, oil, rosemary, pepper, and salt in a mixing bowl and toss well. Cover and place in the fridge for 1 hour.

3.Add marinated prawns into the multi-level air fryer basket.

4.Place basket into the pot. Secure pot with air fryer lid and cook on air fry mode at 350 F for 10 minutes.

5.Serve and enjoy.

Nutritional Value (Amount per Serving):

•Calories 35

- Fat 1.3 g
- Carbohydrates 0.6 g
- Sugar 0 g
- Protein 5 g
- Cholesterol 46 mg

VEGETABLES & SIDE DISHES

250

CRISPY MAC & CHEESE

Preparation Time: 10 minutes

Cooking Time: 9 minutes

Serve: 6

Ingredients:

•2 1/2 cups macaroni

•1/4 tsp garlic powder

•1 sleeve Ritz crackers, crushed

•1/3 cup parmesan cheese, shredded

•2 2/3 cups pepper jack cheese, shredded

•1/2 cup butter, melted

•1 1/4 cup heavy cream

•2 cups vegetable broth

•Pepper

•Salt

Directions:

1.Add 1/4 cup butter, broth, garlic powder, cream, pepper, and salt into the instant pot and stir well.

2.Add macaroni and secure pot with pressure cooking lid and cook on high for 4 minutes.

3.Once done, release pressure using quick release. Remove lid.

4.Add 2 cups pepper jack cheese and stir until cheese is melted.

5.Mix together remaining melted butter and crushed crackers sprinkle on top of macaroni.

6.Sprinkle remaining pepper jack cheese and parmesan cheese on top of macaroni.

7.Secure pot with air fryer lid and cook on air fry mode at 400 F for 5 minutes.

8.Serve and enjoy.

Nutritional Value (Amount per Serving):

•Calories 561

•Fat 41.1 g

•Carbohydrates 29.3 g

•Sugar 1.6 g

•Protein 19.2 g

•Cholesterol 124 mg

251

HEALTHY RATATOUILLE PASTA

Preparation Time: 10 minutes

Cooking Time: 10 minutes

Serve: 4

Ingredients:

- 1 1/4 cups elbow pasta
- 2 cups vegetable stock
- 14 oz can tomatoes, chopped
- 1/2 eggplant, chopped
- 1 red bell pepper, diced
- 1 zucchini, chopped
- 1 tsp olive oil
- 1/2 cup parmesan cheese, shredded
- Pepper
- Salt

Directions:

1.Add oil into the instant pot and set the pot on sauté mode.

2.Add eggplant, bell pepper, zucchini, pepper, and salt, and sauté for 5 minutes. Cancel sauté mode.

3.Add pasta, stock, and tomatoes and stir well.

4.Secure pot with pressure cooking lid and cook on high for 2 minutes.

5.Once done, release pressure using quick release. Remove lid.

6.Sprinkle shredded parmesan cheese on top of pasta.

7.Secure pot with air fryer lid and broil for 4 minutes.

8.Serve and enjoy.

Nutritional Value (Amount per Serving):

•Calories 168

•Fat 4.2 g

•Carbohydrates 26.3 g

•Sugar 8.4 g

•Protein 8.4 g

•Cholesterol 8 mg

252

HEALTHY & CRISPY BROCCOLI

Preparation Time: 10 minutes

Cooking Time: 8 minutes

Serve: 2

Ingredients:

•3 cups broccoli florets

•1/4 tsp garlic powder

•2 tbsp olive oil

•1/8 tsp red chili flakes

•1/4 tsp pepper

•1/4 tsp salt

Directions:

1.Add broccoli florets and remaining ingredients into the mixing bowl and toss to combine.

2.Add broccoli florets into the multi-level air fryer basket.

3.Place basket into the pot. Secure pot with air fryer lid and cook on air fry mode at 375 F for 8 minutes.

4.Serve and enjoy.

Nutritional Value (Amount per Serving):

•Calories 168

- •Fat 14.5 g
- •Carbohydrates 9.5 g
- •Sugar 2.4 g
- •Protein 3.9 g
- •Cholesterol 0 mg

253

CRISPY CAULIFLOWER FLORETS

Preparation Time: 10 minutes

Cooking Time: 10 minutes

Serve: 2

Ingredients:

•3 cups cauliflower florets

•1 tbsp almond flour

•1/4 tsp red chili flakes

•1/4 tsp garlic powder

•1 tbsp olive oil

•1/4 tsp pepper

•Salt

Directions:

1.Add cauliflower florets and remaining ingredients into the bowl and mix well.

2.Add cauliflower florets into the multi-level air fryer basket.

3.Place basket into the pot. Secure pot with air fryer lid and cook on air fry mode at 400 F for 10 minutes.

4.Serve and enjoy.

Nutritional Value (Amount per Serving):

•Calories 179

- Fat 14.2 g
- Carbohydrates 11.4 g
- Sugar 4.2 g
- Protein 6.1 g
- Cholesterol 0 mg

254

CRISPY CAULIFLOWER STEAKS

Preparation Time: 10 minutes

Cooking Time: 15 minutes

Serve: 4

Ingredients:

•1 medium cauliflower head, cut into 1-inch thick slices

•1 tbsp fresh lime juice

•1 tsp garlic, minced

•1/2 tsp paprika

•1/2 tsp turmeric

•1 tbsp olive oil

•1/2 tsp salt

Directions:

1.In a bowl, mix lime juice, garlic, paprika, turmeric, oil, and salt.

2.Add cauliflower slices and coat well and let them sit for 1 hour.

3.Place marinated cauliflower slices into the multi-level air fryer basket.

4.Place basket into the pot. Secure pot with air fryer lid and cook on air fry mode at 375 F for 15 minutes.

5.Serve and enjoy.

Nutritional Value (Amount per Serving):

•Calories 71

•Fat 3.7 g

•Carbohydrates 9.1 g

•Sugar 3.7 g

•Protein 3 g

•Cholesterol 0 mg

255

ROASTED CAULIFLOWER

Preparation Time: 10 minutes

Cooking Time: 10 minutes

Serve: 2

Ingredients:

•3 cups cauliflower florets

•1 tbsp fresh parsley, chopped

•1/2 tsp fresh lime juice

•1/2 tsp dried oregano

•1 1/2 tbsp olive oil

•1 tbsp pine nuts

•Pepper

•Salt

Directions:

1.Add cauliflower florets, olive oil, oregano, pepper, and salt into the bowl and toss well.

2.Add cauliflower florets into the multi-level air fryer basket.

3.Place basket into the pot. Secure pot with air fryer lid and cook on air fry mode at 375 F for 10 minutes.

4.Transfer cauliflower florets into the mixing bowl. Add parsley, lime juice, and pine nuts and toss well.

5.Serve and enjoy.

Nutritional Value (Amount per Serving):

•Calories 161
•Fat 13.7 g
•Carbohydrates 9.8 g
•Sugar 4 g
•Protein 3.7 g
•Cholesterol 0 mg

256

PERFECT MEXICAN CAULIFLOWER

Preparation Time: 10 minutes

Cooking Time: 12 minutes

Serve: 4

Ingredients:

•1 medium cauliflower head, cut into florets

•1 tsp chili powder

•1/2 tsp paprika

•1/2 tsp onion powder

•1/2 tsp turmeric

•2 tsp parsley, chopped

•1 tsp cumin

•2 tbsp olive oil

•1 lime juice

•1 1/2 tsp garlic powder

•Pepper

•Salt

Directions:

1.Add cauliflower florets and remaining ingredients into the mixing bowl and toss well.

2.Add cauliflower florets into the multi-level air fryer basket.

3.Place basket into the pot. Secure pot with air fryer lid and cook on air fry mode at 400 F for 12 minutes.

4.Drizzle with lime juice and serve.

Nutritional Value (Amount per Serving):

•Calories 109

•Fat 7.5 g

•Carbohydrates 10.5 g

•Sugar 4.1 g

•Protein 3.4 g

•Cholesterol 0 mg

257

CRISPY CAULIFLOWER & ALMONDS

Preparation Time: 10 minutes

Cooking Time: 15 minutes

Serve: 4

Ingredients:

•3 cups cauliflower florets

•1 tsp garlic, minced

•1/2 tsp dried thyme

•1/4 cup breadcrumbs

•1/4 cup almonds, chopped

•1/4 cup parmesan cheese, shredded

•3 tsp olive oil

•Pepper

•Salt

Directions:

1.Line multi-level air fryer basket with parchment paper.

2.In a bowl, toss cauliflower florets with oil, garlic, pepper, and salt.

3.Add cauliflower florets into the multi-level air fryer basket.

4.Place basket into the pot. Secure pot with air fryer lid and cook on air fry mode at 360 F for 10 minutes.

5.Transfer cauliflower florets into the mixing bowl. Add thyme, breadcrumbs, almonds, and cheese and toss until well coated.

6.Return cauliflower mixture into the multi-level air fryer basket.

7.Place basket into the pot. Secure pot with air fryer lid and cook on air fry mode at 360 F for 5 minutes more.

8.Serve and enjoy.

Nutritional Value (Amount per Serving):

•Calories 129

•Fat 8.1 g

•Carbohydrates 10.6 g

•Sugar 2.5 g

•Protein 5.5 g

•Cholesterol 4 mg

258

CAULIFLOWER ROAST WITH PEPPERONCINI

Preparation Time: 10 minutes

Cooking Time: 15 minutes

Serve: 2

Ingredients:

•2 cups cauliflower florets

•1/4 tbsp vinegar

•2 tbsp almonds, sliced & toasted

•4 oz jar pepperoncini, drained & chopped

•1/2 tbsp olive oil

•Pepper

•Salt

Directions:

1.Toss cauliflower florets with oil, pepper, and salt.

2.Add cauliflower florets into the multi-level air fryer basket.

3.Place basket into the pot. Secure pot with air fryer lid and cook on roast mode at 400 F for 15 minutes.

4.Transfer roasted cauliflower florets into the bowl. Add vinegar, almonds, and pepperoncini and toss well.

5.Serve and enjoy.

Nutritional Value (Amount per Serving):

- Calories 100
- Fat 6.6 g
- Carbohydrates 8.6 g
- Sugar 2.7 g
- Protein 3.3 g
- Cholesterol 0 mg

259

CRISPY ROSEMARY POTATOES

Preparation Time: 10 minutes

Cooking Time: 15 minutes

Serve: 4

Ingredients:

•4 cups baby potatoes, quartered

•1/2 tsp garlic powder

•1 tbsp fresh rosemary, chopped

•1 tbsp olive oil

•1/4 tsp pepper

•1/2 tsp salt

Directions:

1.Add potatoes and remaining ingredients into the mixing bowl and toss well.

2.Add potatoes into the multi-level air fryer basket.

3.Place basket into the pot. Secure pot with air fryer lid and cook on air fry mode at 400 F for 15 minutes.

4.Serve and enjoy.

Nutritional Value (Amount per Serving):

•Calories 56

- Fat 3.7 g
- Carbohydrates 5.6 g
- Sugar 0.1 g
- Protein 1.1 g
- Cholesterol 0 mg

260

BAKED MUSHROOMS

Preparation Time: 10 minutes

Cooking Time: 20 minutes

Serve: 4

Ingredients:

•1 lb shiitake mushrooms, rinsed & pat dry

•3/4 tsp dried thyme

•1/2 tsp garlic powder

•1 tbsp vinegar

•1/4 cup olive oil

•1/4 tsp pepper

•1/2 tsp salt

Directions:

1.Line multi-level air fryer basket with parchment paper.

2.In a mixing bowl, mix oil, vinegar, garlic powder, thyme, pepper, and salt. Add mushrooms and toss well.

3.Transfer mushrooms into the multi-level air fryer basket.

4.Place basket into the pot. Secure pot with air fryer lid and cook on bake mode at 400 F for 20 minutes.

5.Serve and enjoy.

Nutritional Value (Amount per Serving):

- Calories 172
- Fat 12.9 g
- Carbohydrates 16.1 g
- Sugar 4.2 g
- Protein 1.9 g
- Cholesterol 0 mg

261

CRISPY PARMESAN BRUSSELS SPROUTS

Preparation Time: 10 minutes

Cooking Time: 25 minutes

Serve: 4

Ingredients:

•1 lb Brussels sprouts, trimmed & cut in half

•1/2 cup parmesan cheese, grated

•1/4 cup breadcrumbs

•1/4 cup olive oil

•1 1/2 tsp garlic powder

•1 1/2 tsp pepper

•1/2 tsp salt

Directions:

1.Line multi-level air fryer basket with parchment paper.

2.Add Brussels sprouts and remaining ingredients into the mixing bowl and toss until well coated.

3.Transfer Brussels sprouts into the multi-level air fryer basket.

4.Place basket into the pot. Secure pot with air fryer lid and cook on bake mode at 400 F for 25 minutes. Flip Brussels sprouts after 20 minutes.

5.Serve and enjoy.

Nutritional Value (Amount per Serving):

- Calories 225
- Fat 15.8 g
- Carbohydrates 16.8 g
- Sugar 3.1 g
- Protein 8.7 g
- Cholesterol 8 mg

262

BAGEL SEASONED BRUSSELS SPROUTS

Preparation Time: 10 minutes

Cooking Time: 25 minutes

Serve: 4

Ingredients:

•1 lb Brussels sprouts

•3 tbsp everything bagel seasoning

•1/4 cup parmesan cheese, grated

•2 tbsp olive oil

•2 cups of water

Directions:

1.Add water and Brussels sprouts into the pan, cover, and cook for 10 minutes over medium heat.

2.Drain Brussels sprouts and let it cool completely then cut in half.

3.In a mixing bowl, add Brussels sprouts, bagel seasoning, cheese, and oil and toss well.

4.Line multi-level air fryer basket with parchment paper.

5.Transfer Brussels sprouts into the multi-level air fryer basket.

6.Place basket into the pot. Secure pot with air fryer lid and cook on air fry mode at 375 F for 15 minutes.

7.Serve and enjoy.

Nutritional Value (Amount per Serving):

•Calories 147

•Fat 8.7 g

•Carbohydrates 14.8 g

•Sugar 2.8 g

•Protein 6.4 g

•Cholesterol 4 mg

263

EASY BAKED BROCCOLI

Preparation Time: 10 minutes

Cooking Time: 20 minutes

Serve: 3

Ingredients:

•1 lb broccoli florets

•1/4 cup breadcrumbs

•1/4 cup cheddar cheese, shredded

•1/4 tsp Italian seasoning

•1 garlic, minced

•1 tbsp olive oil

•Pepper

•Salt

Directions:

1.Line multi-level air fryer basket with parchment paper.

2.Toss broccoli florets with Italian seasoning, garlic, oil, pepper, and salt.

3.Add broccoli florets into the multi-level air fryer basket.

4.Place basket into the pot. Secure pot with air fryer lid and cook on air fry mode at 400 F for 15 minutes.

5.Transfer broccoli florets into the mixing bowl and toss with cheese and breadcrumbs.

6.Return broccoli florets into the multi-level air fryer basket.

7.Place basket into the pot. Secure pot with air fryer lid and cook on air fry mode at 400 F for 5 minutes more.

8.Serve and enjoy.

Nutritional Value (Amount per Serving):

•Calories 168

•Fat 8.9 g

•Carbohydrates 17 g

•Sugar 3.2 g

•Protein 7.8 g

•Cholesterol 10 mg

264

HEALTHY ROASTED VEGETABLES

Preparation Time: 10 minutes

Cooking Time: 40 minutes

Serve: 4

Ingredients:

•3 potatoes, diced

•1/4 cup mushrooms, sliced

•1/2 zucchini, sliced

•1/2 yellow summer squash, sliced

•1 carrot, sliced

•1 tsp Italian seasoning

•1 tsp garlic, minced

•2 tbsp olive oil

•1/4 tsp pepper

•1/4 tsp salt

Directions:

1.Line multi-level air fryer basket with parchment paper.

2.Add potatoes, mushrooms, zucchini, squash, carrot, Italian seasoning, garlic, oil, pepper, and salt into the mixing bowl and toss well.

3.Add vegetables into the multi-level air fryer basket.

4.Place basket into the pot. Secure pot with air fryer lid and cook on roast mode at 400 F for 40 minutes.

5.Serve and enjoy.

Nutritional Value (Amount per Serving):

•Calories 189

•Fat 7.6 g

•Carbohydrates 28.5 g

•Sugar 3.5 g

•Protein 3.5 g

•Cholesterol 1 mg

265

CAJUN OKRA FRIES

Preparation Time: 10 minutes

Cooking Time: 30 minutes

Serve: 4

Ingredients:

•15 oz okra, cut the tops & slice lengthwise

•1/2 tsp garlic powder

•1/2 tsp paprika

•1/4 tsp cayenne

•2 tbsp olive oil

•1/2 tsp pepper

•1 tsp kosher salt

Directions:

1.Line multi-level air fryer basket with parchment paper.

2.Add okra, garlic powder, paprika, cayenne, oil, pepper, and salt into the mixing bowl and toss well.

3.Add okra into the multi-level air fryer basket.

4.Place basket into the pot. Secure pot with air fryer lid and cook on roast mode at 375 F for 25-30 minutes.

5.Serve and enjoy.

Nutritional Value (Amount per Serving):

- Calories 105
- Fat 7.3 g
- Carbohydrates 8.5 g
- Sugar 1.7 g
- Protein 2.2 g
- Cholesterol 0 mg

266

ROASTED GREEN BEANS & CARROTS

Preparation Time: 10 minutes

Cooking Time: 20 minutes

Serve: 4

Ingredients:

•1/3 lb green beans, trimmed

•1/2 lb carrots, trimmed, peeled & sliced

•1 tbsp butter

•1/4 cup honey

•1 tbsp olive oil

•1/4 tsp pepper

•1/4 tsp salt

Directions:

1.Line multi-level air fryer basket with parchment paper.

2.In a bowl, add carrots, green beans, olive oil, pepper, and salt and toss well.

3.Add carrots and green beans into the multi-level air fryer basket.

4.Place basket into the pot. Secure pot with air fryer lid and cook on roast mode at 400 F for 20 minutes.

5.Meanwhile, in a small saucepan add butter and honey and cook over medium heat for 2 minutes.

6.Remove roasted carrots and green beans from pot and place into the mixing bowl. Pour honey-butter mixture over roasted vegetables and toss well to coat.

7.Serve and enjoy.

Nutritional Value (Amount per Serving):

•Calories 155

•Fat 6.4 g

•Carbohydrates 25.8 g

•Sugar 20.7 g

•Protein 1.3 g

•Cholesterol 8 mg

267

GREEN BEANS WITH CHERRY TOMATOES

Preparation Time: 10 minutes

Cooking Time: 20 minutes

Serve: 2

Ingredients:

•1/2 lb green beans, trimmed

•1 cup cherry tomatoes, cut in half

•1/4 cup parmesan cheese, shredded

•1/4 cup balsamic vinegar

•1 tbsp olive oil

•1/4 tsp pepper

•1/4 tsp salt

Directions:

1.Line multi-level air fryer basket with parchment paper.

2.In a mixing bowl, add tomatoes, green beans, oil, pepper, and salt and toss well to coat.

3.Add tomatoes and green beans into the multi-level air fryer basket.

4.Place basket into the pot. Secure pot with air fryer lid and cook on roast mode at 400 F for 20 minutes.

5.Meanwhile, in a small saucepan add vinegar and cook until reduced by half.

6.Remove beans and tomatoes from the pot and sprinkle with cheese and drizzle with vinegar.

7.Serve and enjoy.

Nutritional Value (Amount per Serving):

•Calories 154

•Fat 9.7 g

•Carbohydrates 12.4 g

•Sugar 4.1 g

•Protein 6.5 g

•Cholesterol 8 mg

268

BAKED BRUSSELS SPROUTS & ASPARAGUS

Preparation Time: 10 minutes

Cooking Time: 20 minutes

Serve: 3

Ingredients:

•1/2 lb Brussels sprouts, cut in half

•1/2 lb asparagus, trimmed

•2 tbsp parmesan cheese, shredded

•1/2 tsp garlic powder

•2 tbsp olive oil

•Pepper

•Salt

Directions:

1.Line multi-level air fryer basket with parchment paper.

2.In a bowl, toss Brussels sprouts, asparagus, garlic powder, oil, pepper, and salt.

3.Add Brussels sprouts and asparagus into the multi-level air fryer basket.

4.Place basket into the pot. Secure pot with air fryer lid and cook on bake mode at 400 F for 20 minutes. Stir after 15 minutes.

5.Sprinkle parmesan cheese on top of baked vegetables and serve.

Nutritional Value (Amount per Serving):

•Calories 129

•Fat 10.5 g

•Carbohydrates 10.3 g

•Sugar 3.2 g

•Protein 5.6 g

•Cholesterol 3 mg

269

ROASTED ZUCCHINI, TOMATOES & SQUASH

Preparation Time: 10 minutes

Cooking Time: 30 minutes

Serve: 3

Ingredients:

•1/2 lb zucchini, cut into slices

•7 oz cherry tomatoes, cut in half

•1/2 cup parmesan cheese, shredded

•3/4 tsp Italian seasoning

•2 garlic cloves, minced

•1/2 lb yellow squash, cut slices

•1 1/2 tbsp olive oil

•Pepper

•Salt

Directions:

1.Line multi-level air fryer basket with parchment paper.

2.In a large bowl, toss zucchini, tomatoes, squash, Italian seasoning, garlic, cheese, oil, pepper, and salt.

3.Add vegetable mixture into the multi-level air fryer basket.

4.Place basket into the pot. Secure pot with air fryer lid and cook on roast mode at 400 F for 30 minutes.

5.Serve and enjoy.

Nutritional Value (Amount per Serving):

•Calories 151

•Fat 11 g

•Carbohydrates 9 g

•Sugar 4.5 g

•Protein 7.4 g

•Cholesterol 12 mg

270

ROASTED SQUASH & ZUCCHINI

Preparation Time: 10 minutes

Cooking Time: 20 minutes

Serve: 6

Ingredients:

•2 zucchini, diced

•1 tsp garlic salt

•2 tbsp olive oil

•2 squash, diced

•1/2 onion, diced

•1 cup cherry tomatoes, cut in half

•1/3 tsp pepper

•1/2 tsp salt

Directions:

1.Line multi-level air fryer basket with parchment paper.

2.In a mixing bowl, toss squash, zucchini, onion, tomatoes, oil, garlic salt, pepper, and salt.

3.Add vegetable mixture into the multi-level air fryer basket.

4.Place basket into the pot. Secure pot with air fryer lid and cook on roast mode at 400 F for 15-20 minutes.

5.Serve and enjoy.

Nutritional Value (Amount per Serving):

•Calories 72

•Fat 5 g

•Carbohydrates 6.8 g

•Sugar 3.6 g

•Protein 2 g

•Cholesterol 0 mg

271

ROASTED SUMMER ZUCCHINI & TOMATOES

Preparation Time: 10 minutes

Cooking Time: 30 minutes

Serve: 2

Ingredients:

•2 medium zucchini, sliced

•1 cup cherry tomatoes, cut in half

•1/2 tbsp balsamic vinegar

•1 tbsp olive oil

•1/4 tsp pepper

•1/4 tsp salt

Directions:

1.Line multi-level air fryer basket with parchment paper.

2.In a mixing bowl, add zucchini, cherry tomatoes, vinegar, oil, pepper, and salt and toss well.

3.Add zucchini and tomatoes into the multi-level air fryer basket.

4.Place basket into the pot. Secure pot with air fryer lid and cook on roast mode at 375 F for 30 minutes.

5.Serve and enjoy.

Nutritional Value (Amount per Serving):

- •Calories 109
- •Fat 7.5 g
- •Carbohydrates 10.3 g
- •Sugar 5.8 g
- •Protein 3.2 g
- •Cholesterol 0 mg

272

HEALTHY BUTTERNUT SQUASH FRIES

Preparation Time: 10 minutes

Cooking Time: 20 minutes

Serve: 4

Ingredients:

•3 cups butternut squash, peeled and cut into 1-inch cubes

•1/2 tsp paprika

•1 tsp dried oregano

•1 tbsp olive oil

•Salt

Directions:

1.Add butternut squash and remaining ingredients into the bowl and toss well.

2.Add butternut squash into the multi-level air fryer basket.

3.Place basket into the pot. Secure pot with air fryer lid and cook on air fry mode at 400 F for 15-20 minutes.

4.Serve and enjoy.

Nutritional Value (Amount per Serving):

•Calories 79

•Fat 3.7 g

- Carbohydrates 12.7 g
- Sugar 2.4 g
- Protein 1.1 g
- Cholesterol 0 mg

273

SAVORY ROASTED RADISHES

Preparation Time: 10 minutes

Cooking Time: 30 minutes

Serve: 6

Ingredients:

•20 radishes, clean & cut in half

•1/4 tsp dried oregano

•1/2 tsp onion powder

•1/2 tsp dried rosemary

•1 tbsp garlic, minced

•2 tbsp olive oil

•Pepper

•Salt

Directions:

1.Line multi-level air fryer basket with parchment paper.

2.In a mixing bowl, add radishes and remaining ingredients and toss well.

3.Add radishes into the multi-level air fryer basket.

4.Place basket into the pot. Secure pot with air fryer lid and cook on bake mode at 400 F for 25-30 minutes.

5.Serve and enjoy.

Nutritional Value (Amount per Serving):

- Calories 46
- Fat 4.7 g
- Carbohydrates 1.2 g
- Sugar 0.4 g
- Protein 0.2 g
- Cholesterol 0 mg

274

HEALTHY ROASTED YELLOW SQUASH

Preparation Time: 10 minutes

Cooking Time: 15 minutes

Serve: 4

Ingredients:

•2 yellow squash, cut into 1-inch pieces

•1 tsp Italian seasoning

•1 tbsp olive oil

•Pepper

•Salt

Directions:

1.Line multi-level air fryer basket with parchment paper.

2.In a bowl, add squash, Italian seasoning, oil, pepper, and salt and toss well.

3.Add squash into the multi-level air fryer basket.

4.Place basket into the pot. Secure pot with air fryer lid and cook on roast mode at 400 F for 15 minutes.

5.Serve and enjoy.

Nutritional Value (Amount per Serving):

•Calories 49

- •Fat 4 g
- •Carbohydrates 3.4 g
- •Sugar 1.8 g
- •Protein 1.2 g
- •Cholesterol 1 mg

275

DELICIOUS CHICKPEA PATTIES

Preparation Time: 10 minutes

Cooking Time: 35 minutes

Serve: 6

Ingredients:

•14 oz can chickpeas, rinsed & drained

•3 tbsp water

•2 tbsp olive oil

•1 tsp dried parsley

•1 tsp paprika

•1 tsp garlic powder

•1 tbsp nutritional yeast flakes

•4 tbsp shredded carrot

•1/4 cup green onion, chopped

•1/4 cup bell pepper, diced

•1/2 cup breadcrumbs

•1 tsp salt

Directions:

1.Line multi-level air fryer basket with parchment paper.

2.Add chickpeas into the mixing bowl and mash using the potato masher.

3.Add remaining ingredients into the bowl and mix until well combined.

4.Make equal shapes of patties from the mixture and place it into the multi-level air fryer basket.

5.Place basket into the pot. Secure pot with air fryer lid and cook on bake mode at 375 F for 35 minutes.

6.Serve and enjoy.

Nutritional Value (Amount per Serving):

•Calories 168

•Fat 6.1 g

•Carbohydrates 23.9 g

•Sugar 1.3 g

•Protein 5.6 g

•Cholesterol 0 mg

276

HEALTHY SUMMER SQUASH ROAST

Preparation Time: 10 minutes

Cooking Time: 30 minutes

Serve: 4

Ingredients:

•5 cups summer squash, chopped

•1 tbsp Mrs, Dash seasoning

•1 1/2 tbsp olive oil

•1/2 tsp pepper

•1 1/2 tsp salt

Directions:

1.Line multi-level air fryer basket with parchment paper.

2.Add squash and remaining ingredients into the bowl and toss well.

3.Add squash into the multi-level air fryer basket.

4.Place basket into the pot. Secure pot with air fryer lid and cook on roast mode at 400 F for 25-30 minutes.

5.Serve and enjoy.

Nutritional Value (Amount per Serving):

•Calories 76

- Fat 5.7 g
- Carbohydrates 6.3 g
- Sugar 5.6 g
- Protein 1.6 g
- Cholesterol 0 mg

277

SAVORY PESTO TOFU

Preparation Time: 10 minutes

Cooking Time: 40 minutes

Serve: 4

Ingredients:

•1 lb tofu, drained & cut into 1/2-inch cubes

•3 tbsp pesto

•1/4 tsp garlic powder

•1 tbsp olive oil

•1/8 tsp pepper

•1/8 tsp sea salt

Directions:

1.Line multi-level air fryer basket with parchment paper.

2.Add tofu into the mixing bowl. Add pesto, garlic powder, oil, pepper, and salt and stir until tofu is well coated.

3.Place tofu cubes into the multi-level air fryer basket.

4.Place basket into the pot. Secure pot with air fryer lid and cook on bake mode at 350 F for 40 minutes.

5.Serve and enjoy.

Nutritional Value (Amount per Serving):

•Calories 161

- •Fat 13.1 g
- •Carbohydrates 2.9 g
- •Sugar 1.5 g
- •Protein 10.5 g
- •Cholesterol 3 mg

278

CRISPY POTATOES

Preparation Time: 10 minutes

Cooking Time: 15 minutes

Serve: 2

Ingredients:

•2 cups baby potatoes, cut into four pieces each

•1 tsp dried rosemary, minced

•1 1/2 tbsp olive oil

•1/2 tbsp garlic, minced

•Pepper

•Salt

Directions:

1.Line multi-level air fryer basket with parchment paper.

2.In a bowl, add potatoes, garlic, rosemary, oil, pepper, and salt and toss well.

3.Add potatoes into the multi-level air fryer basket.

4.Place basket into the pot. Secure pot with air fryer lid and cook on air fry mode at 400 F for 15 minutes.

5.Serve and enjoy.

Nutritional Value (Amount per Serving):

•Calories 117

- •Fat 10.6 g
- •Carbohydrates 5.8 g
- •Sugar 0 g
- •Protein 1.2 g
- •Cholesterol 0 mg

279

ROASTED CARROTS POTATOES

Preparation Time: 10 minutes

Cooking Time: 40 minutes

Serve: 2

Ingredients:

•1/2 lb carrots, peeled & cut into chunks

•1/2 lb potatoes, cut into 1-inch cubes

•1/2 tsp Italian seasoning

•1/4 tsp garlic powder

•1 tbsp olive oil

•1/2 onion, diced

•Pepper

•Salt

Directions:

1.Line multi-level air fryer basket with parchment paper.

2.In a bowl, toss carrots, potatoes, garlic powder, Italian seasoning, oil, onion, pepper, and salt.

3.Add carrot potato mixture into the multi-level air fryer basket.

4.Place basket into the pot. Secure pot with air fryer lid and cook on roast mode at 400 F for 40 minutes.

5.Serve and enjoy.

Nutritional Value (Amount per Serving):

•Calories 201

•Fat 7.5 g

•Carbohydrates 32 g

•Sugar 8.2 g

•Protein 3.2 g

•Cholesterol 1 mg

280

FRENCH FRIES

Preparation Time: 10 minutes

Cooking Time: 20 minutes

Serve: 4

Ingredients:

•2 large potatoes, scrub and cut into fries shape

•1 tbsp olive oil

•1/4 tsp pepper

•1/2 tsp salt

Directions:

1.Line multi-level air fryer basket with parchment paper.

2.Soak potato fries in water for 15 minutes. Drain well and pat dry.

3.Add potato fries into the bowl. Add oil, pepper, and salt and toss well.

4.Transfer potato fries into the multi-level air fryer basket.

5.Place basket into the pot. Secure pot with air fryer lid and cook on air fry mode at 375 F for 20 minutes. Stir halfway through.

6.Serve and enjoy.

Nutritional Value (Amount per Serving):

- Calories 158
- Fat 3.7 g
- Carbohydrates 29.1 g
- Sugar 2.1 g
- Protein 3.1 g
- Cholesterol 0 mg

281

RANCH POTATOES

Preparation Time: 10 minutes

Cooking Time: 20 minutes

Serve: 2

Ingredients:

•1/2 lb baby potatoes, cut in half

•1/2 tbsp olive oil

•1/4 tsp dill

•1/4 tsp paprika

•1/4 tsp onion powder

•1/4 tsp garlic powder

•1/4 tsp parsley

•Salt

Directions:

1.Line multi-level air fryer basket with parchment paper.

2.Add all ingredients into the bowl and toss well.

3.Add potatoes into the multi-level air fryer basket.

4.Place basket into the pot. Secure pot with air fryer lid and cook on air fry mode at 400 F for 20 minutes. Stir halfway through.

5.Serve and enjoy.

Nutritional Value (Amount per Serving):

•Calories 99

•Fat 3.7 g

•Carbohydrates 14.8 g

•Sugar 0.2 g

•Protein 3.1 g

•Cholesterol 0 mg

282

BROCCOLI FRITTERS

Preparation Time: 10 minutes

Cooking Time: 30 minutes

Serve: 4

Ingredients:

•3 cups broccoli florets, steam & chopped

•2 cups cheddar cheese, shredded

•1/4 cup breadcrumbs

•2 eggs, lightly beaten

•2 garlic cloves, minced

•Pepper

•Salt

Directions:

1.Line multi-level air fryer basket with parchment paper.

2.Add all ingredients into the large bowl and mix until well combined.

3.Make patties from the broccoli mixture and place it into the multi-level air fryer basket.

4.Place basket into the pot. Secure pot with air fryer lid and cook on bake mode at 375 F for 30 minutes. Flip patties halfway through.

5.Serve and enjoy.

Nutritional Value (Amount per Serving):

•Calories 311

•Fat 21.5 g

•Carbohydrates 10.8 g

•Sugar 2.1 g

•Protein 19.8 g

•Cholesterol 141 mg

283

BAKED ZUCCHINI CHUNKS

Preparation Time: 10 minutes

Cooking Time: 20 minutes

Serve: 2

Ingredients:

•3 medium zucchinis, cut into chunks

•2 tbsp olive oil

•1 tsp sweet paprika

•1 tsp garlic powder

•Pepper

•Salt

Directions:

1.Line multi-level air fryer basket with parchment paper.

2.In a bowl, toss zucchini chunks with paprika, garlic powder, oil, pepper, and salt.

3.Spread zucchini into the multi-level air fryer basket.

4.Place basket into the pot. Secure pot with air fryer lid and cook on bake mode at 375 F for 15-20 minutes.

5.Serve and enjoy.

Nutritional Value (Amount per Serving):

•Calories 175

- Fat 14.7 g
- Carbohydrates 11.5 g
- Sugar 5.5 g
- Protein 4 g
- Cholesterol 0 mg

284

ROASTED FROZEN MIXED VEGETABLES

Preparation Time: 10 minutes

Cooking Time: 30 minutes

Serve: 3

Ingredients:

•6 oz mixed frozen vegetables

•1 tbsp olive oil

•1/4 tsp pepper

•1/4 tsp onion powder

•1/4 tsp garlic powder

•1/4 tsp salt

Directions:

1.Line multi-level air fryer basket with parchment paper.

2.In a bowl, toss frozen mixed vegetables with remaining ingredients.

3.Spread vegetables into the multi-level air fryer basket.

4.Place basket into the pot. Secure pot with air fryer lid and cook on bake mode at 390 F for 30 minutes.

5.Serve and enjoy.

Nutritional Value (Amount per Serving):

•Calories 79

- Fat 4.8 g
- Carbohydrates 7.9 g
- Sugar 1.9 g
- Protein 1.7 g
- Cholesterol 0 mg

285

HEALTHY ROOT VEGETABLES

Preparation Time: 10 minutes

Cooking Time: 30 minutes

Serve: 4

Ingredients:

•1 parsnip, cut into 1-inch chunks

•3 medium carrots, cut into 1-inch pieces

•1 onion, cut into wedges

•1 rutabaga, peeled and cut into 1-inch chunks

•2 tsp Italian seasoning

•1 tbsp olive oil

•2 tbsp vinegar

•Pepper

•Salt

Directions:

1.Line multi-level air fryer basket with parchment paper.

2.In a bowl, toss vegetables with remaining ingredients and spread on roasting pan.

3.Add vegetables into the multi-level air fryer basket.

4.Place basket into the pot. Secure pot with air fryer lid and cook on bake mode at 390 F for 25-30 minutes.

5.Serve and enjoy.

Nutritional Value (Amount per Serving):

•Calories 128

•Fat 4.5 g

•Carbohydrates 21.3 g

•Sugar 10.7 g

•Protein 2.3 g

•Cholesterol 2 mg

286

BAKED BABY CARROTS

Preparation Time: 10 minutes

Cooking Time: 30 minutes

Serve: 2

Ingredients:

•12 baby carrots

•1/2 tsp cinnamon

•3 tbsp butter, melted

•2 tbsp brown sugar

•Pepper

•Salt

Directions:

1.Line multi-level air fryer basket with parchment paper.

2.In a bowl, add carrots and remaining ingredients and toss well.

3.Add carrots into the multi-level air fryer basket.

4.Place basket into the pot. Secure pot with air fryer lid and cook on bake mode at 390 F for 25-30 minutes.

5.Serve and enjoy.

Nutritional Value (Amount per Serving):

•Calories 209

- •Fat 17.4 g
- •Carbohydrates 14.3 g
- •Sugar 11.6 g
- •Protein 0.6 g
- •Cholesterol 46 mg

287

ROASTED TASTY SWEET POTATOES

Preparation Time: 10 minutes

Cooking Time: 40 minutes

Serve: 4

Ingredients:

•2 large sweet potatoes, cut into pieces

•1/2 tsp chili powder

•3/4 tsp paprika

•1/4 tsp pepper

•1/4 tsp onion powder

•1/2 tsp garlic powder

•1 tbsp olive oil

•1/2 tsp cumin

•1/2 tsp salt

Directions:

1.Line multi-level air fryer basket with parchment paper.

2.In a bowl, toss sweet potatoes with remaining ingredients until well coated.

3.Spread sweet potatoes into the multi-level air fryer basket.

4.Place basket into the pot. Secure pot with air fryer lid and cook on bake mode at 390 F for 40 minutes.

5.Serve and enjoy.

Nutritional Value (Amount per Serving):

•Calories 85

•Fat 3.7 g

•Carbohydrates 12.8 g

•Sugar 0.4 g

•Protein 0.9 g

•Cholesterol 0 mg

288

CINNAMON BUTTERNUT SQUASH

Preparation Time: 10 minutes

Cooking Time: 40 minutes

Serve: 2

Ingredients:

•1 1/2 lbs butternut squash, peeled & cut into pieces

•1/4 tsp cinnamon

•3/4 tbsp olive oil

•3/4 tbsp maple syrup

•Pepper

•Salt

Directions:

1.Line multi-level air fryer basket with parchment paper.

2.In a mixing bowl, toss squash cubes with remaining ingredients.

3.Spread squash cubes into the multi-level air fryer basket.

4.Place basket into the pot. Secure pot with air fryer lid and cook on roast mode at 400 F for 35-40 minutes.

5.Serve and enjoy.

Nutritional Value (Amount per Serving):

•Calories 219

- Fat 5.6 g
- Carbohydrates 45.1 g
- Sugar 12 g
- Protein 3.4 g
- Cholesterol 0 mg

SNACKS & APPETIZERS

289

CHEESY BROCCOLI BITES

Preparation Time: 10 minutes

Cooking Time: 15 minutes

Serve: 10

Ingredients:

•2 eggs, lightly beaten

•2 cups cheddar cheese, shredded

•2 cups broccoli, cooked & chopped

•2 tbsp water

•1 cup flour

•1 cup breadcrumbs

•1/4 tsp garlic powder

•Pepper

•Salt

Directions:

1.Add all ingredients into the mixing bowl and mix until well combined.

2.Line multi-level air fryer basket with parchment paper.

3.Make small balls from the mixture and press lightly and place them into the basket.

4.Place basket into the pot. Secure pot with air fryer lid and bake at 400 F for 10 minutes.

5.Flip and bake for 5 minutes more or until crispy.

6.Serve and enjoy.

Nutritional Value (Amount per Serving):

•Calories 198

•Fat 9.1 g

•Carbohydrates 18.9 g

•Sugar 1.2 g

•Protein 10 g

•Cholesterol 56 mg

290

CRISPY ARTICHOKE HEARTS

Preparation Time: 10 minutes

Cooking Time: 10 minutes

Serve: 4

Ingredients:

•8.5 oz can artichokes, drained, par dry & quartered

•2 tbsp parmesan cheese, grated

•1/2 cup breadcrumbs

•1/4 cup mayonnaise

•Pepper

•Salt

Directions:

1.Add breadcrumbs, pepper, and salt into the zip-lock bag.

2.In a bowl, mix artichokes with mayonnaise. Transfer artichokes into the zip-lock bag and shake until well coated with breadcrumbs.

3.Place coated artichokes into the multi-level air fryer basket.

4.Place basket into the pot. Secure pot with air fryer lid and air fry at 370 F for 10 minutes.

5.Serve and enjoy.

Nutritional Value (Amount per Serving):

- Calories 154
- Fat 6.6 g
- Carbohydrates 20.6 g
- Sugar 2.4 g
- Protein 4.8 g
- Cholesterol 6 mg

291

PARMESAN CAULIFLOWER FLORETS

Preparation Time: 10 minutes

Cooking Time: 15 minutes

Serve: 6

Ingredients:

•1 medium cauliflower head, cut into 1-inch pieces

•2 tbsp parmesan cheese, grated

•1/2 tsp paprika

•1/2 tsp garlic powder

•2 tbsp olive oil

•1 tsp salt

Directions:

1.Add cauliflower florets and remaining ingredients into the bowl and toss until well coated.

2.Transfer cauliflower florets into the multi-level air fryer basket.

3.Place basket into the pot. Secure pot with air fryer lid and air fry at 390 F for 15 minutes.

4.Serve and enjoy.

Nutritional Value (Amount per Serving):

•Calories 74

- Fat 5.4 g
- Carbohydrates 5.5 g
- Sugar 2.4 g
- Protein 2.8 g
- Cholesterol 2 mg

292

BROCCOLI TOTS

Preparation Time: 10 minutes

Cooking Time: 20 minutes

Serve: 4

Ingredients:

•1 lb broccoli, chopped & cooked

•1/2 tsp garlic powder

•1/2 cup almond flour

•1/4 cup flaxseed meal

•1 tsp salt

Directions:

1.Add broccoli into the food processor and process until the broccoli texture looks like rice.

2.Add broccoli rice and remaining ingredients into the mixing bowl and mix until well combined.

3.Make small tots from the mixture and place it into the multi-level air fryer basket.

4.Place basket into the pot. Secure pot with air fryer lid and bake at 375 F for 20 minutes. Flip tots halfway through.

5.Serve and enjoy.

Nutritional Value (Amount per Serving):

- •Calories 97
- •Fat 4.3 g
- •Carbohydrates 10.5 g
- •Sugar 2.3 g
- •Protein 5.3 g
- •Cholesterol 0 mg

293

CAULIFLOWER CROQUETTES

Preparation Time: 10 minutes

Cooking Time: 13 minutes

Serve: 4

Ingredients:

•2 eggs, lightly beaten

•2 cups cauliflower rice

•1/2 tsp onion powder

•1 tsp dried basil

•1/3 cup breadcrumbs

•1 tsp garlic powder

•4 tbsp mozzarella cheese, shredded

•4 tbsp parmesan cheese, grated

•1/2 cup cheddar cheese, shredded

•1/4 tsp pepper

•1/4 tsp salt

Directions:

1.Add cauliflower rice into the microwave-safe bowl and microwave for 5 minutes.

2.Transfer cauliflower rice and remaining ingredients into the mixing bowl and mix until well combined.

3.Make equal shapes of patties from the mixture and place it into the multi-level air fryer basket.

4.Place basket into the pot. Secure pot with a lid and air fry at 400 F for 8 minutes. Flip halfway through.

5.Serve and enjoy.

Nutritional Value (Amount per Serving):

•Calories 250

•Fat 14.2 g

•Carbohydrates 12.2 g

•Sugar 3.1 g

•Protein 19.1 g

•Cholesterol 115 mg

294

FLAVORS STUFFED MUSHROOMS

Preparation Time: 10 minutes

Cooking Time: 20 minutes

Serve: 12

Ingredients:

•12 large mushrooms, cleaned & remove stems

•1 cup crab meat, cooked and chopped

•2 tbsp fresh parsley, chopped

•1/2 cup parmesan cheese, grated

•1/2 cup green onions, chopped

•1/2 tbsp Worcestershire sauce

•1 tsp garlic, minced

•1/2 cup breadcrumbs

•8 oz cream cheese, softened

Directions:

1.Line multi-level air fryer basket with parchment paper.

2.In a bowl, mix crab meat, parsley, parmesan cheese, green onions, Worcestershire sauce, garlic, breadcrumbs, and cream cheese.

3.Stuff crab meat mixture into the mushroom caps.

4.Place stuffed mushrooms into the multi-level air fryer basket.

5.Place basket into the pot. Secure pot with air fryer lid and cook on bake mode at 375 F for 20 minutes.

6.Serve and enjoy.

Nutritional Value (Amount per Serving):

•Calories 105

•Fat 7.8 g

•Carbohydrates 5.2 g

•Sugar 1 g

•Protein 4.4 g

•Cholesterol 25 mg

295

SPICY BRUSSEL SPROUTS

Preparation Time: 10 minutes

Cooking Time: 30 minutes

Serve: 4

Ingredients:

•1 1/2 lbs Brussel sprouts, trimmed & cut in half

•1/4 tsp cayenne pepper

•1/4 tsp paprika

•1/2 tsp garlic powder

•1 tbsp nutritional yeast

•1 1/2 tbsp hot sauce

•1 1/2 tbsp butter, melted

•Pepper

•Salt

Directions:

1.Line multi-level air fryer basket with parchment paper.

2.In a large bowl, mix cayenne, paprika, garlic powder, nutritional yeast, hot sauce, butter, pepper, and salt.

3.Add Brussel sprouts and toss until well coated.

4.Transfer Brussels sprouts into the multi-level air fryer basket.

5.Place basket into the pot. Secure pot with air fryer lid and cook on roast mode at 375 F for 30 minutes.

6.Serve and enjoy.

Nutritional Value (Amount per Serving):

•Calories 123

•Fat 5.1 g

•Carbohydrates 17.1 g

•Sugar 3.9 g

•Protein 7.1 g

•Cholesterol 11 mg

296

CAULIFLOWER TOTS

Preparation Time: 10 minutes

Cooking Time: 25 minutes

Serve: 4

Ingredients:

•3 cups shredded cauliflower

•1/2 tsp ground mustard

•1/4 cup breadcrumbs

•1 egg, lightly beaten

•4 oz cheddar cheese, shredded

•1 tsp kosher salt

Directions:

1.Line multi-level air fryer basket with parchment paper.

2.Add all ingredients and into the mixing bowl and mix until well combined.

3.Make small tots from cauliflower mixture and place it into the basket.

4.Place basket into the pot. Secure pot with air fryer lid and cook on bake mode at 400 F for 20-25 minutes.

5.Serve and enjoy.

Nutritional Value (Amount per Serving):

- Calories 177
- Fat 11.1 g
- Carbohydrates 9.4 g
- Sugar 2.5 g
- Protein 10.9 g
- Cholesterol 71 mg

297

HONEY MIXED NUTS

Preparation Time: 10 minutes

Cooking Time: 30 minutes

Serve: 8

Ingredients:

•8 oz mixed nuts

•1/2 tsp smoked paprika

•1 tbsp honey

•1 tbsp butter, melted

•1/2 tsp sea salt

Directions:

1.Line multi-level air fryer basket with parchment paper.

2.Add mixed nuts, paprika, honey, butter, and salt into the mixing bowl and toss well.

3.Transfer nuts into the basket.

4.Place basket into the pot. Secure pot with air fryer lid and cook on bake mode at 300 F for 30 minutes. Stir after every 10 minutes.

5.Serve and enjoy.

Nutritional Value (Amount per Serving):

•Calories 195

- •Fat 17.4 g
- •Carbohydrates 8.6 g
- •Sugar 3.4 g
- •Protein 4.5 g
- •Cholesterol 4 mg

298

SAVORY GARLIC ALMONDS

Preparation Time: 10 minutes

Cooking Time: 12 minutes

Serve: 8

Ingredients:

•2 cups almonds

•1/2 tsp garlic powder

•1 tsp Italian seasoning

•2 tsp rosemary, chopped

•1 tbsp olive oil

•1/2 tsp salt

Directions:

1.Line multi-level air fryer basket with parchment paper.

2.Add almonds and remaining ingredients into the mixing bowl and toss well.

3.Add almonds into the basket.

4.Place basket into the pot. Secure pot with air fryer lid and cook on bake mode at 350 F for 12 minutes.

5.Serve and enjoy.

Nutritional Value (Amount per Serving):

•Calories 156

- •Fat 13.6 g
- •Carbohydrates 5.5 g
- •Sugar 1.1 g
- •Protein 5.1 g
- •Cholesterol 0 mg

299

SPICY ALMONDS

Preparation Time: 10 minutes

Cooking Time: 20 minutes

Serve: 6

Ingredients:

•1 1/2 cups almonds

•1/2 tsp cayenne

•1/4 tsp onion powder

•1/4 tsp dried basil

•1/2 tsp garlic powder

•1/2 tsp cumin

•1 1/2 tsp chili powder

•2 tsp Worcestershire sauce

•2 tbsp butter, melted

•1/2 tsp sea salt

Directions:

1.Line multi-level air fryer basket with parchment paper.

2.Add all ingredients except almonds into the mixing bowl and mix well.

3.Add almonds and coat well. Transfer almonds into the basket.

4.Place basket into the pot. Secure pot with air fryer lid and cook on bake mode at 350 F for 18-20 minutes.

5.Serve and enjoy.

Nutritional Value (Amount per Serving):

•Calories 177

•Fat 15.9 g

•Carbohydrates 6.2 g

•Sugar 1.5 g

•Protein 5.2 g

•Cholesterol 10 mg

300

ROASTED CASHEWS

Preparation Time: 10 minutes

Cooking Time: 20 minutes

Serve: 6

Ingredients:

•1 1/2 cups cashews

•2 tsp black pepper

•4 tsp olive oil

•1/2 tsp salt

Directions:

1.Line multi-level air fryer basket with parchment paper.

2.Toss cashews and olive oil. Add cashews into the basket.

3.Place basket into the pot. Secure pot with air fryer lid and cook on bake mode at 350 F for 18-20 minutes.

4.Toss roasted cashews with black pepper and salt.

5.Serve and enjoy.

Nutritional Value (Amount per Serving):

•Calories 225

•Fat 19 g

•Carbohydrates 11.7 g

- Sugar 1.7 g
- Protein 5.3 g
- Cholesterol 0 mg

301

SPICY ROASTED ALMONDS

Preparation Time: 10 minutes

Cooking Time: 15 minutes

Serve: 12

Ingredients:

•3 cups almonds

•1/4 tsp cayenne pepper

•2 tbsp olive oil

•1 tsp sea salt

Directions:

1.Line multi-level air fryer basket with parchment paper.

2.In a bowl, toss almonds with cayenne pepper, oil, and salt.

3.Add almonds into the basket.

4.Place basket into the pot. Secure pot with air fryer lid and cook on bake mode at 350 F for 15 minutes. Stir after 10 minutes.

5.Serve and enjoy.

Nutritional Value (Amount per Serving):

•Calories 158

•Fat 14.2 g

•Carbohydrates 5.1 g

- Sugar 1 g
- Protein 5 g
- Cholesterol 0 mg

302

ROASTED PEANUTS

Preparation Time: 10 minutes

Cooking Time: 20 minutes

Serve: 12

Ingredients:

•3 cups peanuts

•1 tsp garlic powder

•3 tsp cayenne pepper

•3 tbsp hot sauce

•3 tbsp butter, melted

•1 1/2 tsp salt

Directions:

1.Line multi-level air fryer basket with parchment paper.

2.In a bowl, toss peanuts with remaining ingredients until well coated.

3.Add peanuts into the basket.

4.Place basket into the pot. Secure pot with air fryer lid and cook on bake mode at 350 F for 15-20 minutes. Stir after 10 minutes.

5.Serve and enjoy.

Nutritional Value (Amount per Serving):

- Calories 235
- Fat 20.9 g
- Carbohydrates 6.4 g
- Sugar 1.6 g
- Protein 9.6 g
- Cholesterol 8 mg

303

CINNAMON SWEET POTATO FRIES

Preparation Time: 10 minutes

Cooking Time: 15 minutes

Serve: 4

Ingredients:

•2 sweet potatoes, peel & cut into fries shape

•1/2 tsp cinnamon

•2 tbsp sugar

•1 tsp butter, melted

•1 tbsp butter, melted

Directions:

1.Line multi-level air fryer basket with parchment paper.

2.Coat sweet potato fries with 1 tablespoon of melted butter.

3.Add sweet potato fries into the basket.

4.Place basket into the pot. Secure pot with air fryer lid and cook on bake mode at 380 F for 15 minutes.

5.Transfer sweet potato fries into the mixing bowl. Add cinnamon, sugar, and 1 teaspoon melted butter and toss well.

6.Serve and enjoy.

Nutritional Value (Amount per Serving):

•Calories 107

- Fat 3.9 g
- Carbohydrates 18.1 g
- Sugar 6.2 g
- Protein 0.7 g
- Cholesterol 10 mg

304

CRISPY MEXICAN POTATOES

Preparation Time: 10 minutes

Cooking Time: 20 minutes

Serve: 4

Ingredients:

•1 lb baby potatoes, quartered

•1/4 tsp ground coriander

•1/4 tsp cinnamon

•1/2 tsp dried oregano

•1/2 tsp garlic powder

•1/2 tsp chili powder

•1 tbsp olive oil

•1/2 tsp kosher salt

Directions:

1.Line multi-level air fryer basket with parchment paper.

2.Toss potatoes with oil and place them into the basket.

3.Place basket into the pot. Secure pot with air fryer lid and cook on air fry mode at 400 F for 10 minutes.

4.Transfer potatoes into the mixing bowl. Add spices and toss well.

5.Add potatoes into the basket.

6.Place basket into the pot. Secure pot with air fryer lid and cook on air fry mode at 400 F for 10 minutes.

7.Serve and enjoy.

Nutritional Value (Amount per Serving):

•Calories 99

•Fat 3.7 g

•Carbohydrates 14.8 g

•Sugar 0.1 g

•Protein 3 g

•Cholesterol 0 mg

305

SIMPLE & HEALTHY ZUCCHINI CHIPS

Preparation Time: 10 minutes

Cooking Time: 20 minutes

Serve: 6

Ingredients:

•3 cups zucchini slices

•1 tsp garlic powder

•1 tbsp vinegar

•Salt

Directions:

1.Line multi-level air fryer basket with parchment paper.

2.Toss zucchini slices with vinegar.

3.Add zucchini slices into the basket.

4.Place basket into the pot. Secure pot with air fryer lid and cook on air fry mode at 370 F for 20 minutes. Flip zucchini slices halfway through.

5.Season zucchini chips with garlic powder and salt.

6.Serve and enjoy.

Nutritional Value (Amount per Serving):

•Calories 97

- Fat 5.5 g
- Carbohydrates 9.9 g
- Sugar 1.1 g
- Protein 1.1 g
- Cholesterol 0 mg

306

CRISPY ZUCCHINI FRITTERS

Preparation Time: 10 minutes

Cooking Time: 12 minutes

Serve: 8

Ingredients:

•1 egg

•2 1/2 cups shredded zucchini

•1/2 tsp Italian seasoning

•1/2 tsp paprika

•1/4 cup parmesan cheese

•1/2 tsp garlic powder

•1/4 tsp lemon pepper

•1/2 tsp baking powder

•1/2 cup almond flour

•1/2 tsp sea salt

Directions:

1.Line multi-level air fryer basket with parchment paper.

2.Add all ingredients into the mixing bowl and mix until well combined.

3.Make 8 equal shapes of patties from the mixture and place it into the basket.

4.Place basket into the pot. Secure pot with air fryer lid and cook on air fry mode at 380 F for 12 minutes.

5.Serve and enjoy.

Nutritional Value (Amount per Serving):

•Calories 35

•Fat 2.2 g

•Carbohydrates 2.1 g

•Sugar 0.8 g

•Protein 2.5 g

•Cholesterol 23 mg

307

TASTY & CRISPY CHICKPEAS

Preparation Time: 10 minutes

Cooking Time: 15 minutes

Serve: 4

Ingredients:

•14 oz can chickpeas

•1/2 tsp paprika

•1/4 tsp garlic powder

•1 tbsp olive oil

•1/4 tsp onion powder

•1/8 tsp salt

Directions:

1.Line multi-level air fryer basket with parchment paper.

2.In a bowl, toss chickpeas with remaining ingredients.

3.Add chickpeas into the basket.

4.Place basket into the pot. Secure pot with air fryer lid and cook on air fry mode at 390 F for 12-15 minutes.

5.Serve and enjoy.

Nutritional Value (Amount per Serving):

•Calories 201

- Fat 5.2 g
- Carbohydrates 32.4 g
- Sugar 0.1 g
- Protein 7.1 g
- Cholesterol 0 mg

308

HEALTHY BROCCOLI TOTS

Preparation Time: 10 minutes

Cooking Time: 20 minutes

Serve: 12

Ingredients:

•2 cups broccoli, cooked & finely chopped

•1/2 tsp garlic powder

•1 egg, lightly beaten

•1/4 cup onion, minced

•2 potatoes, boiled & mashed

•1/2 tsp pepper

•1/2 tsp salt

Directions:

1.Line multi-level air fryer basket with parchment paper.

2.Add all ingredients and into the mixing bowl and mix until well combined.

3.Make small tots from the mixture and place it into the basket.

4.Place basket into the pot. Secure pot with air fryer lid and cook on bake mode at 400 F for 15-20 minutes.

5.Serve and enjoy.

Nutritional Value (Amount per Serving):
•Calories 37
•Fat 0.5 g
•Carbohydrates 7 g
•Sugar 0.8 g
•Protein 1.5 g
•Cholesterol 14 mg

309

BBQ CHICKPEAS

Preparation Time: 10 minutes

Cooking Time: 25 minutes

Serve: 4

Ingredients:

•14 oz can chickpeas, rinsed & drained

•3/4 tsp sugar

•1/2 tsp garlic powder

•1/2 tsp chili powder

•1/2 tsp paprika

•1 tbsp olive oil

•1/4 tsp salt

Directions:

1.Line multi-level air fryer basket with parchment paper.

2.In a bowl, toss chickpeas with remaining ingredients.

3.Add chickpeas into the basket.

4.Place basket into the pot. Secure pot with air fryer lid and cook on bake mode at 400 F for 25 minutes.

5.Serve and enjoy.

Nutritional Value (Amount per Serving):

•Calories 156

- Fat 4.8 g
- Carbohydrates 24.1 g
- Sugar 1 g
- Protein 5.1 g
- Cholesterol 0 mg

310

FLAVORFUL ROASTED BROCCOLI

Preparation Time: 10 minutes

Cooking Time: 20 minutes

Serve: 4

Ingredients:

•16 oz frozen broccoli florets

•1/4 cup parmesan cheese, grated

•1/4 tsp garlic powder

•1/4 tsp red chili flakes

•2 tbsp olive oil

•1/4 tsp pepper

•1/4 tsp salt

Directions:

1.Line multi-level air fryer basket with parchment paper.

2.In a bowl, add broccoli florets and remaining ingredients and toss well.

3.Add broccoli florets into the basket.

4.Place basket into the pot. Secure pot with air fryer lid and cook on bake mode at 400 F for 18-20 minutes.

5.Serve and enjoy.

Nutritional Value (Amount per Serving):

- Calories 119
- Fat 8.2 g
- Carbohydrates 5.8 g
- Sugar 2.7 g
- Protein 3.2 g
- Cholesterol 4 mg

311

RANCH CHICKPEAS

Preparation Time: 10 minutes

Cooking Time: 50 minutes

Serve: 4

Ingredients:

•14 oz can chickpeas, rinsed & drained

•1/2 tbsp parsley, chopped

•2 tbsp parmesan cheese

•1/4 tsp dried dill

•1/4 tsp onion powder

•1/4 tsp garlic powder

•1 tbsp vinegar

•2 tbsp olive oil

•1 tsp sea salt

Directions:

1.Line multi-level air fryer basket with parchment paper.

2.In a bowl, toss chickpeas with remaining ingredients.

3.Add chickpeas into the basket.

4.Place basket into the pot. Secure pot with air fryer lid and cook on bake mode at 350 F for 40-50 minutes.

5.Serve and enjoy.

Nutritional Value (Amount per Serving):

•Calories 192

•Fat 8.9 g

•Carbohydrates 22.9 g

•Sugar 0.1 g

•Protein 6.1 g

•Cholesterol 3 mg

312

CHEESY ZUCCHINI TOTS

Preparation Time: 10 minutes

Cooking Time: 30 minutes

Serve: 4

Ingredients:

•1 egg

•2 cups grated zucchini

•1/4 tsp onion powder

•1 tsp Italian seasoning

•1/2 cup breadcrumbs

•1/2 cup cheddar cheese, shredded

•Pepper

•Salt

Directions:

1.Line multi-level air fryer basket with parchment paper.

2.Add all ingredients and into the mixing bowl and mix until well combined.

3.Make small tots from the mixture and place it into the basket.

4.Place basket into the pot. Secure pot with air fryer lid and cook on bake mode at 400 F for 25-30 minutes.

5.Serve and enjoy.

Nutritional Value (Amount per Serving):

•Calories 139
•Fat 6.9 g
•Carbohydrates 12.1 g
•Sugar 2.1 g
•Protein 7.4 g
•Cholesterol 57 mg

313

CREAMY QUESO DIP

Preparation Time: 10 minutes

Cooking Time: 5 minutes

Serve: 8

Ingredients:

•4 cup cheddar cheese, shredded

•3/4 cup heavy whipping cream

•4 oz cream cheese

•1/4 tsp black pepper

•1 tsp paprika

•2 tsp cumin

•1/4 cup water

•14 oz can tomatoes

•1 jalapeno, diced

•1/2 onion, diced

•1/4 cup butter

•1 tsp salt

Directions:

1.Set instant pot on sauté mode.

2.Add butter into the pot. Add jalapeno and onion and sauté for 2 minutes. Cancel sauté mode.

3.Add tomatoes and water and stir well.

4.Add paprika, cumin, pepper, and salt and stir to combine.

5.Add cream cheese. Secure pot with pressure cooking lid and cook on high for 1 minute.

6.Once done, release pressure using quick release. Remove lid.

7.Add shredded cheese and heavy cream and stir until cheese is melted.

8.Serve and enjoy.

Nutritional Value (Amount per Serving):

•Calories 386

•Fat 33.8 g

•Carbohydrates 5.7 g

•Sugar 2.7 g

•Protein 16.3 g

•Cholesterol 106 mg

314

SPINACH ARTICHOKE DIP

Preparation Time: 10 minutes

Cooking Time: 3 minutes

Serve: 15

Ingredients:

•1/2 cup parmesan cheese, grated

•8 oz Italian cheese, shredded

•2 tbsp jalapenos, diced

•4 garlic cloves, minced

•6 scallions, chopped

•16 oz cream cheese, cubed

•18 oz jar marinated artichoke, drained & chopped

•10 oz frozen spinach, chopped

•1 1/2 tbsp fresh lemon juice

•1/2 cup vegetable stock

Directions:

1.Add all ingredients except Italian cheese and parmesan cheese into the instant pot and stir well.

2.Secure pot with pressure cooking lid and cook on high for 3 minutes.

3.Once done, allow release pressure naturally for 5 minutes and release remaining using quick release. Remove lid.

4.Add Italian cheese and parmesan cheese and stir well.

5.Serve and enjoy.

Nutritional Value (Amount per Serving):

•Calories 202

•Fat 16.9 g

•Carbohydrates 4.8 g

•Sugar 0.4 g

•Protein 7.9 g

•Cholesterol 46 mg

315

BUFFALO CHICKEN DIP

Preparation Time: 10 minutes

Cooking Time: 15 minutes

Serve: 6

Ingredients:

•1 lb chicken breast, boneless & skinless

•8 oz cream cheese

•16 oz cheddar cheese, shredded

•1 stick butter

•1 cup hot sauce

•1 oz ranch seasoning

Directions:

1.Add all ingredients except cheddar cheese into the instant pot and stir well.

2.Secure pot with pressure cooking lid and cook on high for 15 minutes.

3.Once done, release pressure using quick release. Remove lid.

4.Shred the chicken using a fork.

5.Add cheese and stir until cheese is melted.

6.Serve and enjoy.

Nutritional Value (Amount per Serving):

•Calories 677

•Fat 55.5 g

•Carbohydrates 2.7 g

•Sugar 1 g

•Protein 38.1 g

•Cholesterol 210 mg

316

EGGPLANT CHIPS

Preparation Time: 10 minutes

Cooking Time: 30 minutes

Serve: 2

Ingredients:

•1 eggplant, cut into 1/4-inch slices

•2 tbsp fresh rosemary, chopped

•1/2 cup parmesan cheese, grated

•Pepper

•Salt

Directions:

1.Line multi-level air fryer basket with parchment paper.

2.Toss eggplant slices with rosemary, cheese, pepper, and salt.

3.Add eggplant slices into the basket.

4.Place basket into the pot. Secure pot with air fryer lid and cook on bake mode at 400 F for 30 minutes.

5.Serve and enjoy.

Nutritional Value (Amount per Serving):

•Calories 141

•Fat 5.7 g

- •Carbohydrates 16.4 g
- •Sugar 6.9 g
- •Protein 9.6 g
- •Cholesterol 16 mg

317

CRISPY EGGPLANT CUBES

Preparation Time: 10 minutes

Cooking Time: 20 minutes

Serve: 4

Ingredients:

•1 eggplant, cut into 1-inch pieces

•1/2 tsp Italian seasoning

•1 tsp paprika

•1/2 tsp red pepper

•1 tsp garlic powder

•2 tbsp olive oil

Directions:

1.Line multi-level air fryer basket with parchment paper.

2.Add eggplant pieces and remaining ingredients into the mixing bowl and toss until well coated.

3.Add eggplant pieces into the basket.

4.Place basket into the pot. Secure pot with air fryer lid and cook on air fry mode at 375 F for 20 minutes.

5.Serve and enjoy.

Nutritional Value (Amount per Serving):

•Calories 99

- Fat 7.5 g
- Carbohydrates 8.7 g
- Sugar 4.5 g
- Protein 1.5 g
- Cholesterol 0 mg

318

ROASTED PEPPERS

Preparation Time: 10 minutes

Cooking Time: 13 minutes

Serve: 4

Ingredients:

•3 bell peppers, cut into slices

•2 tbsp olive oil

•Pepper

•Salt

Directions:

1.Line multi-level air fryer basket with parchment paper.

2.In a bowl, toss bell peppers with oil, pepper, and salt.

3.Add bell pepper slices into the basket.

4.Place basket into the pot. Secure pot with air fryer lid and cook on air fry mode at 400 F for 13 minutes.

5.Serve and enjoy.

Nutritional Value (Amount per Serving):

•Calories 89

•Fat 7.2 g

•Carbohydrates 6.8 g

- Sugar 4.5 g
- Protein 0.9 g
- Cholesterol 0 mg

319

ROASTED BEETS

Preparation Time: 10 minutes

Cooking Time: 30 minutes

Serve: 4

Ingredients:

•1 lb beets, peel & cut into 1-inch pieces

•2 tbsp olive oil

•1/2 tsp garlic powder

•Pepper

•Salt

Directions:

1.Line multi-level air fryer basket with parchment paper.

2.In a bowl, toss beets with garlic powder, oil, pepper, and salt.

3.Add beet pieces into the basket.

4.Place basket into the pot. Secure pot with air fryer lid and cook on air fry mode at 390 F for 30 minutes.

5.Serve and enjoy.

Nutritional Value (Amount per Serving):

•Calories 111

•Fat 7.2 g

- •Carbohydrates 11.6 g
- •Sugar 9.1 g
- •Protein 2 g
- •Cholesterol 0 mg

320

AIR FRYER CHERRY TOMATOES

Preparation Time: 10 minutes

Cooking Time: 10 minutes

Serve: 4

Ingredients:

•2 cups cherry tomatoes, cut in half

•1 tsp Italian seasoning

•1 tbsp olive oil

•Pepper

•Salt

Directions:

1.Line multi-level air fryer basket with parchment paper.

2.In a bowl, toss cherry tomatoes with Italian seasoning, oil, pepper, and salt.

3.Add tomatoes into the basket.

4.Place basket into the pot. Secure pot with air fryer lid and cook on air fry mode at 400 F for 10 minutes.

5.Serve and enjoy.

Nutritional Value (Amount per Serving):

•Calories 50

- Fat 4 g
- Carbohydrates 3.7 g
- Sugar 2.5 g
- Protein 0.8 g
- Cholesterol 1 mg

321

PERFECT ROASTED POTATOES

Preparation Time: 10 minutes

Cooking Time: 25 minutes

Serve: 4

Ingredients:

•1 lb potatoes, peel & cut into 1-inch pieces

•1 tbsp olive oil

•1/4 tsp garlic powder

•Pepper

•Salt

Directions:

1.Line multi-level air fryer basket with parchment paper.

2.In a bowl, toss potatoes with oil, garlic powder, pepper, and salt.

3.Add potatoes into the basket.

4.Place basket into the pot. Secure pot with air fryer lid and cook on air fry mode at 400 F for 25 minutes.

5.Serve and enjoy.

Nutritional Value (Amount per Serving):

•Calories 109

- Fat 3.6 g
- Carbohydrates 18 g
- Sugar 1.3 g
- Protein 1.9 g
- Cholesterol 0 mg

322

ACRON SQUASH FRIES

Preparation Time: 10 minutes

Cooking Time: 17 minutes

Serve: 4

Ingredients:

•1 acorn squash, cut into 1-inch wedges

•1 tbsp olive oil

•Pepper

•Salt

Directions:

1.Line multi-level air fryer basket with parchment paper.

2.Toss squash wedges with oil, pepper, and salt.

3.Add squash wedges into the basket.

4.Place basket into the pot. Secure pot with air fryer lid and cook on air fry mode at 400 F for 17 minutes.

5.Serve and enjoy.

Nutritional Value (Amount per Serving):

•Calories 73

•Fat 3.6 g

•Carbohydrates 11.3 g

- Sugar 0 g
- Protein 0.9 g
- Cholesterol 0 mg

323

CRISPY BABY POTATOES

Preparation Time: 10 minutes

Cooking Time: 17 minutes

Serve: 2

Ingredients:

- 1 lb baby potatoes
- 2 tsp steak seasoning
- 1 tsp olive oil
- Pepper
- Salt

Directions:

1. Line multi-level air fryer basket with parchment paper.
2. Add baby potatoes, steak seasoning, oil, pepper, and salt into the mixing bowl and toss well.
3. Add baby potatoes into the basket.
4. Place basket into the pot. Secure pot with air fryer lid and cook on air fry mode at 320 F for 17 minutes.
5. Serve and enjoy.

Nutritional Value (Amount per Serving):

- Calories 207

- Fat 2.3 g
- Carbohydrates 40.1 g
- Sugar 0 g
- Protein 5.3 g
- Cholesterol 0 mg

324

PERFECT AIR FRYER ARTICHOKE HEARTS

Preparation Time: 10 minutes

Cooking Time: 8 minutes

Serve: 4

Ingredients:

•14 oz can artichoke hearts, quartered & drained

•1 tbsp olive oil

•1/8 tsp garlic powder

•1/4 tsp Italian seasoning

•2 tsp parmesan cheese, grated

•Pepper

•Salt

Directions:

1.Line multi-level air fryer basket with parchment paper.

2.Add artichoke hearts and remaining ingredients into the bowl and toss well.

3.Add artichoke hearts into the basket.

4.Place basket into the pot. Secure pot with air fryer lid and cook on air fry mode at 390 F for 8 minutes. Stir halfway through.

5.Serve and enjoy.

Nutritional Value (Amount per Serving):

- •Calories 71
- •Fat 4.3 g
- •Carbohydrates 5.2 g
- •Sugar 0.9 g
- •Protein 2.8 g
- •Cholesterol 3 mg

325

HERB MUSHROOMS

Preparation Time: 10 minutes

Cooking Time: 14 minutes

Serve: 4

Ingredients:

•1 lb mushroom caps

•1 tsp rosemary, chopped

•1 tbsp basil, minced

•1/2 tsp garlic, minced

•1/2 tbsp vinegar

•1/2 tsp ground coriander

•Pepper

•Salt

Directions:

1.Line multi-level air fryer basket with parchment paper.

2.Add all ingredients into the mixing bowl and toss well.

3.Add mushrooms into the basket.

4.Place basket into the pot. Secure pot with air fryer lid and cook on air fry mode at 350 F for 14 minutes.

5.Serve and enjoy.

Nutritional Value (Amount per Serving):

- Calories 26
- Fat 0.4 g
- Carbohydrates 4.1 g
- Sugar 2 g
- Protein 3.6 g
- Cholesterol 0 mg

326

SWEET & SPICY CASHEW

Preparation Time: 10 minutes

Cooking Time: 15 minutes

Serve: 8

Ingredients:

•2 1/2 cups cashew nuts

•1 tsp chili powder

•1/4 cup honey

•2 tbsp sugar

•1/4 tsp cayenne

•1 1/2 tsp sea salt

Directions:

1.Line multi-level air fryer basket with parchment paper.

2.In a microwave-safe bowl add honey and cayenne, chili powder, and microwave for 20-30 seconds. Stir well.

3.Add cashews and honey chili mixture into the mixing bowl and toss to coat.

4.Add cashew into the basket.

5.Place basket into the pot. Secure pot with air fryer lid and cook on roast mode at 325 F for 10-15 minutes.

6.Remove from the oven and let it cool for 5 minutes.

7.Add sugar and salt and toss well.

8.Serve.

Nutritional Value (Amount per Serving):

•Calories 290

•Fat 19.9 g

•Carbohydrates 25.9 g

•Sugar 13.9 g

•Protein 6.6 g

•Cholesterol 0 mg

327

FLAVORFUL POTATO WEDGES

Preparation Time: 10 minutes

Cooking Time: 15 minutes

Serve: 4

Ingredients:

•2 medium potatoes, cut into wedges

•1 1/2 tbsp olive oil

•1/4 tsp pepper

•1/8 tsp cayenne pepper

•1/4 tsp garlic powder

•1/2 tsp paprika

•1 tsp sea salt

Directions:

1.Line multi-level air fryer basket with parchment paper.

2.Soak potato wedges into the cold water for 30 minutes. Drain well and pat dry.

3.In a mixing bowl, toss potato wedges with remaining ingredients.

4.Add potato wedges into the basket.

5.Place basket into the pot. Secure pot with air fryer lid and cook on air fry mode at 400 F for 15 minutes.

6.Serve and enjoy.

Nutritional Value (Amount per Serving):

•Calories 120

•Fat 5.4 g

•Carbohydrates 17.1 g

•Sugar 1.3 g

•Protein 1.9 g

•Cholesterol 0 mg

328

SIMPLE BROCCOLI NUGGETS

Preparation Time: 10 minutes

Cooking Time: 20 minutes

Serve: 4

Ingredients:

•2 cups broccoli florets, cooked until soften

•1 cup cheddar cheese, shredded

•2 egg whites

•1/4 cup Italian breadcrumbs

•1/8 tsp salt

Directions:

1.Line multi-level air fryer basket with parchment paper.

2.Add cooked broccoli to the bowl and using masher mash broccoli into small pieces.

3.Add remaining ingredients to the bowl and mix until well combined.

4.Make small nuggets from the mixture and place it into the basket.

5.Place basket into the pot. Secure pot with air fryer lid and cook on bake mode at 350 F for 20 minutes.

6.Serve and enjoy.

Nutritional Value (Amount per Serving):

•Calories 165

•Fat 9.9 g

•Carbohydrates 8.4 g

•Sugar 1.5 g

•Protein 11 g

•Cholesterol 30 mg

329

CINNAMON MAPLE CHICKPEAS

Preparation Time: 10 minutes

Cooking Time: 12 minutes

Serve: 4

Ingredients:

•14 oz can chickpeas, rinsed, drained and pat dry

•1 tbsp maple syrup

•1 tbsp olive oil

•1/2 tsp ground cinnamon

•Pepper

•Salt

Directions:

1.Line multi-level air fryer basket with parchment paper.

2.Add chickpeas into the basket.

3.Place basket into the pot. Secure pot with air fryer lid and cook on air fry mode at 375 F for 12 minutes.

4.In a large bowl, mix cinnamon, maple syrup, oil, pepper, and salt.

5.Add chickpeas and toss well.

6.Serve and enjoy.

Nutritional Value (Amount per Serving):

- •Calories 162
- •Fat 4.6 g
- •Carbohydrates 26 g
- •Sugar 3 g
- •Protein 4.9 g
- •Cholesterol 0 mg

330

SWEET PECAN HALVES

Preparation Time: 5 minutes

Cooking Time: 6 minutes

Serve: 6

Ingredients:

•2 cups pecan halves

•1 tsp brown sugar

•1 tbsp butter, melted

•Salt

Directions:

1.Line multi-level air fryer basket with parchment paper.

2.Add pecans, butter, and salt in a mixing bowl and toss well.

3.Add pecans into the basket.

4.Place basket into the pot. Secure pot with air fryer lid and cook on air fry mode at 400 F for 6 minutes.

5.Serve and enjoy.

Nutritional Value (Amount per Serving):

•Calories 135

•Fat 13.8 g

•Carbohydrates 2.9 g

- Sugar 1.1 g
- Protein 1.8 g
- Cholesterol 5 mg

331

PARMESAN CARROT FRIES

Preparation Time: 10 minutes

Cooking Time: 15 minutes

Serve: 4

Ingredients:

•4 carrots, peeled and cut into fries

•2 tbsp parmesan cheese, grated

•2 tbsp olive oil

•Pepper

•Salt

Directions:

1.Line multi-level air fryer basket with parchment paper.

2.Add carrots and remaining ingredients into the mixing bowl and toss well.

3.Add carrots fries into the basket.

4.Place basket into the pot. Secure pot with air fryer lid and cook on air fry mode at 350 F for 15 minutes.

5.Serve and enjoy.

Nutritional Value (Amount per Serving):

•Calories 98

- •Fat 7.9 g
- •Carbohydrates 6.2 g
- •Sugar 3 g
- •Protein 1.8 g
- •Cholesterol 3 mg

332

HEALTHY TARO FRIES

Preparation Time: 10 minutes

Cooking Time: 20 minutes

Serve: 2

Ingredients:

•8 small taro, peel and cut into fries shape

•1/4 tsp pepper

•1 tbsp olive oil

•1/2 tsp salt

Directions:

1.Line multi-level air fryer basket with parchment paper.

2.Add taro fries in a bowl and drizzle with olive oil. Season with pepper and salt.

3.Transfer taro slices into the basket.

4.Place basket into the pot. Secure pot with air fryer lid and cook on air fry mode at 400 F for 20 minutes.

5.Serve and enjoy.

Nutritional Value (Amount per Serving):

•Calories 203

•Fat 7.1 g

- Carbohydrates 34.8 g
- Sugar 0.5 g
- Protein 0.6 g
- Cholesterol 0 mg

333

TASTY BAKED OKRA

Preparation Time: 10 minutes

Cooking Time: 15 minutes

Serve: 4

Ingredients:

•1 lb fresh okra, cut into 3/4-inch pieces

•2 tbsp olive oil

•1 tsp smoked paprika

•1/4 tsp chili powder

•1/4 tsp garlic powder

•Salt

Directions:

1.Line multi-level air fryer basket with parchment paper.

2.Add okra, chili powder, paprika, oil, garlic powder, and salt into the bowl and toss well.

3.Add okra into the basket.

4.Place basket into the pot. Secure pot with air fryer lid and cook on bake mode at 390 F for 15 minutes.

5.Serve and enjoy.

Nutritional Value (Amount per Serving):

•Calories 108

- Fat 7.3 g
- Carbohydrates 9 g
- Sugar 1.8 g
- Protein 2.3 g
- Cholesterol 0 mg

334

PAPRIKA CARROT FRIES

Preparation Time: 10 minutes

Cooking Time: 15 minutes

Serve: 2

Ingredients:

•1/2 lb carrots, peeled and cut into fries shape

•1/4 tsp paprika

•1/4 tsp onion powder

•1/4 tsp cumin

•1/2 tbsp olive oil

•1/4 tsp kosher salt

Directions:

1.Line multi-level air fryer basket with parchment paper.

2.In a large bowl, add all ingredients and toss until well coated.

3.Add carrots fries into the basket.

4.Place basket into the pot. Secure pot with air fryer lid and cook on air fry mode at 400 F for 15 minutes.

5.Serve and enjoy.

Nutritional Value (Amount per Serving):

•Calories 79

- •Fat 3.6 g
- •Carbohydrates 11.7 g
- •Sugar 5.7 g
- •Protein 1.1 g
- •Cholesterol 0 mg

335

CRUNCHY BROCCOLI FLORETS

Preparation Time: 10 minutes

Cooking Time: 10 minutes

Serve: 4

Ingredients:

- 1 lb broccoli florets
- 1/2 tsp red chili powder
- 1/4 tsp turmeric powder
- 2 tbsp plain yogurt
- 1 tbsp chickpea flour
- 1/2 tsp salt

Directions:

1. Line multi-level air fryer basket with parchment paper.
2. Add all ingredients to the bowl and toss well.
3. Place marinated broccoli in the fridge for 15 minutes.
4. Place marinated broccoli into the basket.
5. Place basket into the pot. Secure pot with air fryer lid and cook on air fry mode at 400 F for 10 minutes.
6. Serve and enjoy.

Nutritional Value (Amount per Serving):

- Calories 57

- •Fat 0.7 g
- •Carbohydrates 10.2 g
- •Sugar 2.8 g
- •Protein 4.3 g
- •Cholesterol 0 mg

336

CRISPY EGGPLANT FRIES

Preparation Time: 10 minutes

Cooking Time: 20 minutes

Serve: 4

Ingredients:

•1 eggplant, cut into 3-inch pieces

•2 tbsp water

•1 tbsp olive oil

•4 tbsp cornstarch

•Salt

Directions:

1.Line multi-level air fryer basket with parchment paper.

2.In a bowl, mix together water, oil, eggplant, and cornstarch.

3.Place eggplant fries into the basket.

4.Place basket into the pot. Secure pot with air fryer lid and cook on air fry mode at 390 F for 20 minutes.

5.Serve and enjoy.

Nutritional Value (Amount per Serving):

•Calories 89

•Fat 3.7 g

- Carbohydrates 14 g
- Sugar 3.4 g
- Protein 1.1 g
- Cholesterol 0 mg

337

AIR FRYER FISH PATTIES

Preparation Time: 10 minutes

Cooking Time: 15 minutes

Serve: 2

Ingredients:

•1 1/2 cups white fish, cooked

•1/2 tsp sage

•1 tsp parsley

•2 tsp flour

•1 tbsp butter

•1/2 cup mashed potatoes

•1 1/2 tbsp milk

•Pepper

•Salt

Directions:

1.Line multi-level air fryer basket with parchment paper.

2.Add all ingredients to a bowl and mix well.

3.Make patties from mixture and place in the refrigerator for 1 hour.

4.Place patties into the basket.

5.Place basket into the pot. Secure pot with air fryer lid and cook on air fry mode at 400 F for 15 minutes.

6.Serve and enjoy.

Nutritional Value (Amount per Serving):

•Calories 412

•Fat 34.3 g

•Carbohydrates 12.5 g

•Sugar 0.5 g

•Protein 14.7 g

•Cholesterol 17 mg

DEHYDRATE

338

ZUCCHINI CHIPS

Preparation Time: 10 minutes

Cooking Time: 8 hours

Serve: 4

Ingredients:

•2 medium zucchini, wash and cut into 1/4-inch slices

•1/2 tsp garlic powder

•1 tsp olive oil

•1/8 tsp cayenne pepper

•1/8 tsp sea salt

Directions:

1.Add all ingredients into the owl and toss well to coat.

2.Arrange zucchini slices in a multi-level air fryer basket.

3.Place the dehydrating tray in the air fryer basket and arrange the remaining zucchini slices on the dehydrating tray.

4.Place basket into the pot. Secure pot with air fryer lid and cook on dehydrate mode at 135 F for 6-8 hours.

5.Store in an air-tight container.

Nutritional Value (Amount per Serving):

•Calories 27

- Fat 1.4 g
- Carbohydrates 3.6 g
- Sugar 1.8 g
- Protein 1.3 g
- Cholesterol 0 mg

339

EGGPLANT CHIPS

Preparation Time: 10 minutes

Cooking Time: 4 hours

Serve: 4

Ingredients:

•1 medium eggplant, cut into ¼ inch thick slices

•1/4 tsp garlic powder

•1 tsp paprika

•1/4 tsp onion powder

Directions:

1.Add all ingredients into the bowl and toss well.

2.Arrange eggplant slices in a multi-level air fryer basket.

3.Place the dehydrating tray in the air fryer basket and arrange remaining eggplant slices on the dehydrating tray.

4.Place basket into the pot. Secure pot with air fryer lid and cook on dehydrate mode at 145 F for 4 hours.

5.Store in an air-tight container.

Nutritional Value (Amount per Serving):

•Calories 31

•Fat 0.3 g

- Carbohydrates 7.3 g
- Sugar 3.6 g
- Protein 1.3 g
- Cholesterol 0 mg

340

ZUCCHINI CHIPS

Preparation Time: 10 minutes

Cooking Time: 12 hours

Serve: 8

Ingredients:

•4 cups zucchini, sliced thinly

•2 tbsp olive oil

•2 tbsp vinegar

•2 tsp sea salt

Directions:

1.Add olive oil, vinegar, and sea salt to the large bowl and stir well.

2.Add sliced zucchini to the bowl and toss well.

3.Arrange zucchini slices in a multi-level air fryer basket.

4.Place the dehydrating tray in the air fryer basket and arrange the remaining zucchini slices on the dehydrating tray.

5.Place basket into the pot. Secure pot with air fryer lid and cook on dehydrate mode at 135 F for 8-12 hours.

6.Store in an air-tight container.

Nutritional Value (Amount per Serving):

•Calories 40

- •Fat 3.6 g
- •Carbohydrates 1.9 g
- •Sugar 1 g
- •Protein 0.7 g
- •Cholesterol 0 mg

341

CINNAMON CARROTS

Preparation Time: 10 minutes

Cooking Time: 10 hours

Serve: 4

Ingredients:

•10 oz shredded carrots

•2 tbsp coconut oil, melted

•1/2 tsp ground cinnamon

•1 tbsp granulated sugar

•1/2 tsp sea salt

Directions:

1.Add melted coconut oil in a large bowl.

2.Add sugar, cinnamon, and salt to the bowl and stir well.

3.Add shredded carrots to the bowl and toss well.

4.Arrange shredded carrots in a multi-level air fryer basket.

5.Place the dehydrating tray in the air fryer basket and arrange the remaining shredded carrots on the dehydrating tray.

6.Place basket into the pot. Secure pot with air fryer lid and cook on dehydrate mode at 125 F for 8-10 hours.

7.Store in an air-tight container.

Nutritional Value (Amount per Serving):

- Calories 100
- Fat 6.8 g
- Carbohydrates 10.2 g
- Sugar 6.5 g
- Protein 0.6 g
- Cholesterol 0 mg

342

FLAVORS BROCCOLI CHIPS

Preparation Time: 10 minutes

Cooking Time: 12 hours

Serve: 4

Ingredients:

•1 lb broccoli, cut into florets

•1/2 cup vegetable broth

•1/4 cup hemp seeds

•2 tbsp nutritional yeast

•1 tsp onion powder

•1 garlic clove

Directions:

1.Add broccoli florets in a large bowl and set aside.

2.Add remaining ingredients into the blender and blend until smooth.

3.Pour blended mixture over broccoli florets and toss well.

4.Arrange broccoli florets in a multi-level air fryer basket.

5.Place the dehydrating tray in the air fryer basket and arrange the remaining broccoli florets on the dehydrating tray.

6.Place basket into the pot. Secure pot with air fryer lid and cook on dehydrate mode t 115 F for 10-12 hours.

7.Store in an air-tight container.

Nutritional Value (Amount per Serving):

•Calories 106
•Fat 4.3 g
•Carbohydrates 11.2 g
•Sugar 2.2 g
•Protein 8.7 g
•Cholesterol 0 mg

343

TASTY CAULIFLOWER POPCORN

Preparation Time: 10 minutes

Cooking Time: 12 hours

Serve: 4

Ingredients:

•1 cauliflower head, cut into florets

•1 tbsp nutritional yeast

•1 tbsp olive oil

•2 tsp chili powder

•1 tsp cumin powder

•Salt

Directions:

1.Cut cauliflower florets into bite-size pieces and transfer to the bowl.

2.Add remaining ingredients to the bowl and toss until well coated.

3.Arrange cauliflower in the multi-level air fryer basket.

4.Place the dehydrating tray in the air fryer basket and arrange the remaining cauliflower on the dehydrating tray.

5.Place basket into the pot. Secure pot with air fryer lid and cook on dehydrate mode at 115 F for 10-12 hours.

6.Store in an air-tight container.

Nutritional Value (Amount per Serving):

- Calories 61
- Fat 4.1 g
- Carbohydrates 5.6 g
- Sugar 1.7 g
- Protein 2.7 g
- Cholesterol 0 mg

344

SQUASH CHIPS

Preparation Time: 10 minutes

Cooking Time: 12 hours

Serve: 8

Ingredients:

•1 yellow squash, cut into 1/8-inch thick slices

•2 tsp olive oil

•2 tbsp vinegar

•Salt

Directions:

1.Add all ingredients into the bowl and toss well.

2.Arrange squash slices in a multi-level air fryer basket.

3.Place the dehydrating tray in the air fryer basket and arrange remaining squash slices on the dehydrating tray.

4.Place basket into the pot. Secure pot with air fryer lid and cook on dehydrate mode at 115 F for 12 hours.

5.Store in an air-tight container.

Nutritional Value (Amount per Serving):

•Calories 15

•Fat 1.2 g

- •Carbohydrates 0.9 g
- •Sugar 0.4 g
- •Protein 0.3 g
- •Cholesterol 0 mg

345

CINNAMON SWEET POTATO CHIPS

Preparation Time: 10 minutes

Cooking Time: 12 hours

Serve: 2

Ingredients:

•2 sweet potatoes, peel and sliced thinly

•1 tsp coconut oil, melted

•1/8 tsp ground cinnamon

•Seal salt

Directions:

1.Add sweet potato slices in a bowl.

2.Add cinnamon, coconut oil, and salt and toss well.

3.Arrange sweet potato slices in a multi-level air fryer basket.

4.Place the dehydrating tray in the air fryer basket and arrange the remaining sweet potato slices on the dehydrating tray.

5.Place basket into the pot. Secure pot with air fryer lid and cook on dehydrate mode at 125 F for 12 hours.

6.Store in an air-tight container.

Nutritional Value (Amount per Serving):

•Calories 120

- Fat 2.4 g
- Carbohydrates 23.8 g
- Sugar 0.4 g
- Protein 1.3 g
- Cholesterol 23.8 mg

346

AVOCADO CHIPS

Preparation Time: 10 minutes

Cooking Time: 10 hours

Serve: 4

Ingredients:

•4 avocados, halved and pitted

•1/4 tsp sea salt

•1/4 tsp cayenne pepper

•1/2 lemon juice

Directions:

1.Cut avocado into the slices.

2.Drizzle lemon juice over avocado slices. Sprinkle with cayenne pepper and salt.

3.Arrange avocado slices in a multi-level air fryer basket.

4.Place the dehydrating tray in the air fryer basket and arrange the remaining avocado slices on the dehydrating tray.

5.Place basket into the pot. Secure pot with air fryer lid and cook on dehydrate mode at 160 F for 10 hours.

6.Store in an air-tight container.

Nutritional Value (Amount per Serving):

•Calories 412

- Fat 39.3 g
- Carbohydrates 17.5 g
- Sugar 1.1 g
- Protein 3.9 g
- Cholesterol 0 mg

347

DRIED BELL PEPPERS

Preparation Time: 10 minutes

Cooking Time: 24 hours

Serve: 4

Ingredients:

•4 bell peppers, cut in half and de-seed

Directions:

1.Cut bell peppers into strips then cut each strip into 1/2-inch pieces.

2.Arrange bell peppers strips in a multi-level air fryer basket.

3.Place the dehydrating tray in the air fryer basket and arrange the remaining bell pepper strips on the dehydrating tray.

4.Place basket into the pot. Secure pot with air fryer lid and cook on dehydrate mode at 135 F for 12-24 hours.

5.Store in an air-tight container.

Nutritional Value (Amount per Serving):

•Calories 38

•Fat 0.3 g

•Carbohydrates 9 g

•Sugar 6 g

•Protein 1.2 g
•Cholesterol 0 mg

348

DRIED KIWI

Preparation Time: 10 minutes

Cooking Time: 12 hours

Serve: 4

Ingredients:

•4 kiwis, peeled and cut into 1/4-inch thick slices

Directions:

1.Arrange kiwi slices in a multi-level air fryer basket.

2.Place the dehydrating tray in the air fryer basket and arrange the remaining kiwi slices on the dehydrating tray.

3.Place basket into the pot. Secure pot with air fryer lid and cook on dehydrate mode at 135 F for 6-12 hours.

4.Store in an air-tight container.

Nutritional Value (Amount per Serving):

•Calories 46

•Fat 0.4 g

•Carbohydrates 11.1 g

•Sugar 6.8 g

•Protein 0.9 g

•Cholesterol 0 mg

349

CINNAMON CANDIED PECANS

Preparation Time: 10 minutes

Cooking Time: 12 hours

Serve: 4

Ingredients:

•1 cup pecan halves, soaked in water overnight

•1/2 cup maple syrup

•1 tsp cinnamon

•1/8 tsp nutmeg

Directions:

1.Add all ingredients into the bowl and toss well.

2.Arrange pecans in a multi-level air fryer basket.

3.Place the dehydrating tray in the air fryer basket and arrange the remaining pecans on the dehydrating tray.

4.Place basket into the pot. Secure pot with air fryer lid and cook on dehydrate mode at 105 F for 12 hours.

5.Store in an air-tight container.

Nutritional Value (Amount per Serving):

•Calories 192

•Fat 9.1 g

•Carbohydrates 28.7 g
•Sugar 23.9 g
•Protein 1.4 g
•Cholesterol 0 mg

350

DRIED RASPBERRIES

Preparation Time: 10 minutes

Cooking Time: 18 hours

Serve: 4

Ingredients:

•4 cups raspberries, wash and dry

•1/4 cup lemon juice

Directions:

1.Add raspberries and lemon juice in a bowl and toss well.

2.Arrange raspberries in a multi-level air fryer basket.

3.Place the dehydrating tray in the air fryer basket and arrange the remaining raspberries on the dehydrating tray.

4.Place basket into the pot. Secure pot with air fryer lid and cook on dehydrate mode at 135 F for 15-18 hours.

5.Store in an air-tight container.

Nutritional Value (Amount per Serving):

•Calories 68

•Fat 0.9 g

•Carbohydrates 15 g

•Sugar 5.8 g

- Protein 1.6 g
- Cholesterol 0 mg

351

ROSEMARY ALMONDS

Preparation Time: 10 minutes

Cooking Time: 24 hours

Serve: 6

Ingredients:

•2 cups almonds, soak in water overnight

•1 tbsp olive oil

•1 tbsp fresh rosemary, chopped

•1 tsp chili powder

•1/2 tsp kosher salt

Directions:

1.Add all ingredients into the bowl and toss well.

2.Arrange almonds in a multi-level air fryer basket.

3.Place the dehydrating tray in the air fryer basket and arrange the remaining almonds on the dehydrating tray.

4.Place basket into the pot. Secure pot with air fryer lid and cook on dehydrate mode at 125 F for 12-24 hours.

5.Store in an air-tight container.

Nutritional Value (Amount per Serving):

•Calories 206

- Fat 18.3 g
- Carbohydrates 7.4 g
- Sugar 1.4 g
- Protein 6.8 g
- Cholesterol 0 mg

352

DRIED STRAWBERRY SLICES

Preparation Time: 10 minutes

Cooking Time: 12 hours

Serve: 4

Ingredients:

•2 cups strawberries, sliced 1/4-inch thick

Directions:

1.Arrange strawberry slices in a multi-level air fryer basket.

2.Place the dehydrating tray in the air fryer basket and arrange the remaining strawberry slices on the dehydrating tray.

3.Place basket into the pot. Secure pot with air fryer lid and cook on dehydrate mode at 135 F for 8-12 hours.

4.Store in an air-tight container.

Nutritional Value (Amount per Serving):

•Calories 23

•Fat 0.2 g

•Carbohydrates 5.5 g

•Sugar 3.5 g

•Protein 0.5 g

•Cholesterol 0 mg

353

GREEN APPLE CHIPS

Preparation Time: 10 minutes

Cooking Time: 8 hours

Serve: 4

Ingredients:

•4 green apples, cored and sliced 1/8-inch thick

•1/2 lime juice

Directions:

1.Add apple slices and lime juice in a bowl and toss well and set aside for 5 minutes.

2.Arrange apple slices in a multi-level air fryer basket.

3.Place the dehydrating tray in the air fryer basket and arrange the remaining apple slices on the dehydrating tray.

4.Place basket into the pot. Secure pot with air fryer lid and cook on dehydrate mode at 145 F for 8 hours.

5.Store in an air-tight container.

Nutritional Value (Amount per Serving):

•Calories 117

•Fat 0.4 g

•Carbohydrates 31.3 g

- Sugar 23.3 g
- Protein 0.6 g
- Cholesterol 0 mg

354

SNAP PEA CHIPS

Preparation Time: 10 minutes

Cooking Time: 8 hours

Serve: 6

Ingredients:

•3 cups snap peas

•2 tbsp nutritional yeast

•2 tbsp olive oil

•1/2 tsp garlic powder

•1/2 tsp sea salt

Directions:

1.Toss snap peas with oil, garlic powder, nutritional yeast, and salt.

2.Arrange snap peas in a multi-level air fryer basket.

3.Place the dehydrating tray in the air fryer basket and arrange the remaining snap peas on the dehydrating tray.

4.Place basket into the pot. Secure pot with air fryer lid and cook on dehydrate mode at 135 F for 8 hours.

5.Store in an air-tight container.

Nutritional Value (Amount per Serving):

•Calories 111

- Fat 5.1 g
- Carbohydrates 12.2 g
- Sugar 4.2 g
- Protein 5.5 g
- Cholesterol 0 mg

355

DRIED OKRA

Preparation Time: 10 minutes

Cooking Time: 24 hours

Serve: 4

Ingredients:

•10 pods okra, slice into rounds

Directions:

1.Place the cooking tray in the air fryer basket.

2.Arrange okra slices in a multi-level air fryer basket.

3.Place the dehydrating tray in the air fryer basket and arrange remaining okra slices on the dehydrating tray.

4.Place basket into the pot. Secure pot with air fryer lid and cook on dehydrate mode at 130 F for 24 hours.

5.Store in an air-tight container.

Nutritional Value (Amount per Serving):

•Calories 100

•Fat 0.5 g

•Carbohydrates 18.6 g

•Sugar 3.7 g

•Protein 4.8 g

•Cholesterol 0 mg

356

LEMON SLICES

Preparation Time: 10 minutes

Cooking Time: 5 hours

Serve: 6

Ingredients:

•4 lemons, cut into 1/4-inch thick slices

Directions:

1.Place the cooking tray in the air fryer basket.

2.Arrange lemon slices in a multi-level air fryer basket.

3.Place the dehydrating tray in the air fryer basket and arrange remaining lemon slices on the dehydrating tray.

4.Place basket into the pot. Secure pot with air fryer lid and cook on dehydrate mode at 165 F for 5 hours.

5.Store in an air-tight container.

Nutritional Value (Amount per Serving):

•Calories 11

•Fat 0.1 g

•Carbohydrates 3.6 g

•Sugar 1 g

•Protein 0.4 g

•Cholesterol 0 mg

357

DRIED PEAR CHIPS

Preparation Time: 10 minutes

Cooking Time: 8 hours

Serve: 4

Ingredients:

•3 pears, cut into slices

Directions:

1.Arrange pear slices in a multi-level air fryer basket.

2.Place the dehydrating tray in the air fryer basket and arrange remaining pear slices on the dehydrating tray.

3.Place basket into the pot. Secure pot with air fryer lid and cook on dehydrate mode at 130 F for 8 hours.

4.Store in an air-tight container.

Nutritional Value (Amount per Serving):

•Calories 91

•Fat 0.2 g

•Carbohydrates 23.9 g

•Sugar 15.3 g

•Protein 0.6 g

•Cholesterol 0 mg

358

CINNAMON APPLE CHIPS

Preparation Time: 10 minutes

Cooking Time: 8 hours

Serve: 2

Ingredients:

- 1 apple, cut into 1/4-inch thick slices
- 1 tsp cinnamon
- 1 tsp water
- 1 tsp curry powder

Directions:

1. In a small bowl, mix curry powder, cinnamon, and water.
2. Brush apple slices with curry powder mixture.
3. Arrange apple slices in a multi-level air fryer basket.
4. Place the dehydrating tray in the air fryer basket and arrange the remaining apple slices on the dehydrating tray.
5. Place basket into the pot. Secure pot with air fryer lid and cook on dehydrate mode at 135 F for 8 hours.
6. Store in an air-tight container.

Nutritional Value (Amount per Serving):

- Calories 64

- Fat 0.4 g
- Carbohydrates 16.9 g
- Sugar 11.7 g
- Protein 0.5 g
- Cholesterol 0 mg

359

CHILI LIME CAULIFLOWER POPCORN

Preparation Time: 10 minutes

Cooking Time: 12 hours

Serve: 4

Ingredients:

- 1 large cauliflower head, cut into florets
- 1 tbsp chili powder
- 1/4 tsp cayenne
- 1 tbsp olive oil
- 1 lime juice
- 1 tsp sea salt

Directions:

1.Add cauliflower florets into the mixing bowl.

2.Add remaining ingredients and toss well.

3.Arrange cauliflower florets in a multi-level air fryer basket.

4.Place the dehydrating tray in the air fryer basket and arrange the remaining cauliflower florets on the dehydrating tray.

5.Place basket into the pot. Secure pot with air fryer lid and cook on dehydrate mode at 135 F for 12 hours.

6.Store in an air-tight container.

Nutritional Value (Amount per Serving):

- Calories 92
- Fat 4.1 g
- Carbohydrates 13.1 g
- Sugar 5.4 g
- Protein 4.4 g
- Cholesterol 0 mg

360

DEHYDRATED ALMONDS

Preparation Time: 10 minutes

Cooking Time: 18 hours

Serve: 4

Ingredients:

- 1 cup almonds
- 2 cups of water
- 1 tbsp salt

Directions:

1.Add almonds, water, and salt into the bowl. Cover and soak for 24 hours. Drain well.

2.Arrange almonds in a multi-level air fryer basket.

3.Place the dehydrating tray in the air fryer basket and arrange the remaining almonds on the dehydrating tray.

4.Place basket into the pot. Secure pot with air fryer lid and cook on dehydrate mode at 115 F for 18 hours.

5.Store in an air-tight container.

Nutritional Value (Amount per Serving):

- Calories 137
- Fat 11.9 g

•Carbohydrates 5.1 g
•Sugar 1 g
•Protein 5 g
•Cholesterol 0 mg

361

ORANGE SLICES

Preparation Time: 10 minutes

Cooking Time: 7 hours

Serve: 2

Ingredients:

•2 oranges, cut into 1/4-inch thick slices

Directions:

1.Arrange orange slices in a multi-level air fryer basket.

2.Place the dehydrating tray in the air fryer basket and arrange the remaining orange slices on the dehydrating tray.

3.Place basket into the pot. Secure pot with air fryer lid and cook on dehydrate mode at 135 F for 7 hours.

4.Store in an air-tight container.

Nutritional Value (Amount per Serving):

•Calories 86

•Fat 0.2 g

•Carbohydrates 21.6 g

•Sugar 17.2 g

•Protein 1.7 g

•Cholesterol 0 mg

362

RADISH CHIPS

Preparation Time: 10 minutes

Cooking Time: 5 hours

Serve: 4

Ingredients:

•3 radishes, cut into 1/8-inch thick slices

•Salt

Directions:

1.Arrange radish slices in a multi-level air fryer basket.

2.Place the dehydrating tray in the air fryer basket and arrange remaining radish slices on the dehydrating tray.

3.Place basket into the pot. Secure pot with air fryer lid and cook on dehydrate mode at 125 F for 5 hours.

4.Store in an air-tight container.

Nutritional Value (Amount per Serving):

•Calories 1

•Fat 0 g

•Carbohydrates 0.1 g

•Sugar 0.1 g

•Protein 0 g

•Cholesterol 0 mg

363

DRIED CARROT SLICES

Preparation Time: 10 minutes

Cooking Time: 6 hours

Serve: 4

Ingredients:

•2 carrots, peel & 1/8-inch thick slices

Directions:

1.Arrange carrot slices in a multi-level air fryer basket.

2.Place the dehydrating tray in the air fryer basket and arrange the remaining carrot slices on the dehydrating tray.

3.Place basket into the pot. Secure pot with air fryer lid and cook on dehydrate mode at 125 F for 6 hours.

4.Store in an air-tight container.

Nutritional Value (Amount per Serving):

•Calories 13

•Fat 0 g

•Carbohydrates 3 g

•Sugar 1.5 g

•Protein 0.3 g

•Cholesterol 0 mg

364

DRIED APRICOTS

Preparation Time: 10 minutes

Cooking Time: 20 hours

Serve: 12

Ingredients:

•12 apricots, cut in half & remove pits

•1 cup lemon juice

•4 cups of water

Directions:

1.In a large bowl, add water and lemon juice. Add apricots.

2.Remove apricots from water and pat dry.

3.Arrange apricots in a multi-level air fryer basket.

4.Place the dehydrating tray in the air fryer basket and arrange the remaining apricots on the dehydrating tray.

5.Place basket into the pot. Secure pot with air fryer lid and cook on dehydrate mode at 135 F for 20 hours.

6.Store in an air-tight container.

Nutritional Value (Amount per Serving):

•Calories 22

•Fat 0.4 g

- Carbohydrates 4.3 g
- Sugar 3.6 g
- Protein 0.6 g
- Cholesterol 0 mg

365

PARMESAN TOMATO CHIPS

Preparation Time: 10 minutes

Cooking Time: 8 hours

Serve: 6

Ingredients:

•8 tomatoes, cut into 1/4-inch thick slices

•1/2 tsp basil

•1/4 cup parmesan cheese, grated

•1/2 tsp oregano

•1/2 tsp pepper

•1/2 tsp salt

Directions:

1.Sprinkle cheese over tomato slices and season with oregano, pepper, basil, and salt.

2.Arrange tomato slices in a multi-level air fryer basket.

3.Place the dehydrating tray in the air fryer basket and arrange the remaining tomato slices on the dehydrating tray.

4.Place basket into the pot. Secure pot with air fryer lid and cook on dehydrate mode at 155 F for 8 hours.

5.Store in an air-tight container.

Nutritional Value (Amount per Serving):

- •Calories 42
- •Fat 1.2 g
- •Carbohydrates 6.7 g
- •Sugar 4.3 g
- •Protein 2.7 g
- •Cholesterol 3 mg

366

SPICY ALMONDS

Preparation Time: 10 minutes

Cooking Time: 24 hours

Serve: 6

Ingredients:

•2 cups almonds, soak in water overnight

•1 tbsp fresh rosemary, chopped

•1/4 tsp cayenne

•1 tsp chili powder

•1 tbsp olive oil

•3/4 tsp kosher salt

Directions:

1.Add all ingredients into the mixing bowl and toss well.

2.Spread almonds in the multi-level air fryer basket.

3.Place the dehydrating tray in the air fryer basket and arrange the remaining almonds on the dehydrating tray.

4.Place basket into the pot. Secure pot with air fryer lid and cook on dehydrate mode at 125 F for 24 hours.

5.Store in an air-tight container.

Nutritional Value (Amount per Serving):

•Calories 207

- •Fat 18.3 g
- •Carbohydrates 7.4 g
- •Sugar 1.4 g
- •Protein 6.8 g
- •Cholesterol 0 mg

DESSERTS

367

DELICIOUS ORANGE CUPCAKES

Preparation Time: 10 minutes

Cooking Time: 20 minutes

Serve: 6

Ingredients:

•2 eggs

•1/2 tsp baking soda

•1 orange zest

•1/2 orange juice

•1/4 cup butter, melted

•1 1/2 cups almond flour

Directions:

1.Place the dehydrating tray in a multi-level air fryer basket.

2.Add all ingredients into the large bowl and mix until well combined.

3.Pour mixture into the six silicone molds and place molds on dehydrating tray.

4.Place basket into the pot. Secure pot with air fryer lid and cook on bake mode at 350 F for 15-20 minutes.

5.Serve and enjoy.

Nutritional Value (Amount per Serving):

- Calories 133
- Fat 12.6 g
- Carbohydrates 2.6 g
- Sugar 1 g
- Protein 3.5 g
- Cholesterol 75 mg

368

STRAWBERRY COBBLER

Preparation Time: 10 minutes

Cooking Time: 15 minutes

Serve: 6

Ingredients:

•1 egg, lightly beaten

•1 cup almond flour

•2 tsp swerve

•1/2 tsp vanilla

•1 cup strawberries, sliced

•1 tbsp butter, melted

Directions:

1.Add strawberries into the greased cake pan and sprinkle with sweetener.

2.Mix together almond flour, vanilla, and butter in the bowl.

3.Add egg in almond flour mixture and stir to combine.

4.Spread almond flour mixture over sliced strawberries.

5.Place multi-functional rack into the instant pot.

6.Place pan on top of the rack in the pot.

7.Secure pot with air fryer lid and cook on bake mode at 350 F for 10-15 minutes.

8.Serve and enjoy.

Nutritional Value (Amount per Serving):

•Calories 65

•Fat 5.1 g

•Carbohydrates 3.6 g

•Sugar 1.5 g

•Protein 2.1 g

•Cholesterol 32 mg

369

HEALTHY BROWNIE

Preparation Time: 10 minutes

Cooking Time: 20 minutes

Serve: 6

Ingredients:

•2 eggs, lightly beaten

•1 medium zucchini, shredded and squeeze out all liquid

•1/4 cup almond milk

•1/4 cup maple syrup

•1 cup sunbutter

•1/4 cup almond flour

•1/2 cup cocoa powder

Directions:

1.In a large bowl, mix together sunbutter, milk, eggs, and maple syrup.

2.Add almond flour, zucchini, and cocoa powder and stir to combine.

3.Pour batter into a greased cake pan.

4.Place multi-functional rack into the instant pot.

5.Place pan on top of the rack in the pot.

6.Secure pot with air fryer lid and cook on bake mode at 350 F for 20 minutes.

7.Slice and serve.

Nutritional Value (Amount per Serving):

•Calories 373

•Fat 26.8 g

•Carbohydrates 24.1 g

•Sugar 13 g

•Protein 13.4 g

•Cholesterol 55 mg

370

COCONUT ALMOND BUTTER BROWNIE

Preparation Time: 10 minutes

Cooking Time: 10 minutes

Serve: 2

Ingredients:

•1 egg, lightly beaten

•2 tbsp coconut flour

•2 tbsp cocoa powder

•1/4 cup maple syrup

•1/2 cup almond butter

•1/2 tsp vanilla

•1/4 tsp salt

Directions:

1.In a bowl, mix together almond butter, egg, vanilla, maple syrup, and salt.

2.Add coconut flour and cocoa powder and stir to combine.

3.Pour batter into a greased cake pan.

4.Place multi-functional rack into the instant pot.

5.Place pan on top of the rack in the pot.

6.Secure pot with air fryer lid and cook on bake mode at 350 F for 10 minutes.

7.Slice and serve.

Nutritional Value (Amount per Serving):

•Calories 209

•Fat 7 g

•Carbohydrates 34.9 g

•Sugar 25.5 g

•Protein 6.1 g

•Cholesterol 82 mg

371

CHOCOLATE WALNUT BROWNIES

Preparation Time: 10 minutes

Cooking Time: 40 minutes

Serve: 12

Ingredients:

•3 eggs

•3/4 cup cocoa powder

•1 1/4 cups almond flour

•1 cup butter, melted

•1 tsp vanilla

•3/4 cup Swerve

•1/2 cup walnuts, chopped

•2 tbsp proteins collagen

•1/4 tsp baking soda

•1/2 tsp vinegar

•1/2 cup milk

•Pinch of salt

Directions:

1.Add eggs, vanilla, vinegar, milk, and sweetener into the large bowl and beat using a hand mixer until well blended.

2.In a separate bowl, whisk butter, protein collagen, baking soda, cocoa powder, almond flour, and salt until combined.

3.Add egg mixture and stir until well combined.

4.Add walnuts and fold well.

5.Pour batter into the greased cake pan.

6.Place multi-functional rack into the instant pot.

7.Place pan on top of the rack in the pot.

8.Secure pot with air fryer lid and cook on bake mode at 350 F for 35-40 minutes.

9.Slice and serve.

Nutritional Value (Amount per Serving):

•Calories 229

•Fat 21.9 g

•Carbohydrates 4.9 g

•Sugar 0.8 g

•Protein 7.2 g

•Cholesterol 82 mg

372

BAKED CINNAMON APPLE SLICES

Preparation Time: 10 minutes

Cooking Time: 20 minutes

Serve: 6

Ingredients:

•4 large sweet apples, cut into 1/4-inch thick slices

•2 tbsp water

•2 tbsp fresh lemon juice

•2 tsp cinnamon

Directions:

1.Add all ingredients to the large bowl and toss until apple are well coated.

2.Transfer apple slices to the greased cake pan.

3.Place multi-functional rack into the instant pot.

4.Place pan on top of the rack in the pot.

5.Secure pot with air fryer lid and cook on bake mode at 350 F for 30-35 minutes.

6.Serve warm and enjoy.

Nutritional Value (Amount per Serving):

•Calories 80

- Fat 0.3 g
- Carbohydrates 21.3 g
- Sugar 15.6 g
- Protein 0.5 g
- Cholesterol 0 mg

373

LEMON BLUEBERRY MUFFINS

Preparation Time: 10 minutes
Cooking Time: 25 minutes
Serve: 4
Ingredients:
•2 eggs
•1/4 cup blueberries
•1/2 tsp baking powder
•1 1/2 tbsp swerve
•1 cup almond flour
•1/2 tbsp lemon juice
•1/2 tsp vanilla
•1/4 cup heavy whipping cream
•1/4 cup coconut oil, melted
Directions:
1.Place the dehydrating tray in a multi-level air fryer basket.
2.In a large bowl, whisk eggs with lemon juice, vanilla, heavy whipping cream, and coconut oil.
3.In a separate bowl, mix almond flour, swerve, and baking powder.

4.Add almond flour mixture to the egg mixture and mix until well combined.

5.Add blueberries and fold well.

6.Pour mixture into the four silicone molds and place molds on dehydrating tray.

7.Place basket into the pot. Secure pot with air fryer lid and cook on bake mode at 350 F for 20-25 minutes.

8.Serve and enjoy.

Nutritional Value (Amount per Serving):

•Calories 225

•Fat 22.2 g

•Carbohydrates 4.4 g

•Sugar 1.4 g

•Protein 4.5 g

•Cholesterol 92 mg

374

MOIST PUMPKIN MUFFINS

Preparation Time: 10 minutes

Cooking Time: 35 minutes

Serve: 6

Ingredients:

•1 egg

•1/2 tsp pumpkin pie spice

•1 cups all-purpose flour

•1/4 cup of chocolate chips

•1/2 cup can pumpkin puree

•1/4 cup olive oil

•1/4 cup maple syrup

•1/2 tsp baking soda

•Salt

Directions:

1.Place the dehydrating tray in a multi-level air fryer basket.

2.In a bowl, add flour, baking soda, spice, and salt and mix well.

3.In another bowl, whisk together eggs, pumpkin puree, oil, and maple syrup.

4.Slowly add dry mixture to the wet mixture and mix well.

5.Add chocolate chips and fold well.

6.Pour mixture into the six silicone molds and place molds on dehydrating tray.

7.Place basket into the pot. Secure pot with air fryer lid and cook on bake mode at 350 F for 30-35 minutes.

8.Serve and enjoy.

Nutritional Value (Amount per Serving):

•Calories 234

•Fat 11.5 g

•Carbohydrates 29.9 g

•Sugar 11.9 g

•Protein 3.7 g

•Cholesterol 29 mg

375

HEALTHY OAT FLOUR BROWNIE

Preparation Time: 10 minutes

Cooking Time: 20 minutes

Serve: 1

Ingredients:

•1 tbsp oat flour

•1/2 banana, mashed

•2 tbsp cocoa powder

•1/4 tsp baking powder

•1 tbsp maple syrup

•3 tbsp coconut milk

•Pinch of salt

Directions:

1.Add all ingredients into the bowl and stir to combine.

2.Pour bowl mixture into the greased cake pan.

3.Place multi-functional rack into the instant pot.

4.Place pan on top of the rack in the pot.

5.Secure pot with air fryer lid and cook on bake mode at 300 F for 20 minutes.

6.Serve and enjoy.

Nutritional Value (Amount per Serving):

- Calories 256
- Fat 12.8 g
- Carbohydrates 39.8 g
- Sugar 20.8 g
- Protein 4.4 g
- Cholesterol 0 mg

376

BANANA ALMOND BUTTER BROWNIES

Preparation Time: 10 minutes

Cooking Time: 20 minutes

Serve: 4

Ingredients:

•1 scoop protein powder

•1/2 cup almond butter, melted

•1 cup bananas, overripe

•2 tbsp cocoa powder

•1/2 tsp vanilla

Directions:

1.Add all ingredients into the blender and blend until smooth.

2.Pour batter into the greased cake pan.

3.Place multi-functional rack into the instant pot.

4.Place pan on top of the rack in the pot.

5.Secure pot with air fryer lid and cook on bake mode at 350 F for 20 minutes.

6.Serve and enjoy.

Nutritional Value (Amount per Serving):

•Calories 83

- Fat 2.1 g
- Carbohydrates 11.4 g
- Sugar 5 g
- Protein 6.9 g
- Cholesterol 16 mg

377

MOIST BANANA MUFFINS

Preparation Time: 10 minutes

Cooking Time: 10 minutes

Serve: 2

Ingredients:

•4 tbsp flour

•1/4 cup oats

•1/4 cup banana, mashed

•1 tbsp walnuts, chopped

•1/2 tsp baking powder

•1/4 cup powdered sugar

•1/4 cup butter

Directions:

1.Place the dehydrating tray in a multi-level air fryer basket.

2.In a bowl, mix together mashed banana, walnuts, sugar, and butter.

3.In a separate bowl, mix flour, baking powder, and oats.

4.Add flour mixture to the banana mixture and mix well.

5.Pour mixture into the two silicone molds and place molds on dehydrating tray.

6.Place basket into the pot. Secure pot with air fryer lid and cook on air fry mode at 320 F for 10 minutes.

7.Serve and enjoy.

Nutritional Value (Amount per Serving):

•Calories 399

•Fat 26.2 g

•Carbohydrates 39.1 g

•Sugar 17.2 g

•Protein 4.3 g

•Cholesterol 61 mg

378

CHOCOLATE LAVA CAKE

Preparation Time: 10 minutes
Cooking Time: 8 minutes
Serve: 2
Ingredients:
•1 egg
•1 tbsp flax meal
•1/8 tsp stevia
•2 tbsp erythritol
•2 tbsp water
•2 tbsp cocoa powder
•1/2 tsp baking powder
•1 tbsp butter, melted
•1/8 tsp vanilla
•Pinch of salt
Directions:
1.Place the dehydrating tray in a multi-level air fryer basket.
2.Spray two ramekins with cooking spray and set aside.
3.Add all ingredients to the bowl and whisk well.
4.Pour batter into the greased ramekins.
5.Place ramekins on dehydrating tray.

6.Place basket into the pot. Secure pot with air fryer lid and cook on air fry mode at 350 F for 8 minutes.

7.Serve and enjoy.

Nutritional Value (Amount per Serving):

•Calories 111

•Fat 9.9 g

•Carbohydrates 4.8 g

•Sugar 0.3 g

•Protein 4.6 g

•Cholesterol 97 mg

379

CINNAMON PINEAPPLE WEDGES

Preparation Time: 10 minutes

Cooking Time: 10 minutes

Serve: 2

Ingredients:

•1/2 small pineapple, peeled, cored, and cut into wedges

•1 tsp cinnamon

•1/4 cup brown sugar

•1 1/2 tbsp butter, melted

Directions:

1.Line multi-level air fryer basket with parchment paper.

2.In a small bowl, mix cinnamon and sugar.

3.Brush pineapple wedges with butter and sprinkle with brown sugar mixture.

4.Place pineapple wedges into the basket.

5.Place basket into the pot. Secure pot with air fryer lid and cook on air fry mode at 400 F for 10 minutes.

6.Serve and enjoy.

Nutritional Value (Amount per Serving):

•Calories 210

- Fat 8.8 g
- Carbohydrates 35.1 g
- Sugar 29.9 g
- Protein 0.8 g
- Cholesterol 23 mg

380

APPLE RICE PUDDING

Preparation Time: 10 minutes

Cooking Time: 15 minutes

Serve: 6

Ingredients:

•3/4 cup Arborio rice

•1/2 cup water

•1 1/2 cup milk

•1 tsp cinnamon

•1/4 apple, peeled and chopped

•2 rhubarb stalks, chopped

•1 cinnamon stick

•1 tsp vanilla

Directions:

1.Add all ingredients into the instant pot and stir well.

2.Secure pot with pressure cooking lid and cook on high for 15 minutes.

3.Once done, release pressure using quick release. Remove lid.

4.Stir well and serve.

Nutritional Value (Amount per Serving):

- Calories 127
- Fat 1.4 g
- Carbohydrates 24.3 g
- Sugar 4 g
- Protein 3.8 g
- Cholesterol 5 mg

381

CINNAMON PECAN APPLES

Preparation Time: 10 minutes

Cooking Time: 4 minutes

Serve: 6

Ingredients:

•6 apples, cored and cut into wedges

•1 cup red wine

•1/4 cup pecans, chopped

•1/4 cup raisins

•1/4 tsp nutmeg

•1 tsp cinnamon

•1/3 cup honey

Directions:

1.Add all ingredients into the instant pot and stir well.

2.Secure pot with pressure cooking lid and cook on high for 4 minutes.

3.Once done, allow to release pressure naturally for 10 minutes then release remaining using quick release. Remove lid.

4.Stir well and serve.

Nutritional Value (Amount per Serving):

•Calories 260

- Fat 4 g
- Carbohydrates 53.2 g
- Sugar 42.8 g
- Protein 1.5 g
- Cholesterol 0 mg

382

HEALTHY OATS COOKIES

Preparation Time: 10 minutes

Cooking Time: 15 minutes

Serve: 6

Ingredients:

•2 cups quick oats

•4 ripe bananas, mashed

•1/4 cup milk

•1/4 cup coconut shredded

Directions:

1.Line multi-level air fryer basket with parchment paper.

2.Add all ingredients into the bowl and mix well to combine.

3.Spoon cookie dough onto parchment-lined air fryer basket.

4.Place basket into the pot. Secure pot with air fryer lid and cook on air fry mode at 350 F for 15 minutes.

5.Serve and enjoy.

Nutritional Value (Amount per Serving):

•Calories 198

•Fat 3.6 g

•Carbohydrates 38.8 g

- Sugar 12 g
- Protein 4.9 g
- Cholesterol 1 mg

383

CREAMY RICE PUDDING

Preparation Time: 10 minutes

Cooking Time: 7 minutes

Serve: 8

Ingredients:

•2 cups white rice

•1/2 cup sugar

•6 1/2 cups milk

•10.5 oz condensed milk

•2 cinnamon stick

•1/4 tsp lime zest

•Pinch of salt

Directions:

1.Add 6 cups of milk, rice, cinnamon sticks, lime zest, sugar, and salt into the instant pot and stir well.

2.Secure pot with pressure cooking lid and cook on high for 2 minutes.

3.Once done, allow to release pressure naturally for 10 minutes then release remaining using quick release. Remove lid.

4.Add condensed milk and stir well and set the pot on sauté mode for 5 minutes.

5.Add remaining milk and stir well.
6.Serve and enjoy.

Nutritional Value (Amount per Serving):

•Calories 436
•Fat 7.6 g
•Carbohydrates 80 g
•Sugar 41.8 g
•Protein 12.8 g
•Cholesterol 29 mg

384

DELICIOUS APPLE CRISP

Preparation Time: 10 minutes

Cooking Time: 9 minutes

Serve: 4

Ingredients:

•2 cups apples, peeled and chopped

•1 tsp vanilla

•1/2 tsp cinnamon

•1/4 tsp cornstarch

•1/4 cup brown sugar

•For topping:

•1/3 cup flour

•2 tbsp butter

•1 tsp vanilla

•1/4 cup brown sugar

•Pinch of salt

Directions:

1.Add apples, cornstarch, vanilla, brown sugar, and cinnamon into the greased cake pan and mix well.

2.Pour 1 cup of water into the instant pot.

3.Place multi-functional rack into the instant pot.

4.Place cake pan on rack.

5.Secure pot with pressure cooking lid and cook on high for 4 minutes.

6.Once done, release pressure using quick release. Remove lid.

7.Remove cake pan from the pot and clean the pot. Again place the multi-functional rack into the instant pot.

8.Place cake pan on rack.

9.Mix together all topping ingredients and pour over apple mixture into the cake pan.

10. Secure pot with air fryer lid and cook on broil mode for 5 minutes.

11. Serve with ice cream and enjoy it.

Nutritional Value (Amount per Serving):

•Calories 223

•Fat 6.1 g

•Carbohydrates 41.8 g

•Sugar 29.5 g

•Protein 1.5 g

•Cholesterol 15 mg

385

CREAM CHEESE MUFFINS

Preparation Time: 10 minutes

Cooking Time: 16 minutes

Serve: 5

Ingredients:

•1 egg

•1/4 cup erythritol

•4 oz cream cheese

•1/2 tsp ground cinnamon

•1/4 tsp vanilla

Directions:

1.Place the dehydrating tray in a multi-level air fryer basket.

2.In a bowl, mix cream cheese, vanilla, erythritol, and eggs until soft.

3.Pour mixture into the five silicone molds and sprinkle cinnamon on top. Place molds on dehydrating tray.

4.Place basket into the pot. Secure pot with air fryer lid and cook on bake mode at 325 F for 16 minutes.

5.Serve and enjoy.

Nutritional Value (Amount per Serving):

•Calories 105

- Fat 8.8 g
- Carbohydrates 8.1 g
- Sugar 0.2 g
- Protein 2.8 g
- Cholesterol 58 mg

386

BAKED DONUTS

Preparation Time: 10 minutes

Cooking Time: 15 minutes

Serve: 6

Ingredients:

•1 egg

•1/4 tsp vanilla

•1/2 tsp baking powder

•6 tbsp sugar

•1/4 cup buttermilk

•1/8 cup vegetable oil

•1/2 cup all-purpose flour

•1/4 tsp salt

Directions:

1.Place the dehydrating tray in a multi-level air fryer basket.

2.In a bowl, mix together oil, vanilla, baking powder, sugar, eggs, buttermilk, and salt until well combined.

3.Stir in flour and mix until smooth.

4.Pour batter into the six silicone donut molds.

5.Place molds on dehydrating tray.

6.Place basket into the pot. Secure pot with air fryer lid and cook on bake mode at 350 F for 15 minutes.

7.Serve and enjoy.

Nutritional Value (Amount per Serving):

•Calories 139

•Fat 5.5 g

•Carbohydrates 20.7 g

•Sugar 12.6 g

•Protein 2.3 g

•Cholesterol 28 mg

387

MOIST BUTTER CAKE

Preparation Time: 10 minutes

Cooking Time: 30 minutes

Serve: 8

Ingredients:

•1 egg, beaten

•1/2 cup butter, softened

•1 cup all-purpose flour

•3/4 cup sugar

•1/2 tsp vanilla

Directions:

1.In a mixing bowl, mix together sugar and butter.

2.Add egg, flour, and vanilla and mix until combined.

3.Pour batter into the greased cake pan.

4.Place multi-functional rack into the instant pot.

5.Place pan on top of the rack in the pot.

6.Secure pot with air fryer lid and cook on bake mode at 350 F for 30 minutes.

7.Slice and serve.

Nutritional Value (Amount per Serving):

•Calories 238

- Fat 12.2 g
- Carbohydrates 30.8 g
- Sugar 18.9 g
- Protein 2.4 g
- Cholesterol 51 mg

388

PEANUT BUTTER MUFFINS

Preparation Time: 10 minutes

Cooking Time: 20 minutes

Serve: 6

Ingredients:

•1/2 cup peanut butter

•1/2 cup applesauce

•1/4 cup maple syrup

•1/4 cup of cocoa powder

•1/2 tsp baking soda

•1/2 tsp vanilla

Directions:

1.Place the dehydrating tray in a multi-level air fryer basket.

2.Add all ingredients into the blender and blend until smooth.

3.Pour mixture into the six silicone molds and place molds on dehydrating tray.

4.Place basket into the pot. Secure pot with air fryer lid and cook on bake mode at 350 F for 20 minutes.

5.Serve and enjoy.

Nutritional Value (Amount per Serving):

•Calories 178

- Fat 11.3 g
- Carbohydrates 17.3 g
- Sugar 12 g
- Protein 6.1 g
- Cholesterol 0 mg

389

VANILLA BANANA BROWNIES

Preparation Time: 10 minutes
Cooking Time: 20 minutes
Serve: 12
Ingredients:
•1 egg
•1/4 cup butter
•1 tsp vanilla
•1/2 cup sugar
•1 cup all-purpose flour
•2 medium bananas, mashed
•4 oz white chocolate
•1/4 tsp salt
Directions:
1.Add white chocolate and butter in microwave-safe bowl and microwave for 30 seconds. Stir until melted.
2.Stir in sugar. Add mashed bananas, eggs, vanilla, and salt and mix until combined.
3.Add flour and stir to combine.
4.Pour batter into the greased cake pan.
5.Place multi-functional rack into the instant pot.

6.Place pan on top of the rack in the pot.

7.Secure pot with air fryer lid and cook on bake mode at 350 F for 20 minutes.

8.Slice and serve.

Nutritional Value (Amount per Serving):

•Calories 178

•Fat 7.4 g

•Carbohydrates 26.4 g

•Sugar 16.4 g

•Protein 2.3 g

•Cholesterol 26 mg

390

CRANBERRY MUFFINS

Preparation Time: 10 minutes

Cooking Time: 30 minutes

Serve: 6

Ingredients:

•2 eggs

•1/4 cup sour cream

•1 tsp baking powder

•1/4 cup Swerve

•1 1/2 cups almond flour

•1/2 cup cranberries

•1/4 tsp cinnamon

•1 tsp vanilla

•Pinch of salt

Directions:

1.Place the dehydrating tray in a multi-level air fryer basket.

2.In a bowl, beat sour cream, vanilla, and eggs.

3.Add remaining ingredients except for cranberries and beat until smooth.

4.Add cranberries and fold well.

5.Pour mixture into the six silicone molds and place molds on dehydrating tray.

6.Place basket into the pot. Secure pot with air fryer lid and cook on bake mode at 325 F for 30 minutes.

7.Serve and enjoy.

Nutritional Value (Amount per Serving):

•Calories 90

•Fat 7 g

•Carbohydrates 3.5 g

•Sugar 0.8 g

•Protein 3.7 g

•Cholesterol 59 mg

391

BROWNIE MUFFINS

Preparation Time: 10 minutes

Cooking Time: 15 minutes

Serve: 6

Ingredients:

•3 eggs

•1/3 cup cocoa powder

•1/2 cup Swerve

•1 cup almond flour

•1 tbsp gelatin

•1/3 cup butter, melted

Directions:

1.Place the dehydrating tray in a multi-level air fryer basket.

2.Add all ingredients into the mixing bowl and stir until well combined.

3.Pour mixture into the six silicone molds and place molds on dehydrating tray.

4.Place basket into the pot. Secure pot with air fryer lid and cook on bake mode at 350 F for 10-15 minutes.

5.Serve and enjoy.

Nutritional Value (Amount per Serving):

- Calories 284
- Fat 12.8 g
- Carbohydrates 38.8 g
- Sugar 12.8 g
- Protein 4.8 g
- Cholesterol 52 mg

392

BLUEBERRY CAKE

Preparation Time: 10 minutes

Cooking Time: 45 minutes

Serve: 8

Ingredients:

•1 egg

•2 cups all-purpose flour

•1/2 cup milk

•2 tsp baking powder

•2 cups blueberries

•1/2 cup butter, melted

•1/3 cup sugar

•Pinch of salt

Directions:

1.In a large bowl, mix together baking powder, all-purpose flour, sugar, and salt.

2.In a separate bowl, whisk egg, butter, and milk.

3.Add flour mixture into the egg mixture and mix until combined.

4.Pour batter into the greased cake pan.

5.Place multi-functional rack into the instant pot.

6.Place pan on top of the rack in the pot.

7.Secure pot with air fryer lid and cook on bake mode at 350 F for 45 minutes.

8.Slice and serve.

Nutritional Value (Amount per Serving):

•Calories 284

•Fat 12.8 g

•Carbohydrates 38.8 g

•Sugar 12.8 g

•Protein 4.8 g

•Cholesterol 52 mg

393

CHOCOLATE CHEESECAKE MUFFINS

Preparation Time: 10 minutes

Cooking Time: 20 minutes

Serve: 6

Ingredients:

•1 egg

•1/4 cup Swerve

•8 oz cream cheese

•1/4 tsp vanilla

•3 tbsp cocoa powder

Directions:

1.Place the dehydrating tray in a multi-level air fryer basket.

2.In a mixing bowl, beat cream cheese until smooth.

3.Add remaining ingredients and beat until well combined.

4.Pour mixture into the six silicone molds and place molds on dehydrating tray.

5.Place basket into the pot. Secure pot with air fryer lid and cook on bake mode at 350 F for 18-20 minutes.

6.Serve and enjoy.

Nutritional Value (Amount per Serving):

•Calories 149

- Fat 14.3 g
- Carbohydrates 2.7 g
- Sugar 0.2 g
- Protein 4.3 g
- Cholesterol 69 mg

394

DELICIOUS RASPBERRY CAKE

Preparation Time: 10 minutes

Cooking Time: 25 minutes

Serve: 12

Ingredients:

•3 eggs

•1 tbsp vanilla

•1/3 cup almond milk

•1/3 cup coconut oil, melted

•2 1/2 cups almond flour

•1/2 cup erythritol

•1/4 cup raspberries

•1 tbsp baking powder

•Pinch of salt

Directions:

1.In a large bowl, mix together almond milk, sweetener, coconut oil, and vanilla.

2.Add baking powder, salt, and almond flour and stir until well combined.

3.Add raspberries and fold well.

4.Pour batter into the greased cake pan.

5.Place multi-functional rack into the instant pot.

6.Place pan on top of the rack in the pot.

7.Secure pot with air fryer lid and cook on bake mode at 350 F for 25 minutes.

8.Slice and serve.

Nutritional Value (Amount per Serving):

•Calories 122

•Fat 11.7 g

•Carbohydrates 2.7 g

•Sugar 0.8 g

•Protein 2.8 g

•Cholesterol 41 mg

395

ZUCCHINI MUFFINS

Preparation Time: 10 minutes

Cooking Time: 30 minutes

Serve: 6

Ingredients:

•1 egg

•1/8 cup sour cream

•1/8 cup butter, melted

•1/4 cup Swerve

•1/8 cup coconut flour

•1/2 cup almond flour

•1/4 cup chocolate chips

•1/2 cup shredded zucchini

•1/2 tbsp baking powder

•1/2 tsp vanilla

Directions:

1.Place the dehydrating tray in a multi-level air fryer basket.

2.Add all ingredients except chocolate chips and shredded zucchini into the mixing bowl and stir until smooth.

3.Add chocolate chips and shredded zucchini and stir well.

4.Pour mixture into the six silicone molds and place molds on dehydrating tray.

5.Place basket into the pot. Secure pot with air fryer lid and cook on bake mode at 350 F for 25-30 minutes.

6.Serve and enjoy.

Nutritional Value (Amount per Serving):

•Calories 121

•Fat 9.4 g

•Carbohydrates 7.5 g

•Sugar 4.5 g

•Protein 2.8 g

•Cholesterol 41 mg

30-DAY MEAL PLAN

Day 1

Breakfast- Spinach Mushroom Frittata
Lunch- Greek Pesto Salmon
Dinner- Baked Beef & Broccoli

Day 2

Breakfast- Easy Mexican Frittata
Lunch- Easy Chicken Fajitas
Dinner- Tasty Beef Fajitas

Day 3

Breakfast- Greek Spinach Tomato Frittata
Lunch- White Fish Fillet with Roasted Pepper
Dinner- Parmesan Paprika Pork Chops

Day 4

Breakfast- Stuffed Omelet Peppers
Lunch- Creamy Jalapeno Chicken Breasts
Dinner- Flavorful Steak Fajitas

Day 5

Breakfast- Bacon Cheese Quiche
Lunch- Blackened Baked Fish Fillets
Dinner- Garlic Air Fryer Steak

Day 6
Breakfast- Spinach Breakfast Quiche
Lunch- Buffalo Chicken Breasts
Dinner- Paprika Pork Chops
Day 7
Breakfast- Healthy Broccoli Quiche
Lunch- Easy Baked Halibut
Dinner- Easy Pork with Mushrooms
Day 8
Breakfast- Artichoke Spinach Quiche
Lunch- Flavorful Salsa Chicken
Dinner- Flavorful Steak Fajitas
Day 9
Breakfast- Light & Fluffy Baked Omelett e
Lunch- Lemon Pepper Fish Fillets
Dinner- Tasty Beef Roast
Day 10
Breakfast- Mexican Breakfast Casserole
Lunch- Herb Lemon Orange Chicken
Dinner- Sirloin Steaks
Day 11
Breakfast- Cheesy Breakfast Casserole
Lunch- Shrimp with Zucchini & Peppers
Dinner- Beef & Broccoli
Day 12
Breakfast- Tomato Breakfast Quiche
Lunch- Creamy Chicken Breasts
Dinner- Flavorful Rib Eye Steak
Day 13
Breakfast- Easy Cheese Egg Muffins
Lunch- Air Fry Shrimp Sausage & Pepper
Dinner- Cheesy Pork Chops
Day 14
Breakfast- Pepper Onion Egg Muffins
Lunch- Italian Chicken Breasts
Dinner- Dijon Lamb Chops

Day 15
Breakfast- Caprese Egg Cups
Lunch- Simple Air Fryer Sriracha Salmon
Dinner- Lemon Pepper Pork Chops
Day 16
Breakfast- Spinach Mushroom Frittata
Lunch- Greek Pesto Salmon
Dinner- Baked Beef & Broccoli
Day 17
Breakfast- Easy Mexican Frittata
Lunch- Easy Chicken Fajitas
Dinner- Tasty Beef Fajitas
Day 18
Breakfast- Greek Spinach Tomato Frittata
Lunch- White Fish Fillet with Roasted Pepper
Dinner- Parmesan Paprika Pork Chops
Day 19
Breakfast- Stuffed Omelet Peppers
Lunch- Creamy Jalapeno Chicken Breasts
Dinner- Flavorful Rib Eye Steak
Day 20
Breakfast- Bacon Cheese Quiche
Lunch- Blackened Baked Fish Fillets
Dinner- Garlic Air Fryer Steak
Day 21
Breakfast- Spinach Breakfast Quiche
Lunch- Buffalo Chicken Breasts
Dinner- Paprika Pork Chops
Day 22
Breakfast- Healthy Broccoli Quiche
Lunch- Easy Baked Halibut
Dinner- Easy Pork with Mushrooms
Day 23
Breakfast- Artichoke Spinach Quiche
Lunch- Flavorful Salsa Chicken
Dinner- Flavorful Steak Fajitas

Day 24
Breakfast- Light & Fluffy Baked Omelette
Lunch- Lemon Pepper Fish Fillets
Dinner- Tasty Beef Roast
Day 25
Breakfast- Mexican Breakfast Casserole
Lunch- Herb Lemon Orange Chicken
Dinner- Sirloin Steaks
Day 26
Breakfast- Cheesy Breakfast Casserole
Lunch- Shrimp with Zucchini & Peppers
Dinner- Beef & Broccol i
Day 27
Breakfast- Tomato Breakfast Quiche
Lunch- Creamy Chicken Breasts
Dinner- Flavorful Rib Eye Steak
Day 28
Breakfast- Easy Cheese Egg Muffins
Lunch- Air Fry Shrimp Sausage & Pepper
Dinner- Cheesy Pork Chops
Day 29
Breakfast- Pepper Onion Egg Muffins
Lunch- Italian Chicken Breasts
Dinner- Dijon Lamb Chops
Day 30
Breakfast- Caprese Egg Cups
Lunch- Simple Air Fryer Sriracha Salmon
Dinner- Lemon Pepper Pork Chops

CONCLUSION

In this cookbook, we have introduced a new member which comes from the instant pot family known as instant pot pro crisp air fryer. It works on two different cooking techniques one is used for pressure cooking purposes and the other is used for air frying. The instant pot pro crisp air fryer comes with two lids one is for pressure cooker lid and another is an air fryer lid. It is one of the advanced cooking appliances loaded with 11 cooking functions.

The Cookbook contains healthy, delicious, and mouth-watering recipes. The book includes all type of recipes start from breakfast and end with desserts. The recipes written in this cookbook are unique and written with step by step instructions. All the recipes written with their perfect preparation and cooking time. Every recipe ends with their exact nutritional values.

CPSIA information can be obtained
at www.ICGtesting.com
Printed in the USA
LVHW080903220621
690766LV00002B/239